Opus Maledictorum

A Book of Bad Words

Reinhold Aman

Marlowe & Company
New York

First Marlowe & Company edition, 1996

Published by
Marlowe & Company
632 Broadway, Seventh Floor
New York, N.Y. 10012

Manufactured in the United States of America

ISBN 1-56924-836-2

Table of Contents

MALAS PALABRAS: TALKING DIRTY IN CUBAN SPANISH

A. P. *and* G. M.

[*Editor's Note:* We wish to thank *Señor P.* for submitting the Cuban material, and express our gratitude to *Professor M.* for his help in translating and annotating the Spanish material.]

1. *The Feminine Pudenda: 'Cunt'*
Bollo "bun"
Chocha "woodcock" [a game bird]
Papaya "papaya" [a large oblong edible fruit]

2. *The Male Organ: 'Prick'*
Bicho "beast; bug; vermin"
Caoba "mahogany tree/wood"
Cuero "leather strap"
Leña "firewood; beating, whipping (coll.)"
Mandarria "sledge hammer"
Nabo "turnip"
Picha [literal meaning unknown]
Pinga "shoulder yoke" [for carrying loads]
Tolete "club, cudgel; oarlock; fool, clod"
Tranca "bat, cudgel; pole, crossbar"

3. *Aggressive Phrases Used to Express Displeasure*
¡Vete a la reverenda mierda! "Go to holy shit!" : Get lost!
¡Vete a la casa del carajo! "Go to the prick's house!" : Get the hell out of here!
¡A la puñeta! "Go to masturbation!" : Go jerk off!
¡Vete por ahí a que te den por el culo! "Go where you'll get it up the ass!" : Get fucked!
¡Vete al coño de tu madre! "Go to your mother's cunt!"

4. *Phrases Descriptive of Actions Arising out of Utter Male Arrogance*
¡Esto lo hago por mis santos cojones! "I'll do it by my saintly balls!"
¡Así . . . por mis timbales! "I'll do it thus . . . by my balls!" [*timbal* "kettledrum"]
¡Dé a Pepe cojones! "Give Pepe balls!"
¡A mi hay que mamarmela! "They should suck my cock!"

5. Phrases Indicative of a Negative Response

¡Por aquí! "Here, these are for you!" [said while holding one's testicles]

¡Leche! "Milk!" : Semen, 'come'

¡Tarros en almibar! "Jars of preserves in heavy syrup!" : Whatever you're asking, however trivial, I consider it outrageous!

6. Phrases Which Refer to One's Being out of Sorts or One's Lack of Money

Estar jodido "To be fucked"

Estar de madre "To be like a mother" [in the sense of the negative biological and psychological aspects ascribed to pregnancy and childbirth]

Estar de culo "To be like an asshole"

Esto está de pinga "This is a prickish thing"

Hoy tengo la leche cortada "Today I have curdled milk [semen] "

Hoy tengo la leche agria "Today I have sour milk [semen] "

7. An Exchange of Insults between Children

¡El coño de tu madre! "Your mother's cunt!"

¡La tuya! "Yours!" : Your mother's, too!

¡La rebombia la tuya . . . y toco madera! "It goes double for your mother ... and I knock on wood!" [magical prophylaxis]

¡Hijo de puta! "(You) son of a whore!"

¡Ese es un H.P.! "This guy is a son of a whore!" [said to a third party, using the euphemistic acronym]

8. Phrases Referring to Sexual Relations

Echar un palo "To strike a blow" : to fuck

Te voy a poner el tolete "I'm going to put the club in you"

Voy a romper el coco que tengo contigo "I'm going to break the coconut that we share" : I'm going to fuck you

Singar "To pole; to propel with an oar" : to fuck. Variant of →

Chingar "To fuck" — the standard term. Chingar is of Gypsy origin, according to Corominas (1954:56-57) who provides an interesting semantic interpretation of the word: its original Gypsy meaning was "to fight, to reprimand", which he suggests belongs to the same semantic domain as "to bother, to molest; to have sexual relations."

Te voy a singar a 'mira quien viene' "I'm going to fuck you (playing) 'look who's coming.'" The phrase describes male rear entry of the woman who while bent forward in the standing position can see the man from between her legs.

Anda, neñita, no seas mala y dame 'el siete' "Come on, baby, don't be bad—give me 'the seven.'" *El siete* is a numerical icon with a sexual-anatomical referent inasmuch as 7 represents a woman bent forward, presenting herself for rear entry intercourse.

Chúpamele, pero no escupas después a mis hijitos "Suck it for me, but afterwards don't spit out my children"

Hacer el sesenta y nueve "To play sixty-nine." 69 refers to the internationally recognized numerical icon for mutual oral-genital stimulation.

¡Me pasmaste el palo! "You chilled my stick!" *Palo* refers to a stick or a blow with a stick, and is euphemistic for sexual intercourse. *Pasmo* is a psychosomatically induced folk disease universal to Latin America, involving local swelling attributed to a sudden and severe change in actual or qualitative body temperature (cf. Wolf 1956:216; Mulcahy 1967, p. 25). The verb is *pasmar.* In this instance, someone has interrupted the speaker's sex act, chilling the heat it generated.

¡Clávatela! "Nail yourself with it!" A passionate phrase said to a woman, indicating that she should violently introduce her partner's phallus into herself.

Te la voy a meter hasta los cojones "I'm going to put it into you right up to the balls."

9. Sexually Abusive Usages Directed at Women

Puta "Whore" — the standard Spanish term

¡Eres una sata! "You're a stray bitch!" : You whore! *Sata* is a dog without pedigree; a mongrel, mutt

Fletera "Freighter" : a prostitute who has nowhere to take her clients; one who has no connections with a bordello or hotel

¡Estás por la libre! "You give it away free!" Said to a promiscuous woman

Se botó por la calle por medio "She got to the street from the middle" Said of a previously 'decent' woman who turned prostitute

Cundanga : a woman who takes it up the ass. [Related to *cunda* 'happy-go-lucky person'?]

Pailera : an AC/DC woman; a lesbian. [*Paila* "sugar pan; evaporator"]

Tortillera "Tortilla maker *or* seller" : a lesbian

ON CHRISTIAN-MOSLEM RELATIONS IN THE BALKANS

*Boris Sukitch Razvratnikov

An interesting piece of evidence on the nature of relations between Christians and Moslems in the Balkans is the following poem, which was taught to the author in Turkish by an Albanian living in Macedonia. The poem is given below in the original Turkish with a translation.

Am karakaşlı	Black-browed cunt
Sik soğan başlı.	Onion-headed prick.
Am dedi "kaçarım."	Cunt said, "I flee."
Sik dedi "koçarım:	Prick said, "I pursue:
Nerede tutarım,	Where I catch,
Orada sikerim."	There I fuck."

Clearly, this verse originates in the centuries-old Balkan tradition of Moslem men raping infidel women. As Moslem women depilate their pubic region, an *am* which is *karakaşlı* can only be non-Moslem. The description of the *sik* as *soğan başlı* indicates an exposed glans—the result of circumcision. It must therefore be Moslem, as a Christian would be uncircumcised. The remainder of the rhyme describes the drama so frequently played out by the characters described in the first two lines.

✳✳✳✳✳✳✳✳✳✳✳✳✳✳✳✳✳✳✳✳✳✳✳✳✳✳✳✳✳✳

⇒ *Kindly tell your acquisitions librarian to move his/her rosy butt*
⇒ *and request a standing order for our Journal and the Monographs.*

MALEDICTION AND PSYCHO-SEMANTIC THEORY
THE CASE OF YIDDISH

James A. Matisoff

[*Editor's Note:* This article is a condensation of Matisoff's monograph published in Hebrew in *Ha-sifrut* (Tel Aviv), no. 18-19 (December 1974), 181-223. The full-length revised English version, *Blessings, Curses, Hopes and Fears: Psycho-ostensive Expressions in Yiddish*, will be published as a *Maledicta Press Publication*, vol. 2, later in 1977.]

Ever since the 1930s, American linguistics has placed an undue emphasis on the "rule-governed" aspects of language use. Orthodox generative grammar viewed a language as "an infinite set of well-formed sentences"—a little like defining a human being as "a featherless biped composed largely of water."

More recently, work on linguistic variation has undercut the overly rigid Chomskyan dichotomy between "competence" and "performance" to the point where it is no longer clear in what sense we can speak of a "rule of grammar" at all. Linguists have now plunged into the study of *semantics*, from a variety of theoretical points of view. Sentences are no longer considered in artificial isolation, but are increasingly being analyzed in terms of their situational or "extra-linguistic" context (here the influence of the British "philosophers of ordinary language" is apparent), as well as their position within the larger linguistic context or "discourse" (here we are rediscovering the joys of literary criticism).

We would now like to go one step further, turning our attention inward to the *mental states* of the speaker and hearer. The real communication that goes on during interpersonal exchanges often has little to do with the actual words that are spoken. Any utterance may in fact be associated with an indefinite number of psychic states. To this area of the study of meaning let us give the name *psycho-semantics*.

Yiddish is an ideal language to start with. Among its arsenal of expressive devices, Yiddish has certain well-defined classes of ready-made phrases or formulas that are typically inserted parenthetically into larger sentences, and whose only function is to give vent to the speaker's emotional attitude toward what he is talking about. These *psycho-ostensive expressions*[1] purport to be direct reflections of the inner state of mind of the speaker. In the simplest cases (barring irony or hypocrisy) they are intended by the speaker to be accepted as the faithful linguistic manifestation of his psychic state of the moment.

Some random examples:

(1) *Mayn zun, zol er zayn gezunt un shtark, vet mir dos shikn aher.* — "My son, *may he be healthy and strong*, will send it here to me."

(2) *Governer Reygn, zol er oysgemekt vern, git mayn zun dem profesor, a gezunt tsu im, keyn hesofe nit hayyor.* — "Governor Reagan, *may he be erased*, isn't giving any raise this year to my son the professor, *a health to him*."

(3) *Mayn feter Khaim-Yankl, olevasholem, flegt dos alemol zogn.* — "My uncle Chaim-Yankl, *upon him peace*, used to say that all the time."

The formation of these expressions is a productive process among fully fluent Yiddish speakers.[2] Virtuosity in concocting new linguistic variations on the old emotive themes is highly prized. Yet Yiddish psycho-ostensives, despite their richness and variety, all seem to fall into a few large psycho-semantic categories, all having to do basically with attitudes toward *good* and *evil*. These include expressions where the speaker is wishing for good things for himself or his family, or altruistically for people in the outgroup; expressions of gratitude for good things received, or lamentations for one's troubles; apotropaic locutions used to ward off evil, including phrases that are meant to appease the dead; formulas for calling down evil (death, disease, misfortune) on others; oaths one uses to swear to the truth, sometimes taking the form of wishing evil to oneself in order to convince others of one's veracity.

The various subtypes of psycho-ostensives may be meaningfully categorized according to the psychic stance of the speaker toward the good or evil that may befall himself or others. Sometimes this is a passive attitude of acceptance or recognition that a "good thing" or a "bad thing" has occurred. At least as often, the speaker assumes a more active psychic stance, expressing his desire, wish, seeking for the good; or conversely, his abhorrence, fear, shunning of the evil; or, perversely, his wish that evil may strike his fellow man or himself.

The relatively passive attitude of acceptance of good or evil we call *recognitive*; the more active attitude of seeking or desiring we call *petitive*; and the more active attitude of shunning or fearing we call *fugitive*. If we add to these the Greek roots for "self" and "others" (*auto-* and *allo-*), and the Latin roots for "good" and "evil" (*bono-* and *malo-*), we have all the technical terminology we need. Thus, e.g. *auto-malo-recognitive* means "recognizing that evil has come to oneself"; *allo-bono-petitive* means "wishing for good to come to others," etc.

These categories, like all others in linguistics, are not mutually exclusive and shade into one another, but they will do as a basis for discussion.[3]

A. Bono-recognition: Thanks and Congratulations
To give thanks is to "recognize that good has come to oneself" (*auto-bono-recognition*). In Yiddish this often takes the form of blessing God's name:

(4) *Ikh bin, borkhashem, gezunt, un di gesheftn geyen gut.* — "I am, *bless God*, healthy, and business is good."

To congratulate someone is to "recognize that good has come to another" (*allo-bono-recognition*):

(5) *Yankele, Got hot dir geholfn, zol zayn mit glik! Efsher voltst mir gekent layen a finef rubl?* — "Yankele, God has been good to you, *congratulations* (lit. "may it be with luck")! Maybe you could lend me five rubles?"

B. Malo-recognition: Lamentation and Sympathy
To lament one's own fate is to "recognize that evil has come to oneself" (*auto-malo-recognition*):

(6) *Itst vet zi khásene hobn mit a frantsóyz, vey iz tsu mir!* — "Now she's going to marry a Frenchman, *woe is me!*"

To express sympathy is to "recognize that evil has come to another" (*allo-malo-recognition*):

(7) *Er hot farlorn beyde hent in der milkhome, az okh un vey tsu im.* — "He lost both his hands in the war, *alas and alack to him!*"

(8) *Fregt der tate, nebekh a toyber, "Ah, vos iz gevorn?"* — "Then the father asked—he was deaf, *poor man (nebekh)* —'Eh? What happened?'"

C. Petitive Attitudes

Some Yiddish constructions express general attitudes of wishing, and are usable equally well regardless of whether it is a good or evil that is desired. Other petitive psycho-ostensives are more specialized in function.

One may wish for good things for oneself (*auto-bono-petition*):

(9) *Aza sheyne heym hot er, oyf mir gezogt gevorn!* — "I wish *I* had such a beautiful home as he does!" (lit. "Such a beautiful home he has, *of me it should be said!*"

More altruistically one may wish for good things for others (*allo-bono-petition*). These locutions are more simply referred to as *blessings*.

Blessing people is a fine art in Yiddish. It is possible to weave infinite variations on the various benedictive themes, revolving around certain key desiderata in Jewish culture:

(10) *Zolstu derlebn tsu firn dayne kinder un kinds kinder tsu der khupe!* — "May you live to lead your children and children's children to the wedding canopy!"

(11) *Zolstu hobn a sakh nakhes fun di eyneklekh!* — "May you have a lot of *nakhes*[4] from your grandchildren!"

"Existential blessings" may be inserted parenthetically into sentences:

(12) *Shver, lebn zolt ir, haynt hobn mir yontev.* — "Father-in-law, *may you live*, today is a holiday."

Sometimes, however, these parenthetical blessings are more "palliative" than benedictive in function, serving merely to soften a reproach, or to take the sting out of one's contradiction of another's words, or to apologize for something unpleasant that must be said ("despite the unwelcomeness of the message I must give you, I am still fundamentally well-disposed towards you"):

(13) *Oy, Raynhold, zolstu gezunt zayn, vos far a patshkeráy hostu do gemakht!* — "Oh, Reinhold, *may you be healthy*, what a mess you've made here!"

One subtype of bono-petitive expressions are phrases which invoke success in the performance of a particular action (verb + *gezunterheyt* = "verb *in good health*"):

(14) *For gezunterheyt, un hit zikh op far shikurim!*— "Drive in good health, and watch out for drunks!"

From one point of view, the ritual blessings of God's name which intervene at specified points during the recitation of Hebrew prayers also belong in this category. We may call these *theo-bono-petitives*:

(15) *Borukh ato adoynoy — borukh hu u-vorukh shemoy — eloyhenu melekh ho-oylom, malbish arumim.* — "Blessed art Thou, Oh Lord — *blessed be He and blessed be His name* — our God, King of the Universe, who clothest the naked."

Yiddish abounds in proverbs which express an ironical attitude toward the bono-petitive stance:

(16) *Oyb di bobe volt gehat eyer, volt zi geven a zeyde.* — "If grandmother had had balls, she would have been a grandfather." That is, "wishing doesn't make it so."[5]

D. Malo-fugition: Deliver Us from Evil!

Yiddish malo-fugitive expressions reflect a variety of techniques for the avoidance of evil, either from oneself (*auto-malo-fugition*) or from others (*allo-malo-fugition*).

Sometimes a formula is recited with the intention of banishing the evil from one's consciousness (cf. "See no evil, hear no evil, speak no evil"):

(17) *Zaynen oysgeshtorbn, nit far aykh gedakht, ale tsign in shtot.* — "So every goat in town—*may it be unthinkable in your case*—died."

Often *euphemisms* are resorted to. Alternatively, magic words like *kholile* (which we conventionally translate "horrors!") may be pronounced:

(18) *Di mume hot ongehoybn moyre tsu hobn, tsi iz der bokher kholile nit baym zinen.* — "The aunt began to be

afraid that the young man might be—*horrors!*—out of his mind."

God's aid is sometimes directly invoked, or else a formula is recited to reassure God that we know that our fate is utterly in His hands:

(19) *Morgn, a m'et lebn, vel ikh geyn koyfn hinerfleysh oyf shabes.* — "Tomorrow, *if I live*, I'll go buy some chicken for the Sabbath."

The Eastern European preoccupation with the "Evil Eye" manifests itself in contexts where one mentions somebody's good fortune. To say *keyn ayn-hore* ("no evil eye!") is to protect oneself or others from the "demons of misfortune" who delight in turning human happiness into grief:

(20) *Hayntiksyor bin ikh gevorn, keyn aynore, akht-un-zibetsik yor alt.* — "This year I became—*no evil eye*—78 years old."

Finally, the "scapegoat approach" may be resorted to, whereby the evil intended for one person is deflected unto another being, human or animal:

(21) *Mir zol zayn far dayne beyndelekh!* — "If only *I* could be the one to suffer instead of your little bones!" (lit. "May it be to me for your little bones!")

E. Psycho-ostensives Relating to the Dead

Expressions of this type reflect a variety of emotions which the living may feel for the dead: love, fear, hatred.

Usually the mention of a dead person's name is accompanied by a blessing (*morto-bono-petitive*).[6]

Sometimes, however, the visceral fear which the living feel for the dead finds expression in "vivo-bono-petitive" (or "vivo-malo-fugitive") formulas, designed to ensure that the speaker and hearer will not be enticed to die before their time by the blandishments of the dead:

(22) *Azoy flegt es kokhn mayn shviger, undz tsu lange yor.* — "That's how my mother-in-law used to cook it—*may we live long years.*"

Occasionally a dead person's name is accompanied by a curse (*morto-malo-petitive*):

(23) *Dos iz geven di arbet fun Hitlern, yimakh shemoy.* — "That was the work of Hitler, *may his name be erased.*"

F. Allo-malo-petition

This leads us to the ramified topic of cursing or "malediction," which in our terminology is called *allo-malo-petition*: wishing for evil to come to others.

At its simplest level, Yiddish verbal abuse takes the form of cusswords or epithets (*zidlverter*) that the speaker applies to his antagonist. These are unlimited in number, since the speaker has the whole arsenal of Germanic, Hebrew, and Slavic insults at his disposal, along with many original Yiddish *trouvailles*.

More interesting than individual lexical items are ritualized curses (*kloles*): petitive expressions that call down misfortune, disease, or death on their intended victims. Taken at their face value these often appear very virulent indeed:

(24) *Zol zi geshvoln vern vi a barg!* — "May she swell up like a mountain!"

(25) *A kholerye zol im khapn!* — "May the cholera seize him!" Yet, needless to say, the malo-petitioner would usually be appalled if the dire eventuality actually came to pass.[7] *Kloles* are to be viewed as the overt linguistic manifestation of a (possibly momentary) psychic state: hostility.

Furthermore, Yiddish curses are often delivered in an elegant, eloquent, or humorous way, so that their harshness is greatly mitigated:

(26) *A ziser toyt zol er hobn—a trok mit tsuker zol im iber-forn!* — "May he have a sweet death—run over by a sugar-truck!"

(27) *Zol im vaksn burikes in pupik, un zol er pishn mit borsht!* — "May beets grow in his navel so that he pisses borscht!"

Allo-malo-petitives may paradoxically be considered the most appealing sort of psycho-ostensive expressions in Yiddish, due to the free rein that speakers give to their imagination in this area.

G. Swearing Oaths

These are complicated speech acts that may reflect several different psycho-ostensive stances: bono-petitive (28), auto-malo-petitive (29), or malo-fugitive (30):

(28) *Zoln mir beyde azoy lebn, vi ikh bin nit shuldik!* — "*May we both live so long,* I'm not guilty!"

(29) *Zol ikh azoy visn fun beyz, vi ikh farshtey epes in maslines.* — "*So may I know of evil,* the way I understand anything about olives."

(30) *Zol ikh nit visn fun beyz, vi ikh veys, vos iz gevorn fun ayer gelt.* — "*So may I not know of evil,* the way I know what happened to your money." (i.e. "I swear I don't know what happened to it.")

Oaths are particularly susceptible of being manipulated for devious motives, both benign and hypocritical.

Conclusion

It is to be emphasized that the psycho-semantic categories set up in this study are not conceived of as mutually exclusive, and that psychic states do not necessarily occur in absolutely "pure" form. Feelings shade into one another in so complex a way that they cannot be forced into any rigid conceptual model in principle.

Yiddish psycho-ostensives are usable on many different levels. Often they are to be taken at face value, as faithful representations of the speaker's dominant state of mind at the moment. Yet they may also be used by pure reflex action, with little genuine feeling at all. In extreme cases they may be used cynically or hypocritically, as a mask for one's true feelings. Yiddish speakers are well aware of the humorous possibilities inherent in the manipulation of psycho-ostensives for special effects, which proves that their "normal" functions are well understood by all native speakers.

The Yiddish language owes much of its rich expressive flavor to psycho-ostensive locutions. This is an area where linguistics, psychology, cultural anthropology, and the history of ideas can all contribute much to one another.

It is to be hoped that the conceptual framework outlined here for Yiddish will prove to have applicability (*mutatis mutandis*) to other languages with a highly developed psycho-ostensive apparatus. Perhaps, indeed, all languages might profitably be studied from this point of view.

Notes

[1] "Soul-showing" expressions.

[2] Who, alas, are growing ever less numerous.

[3] The remainder of this paper will consist of brief examples of the various subtypes of Yiddish psycho-ostensive expressions, chosen for their relatively clearcut quality. For fuller discussions of the various sociolinguistic, syntactic, and psycho-semantic issues raised by these expressions, including the interrelationships among the categories and some 325 illustrative sentences, the reader is referred to the full monograph (see *Editor's Note*).

[4] *Nakhes* is something like "the satisfaction parents get from the accomplishments of their children."

[5] Reinhold Aman cites a similar German proverb: *Wenn der Hund nicht geschissen hätt', dann hätt' er den Hasen erwischt.* — "If the dog hadn't [stopped to] shit, he would have caught the hare."

[6] See sentence (3) above.

[7] Just as we English speakers would not like it if people obligingly expired every time we said "Drop dead!" to them.

אאאאאא

¶ Please help spread the Good Word: Tell your colleagues about MALEDICTA, or send a flyer to appropriate chairpersons for departmental announcements.

AGGRESSION IN CHILDREN'S JOKES

Sandra McCosh

Aggression in children's jokes can be divided into two main categories: the actual aggression expressed in the content or action of the jokes, and the aggression displayed by the teller toward the listener, real or implied. Although both categories can be found in the same joke in some combination, I will discuss them separately as two different phenomena. Most jokes can be seen as aggressive towards the listener in some degree, but not all jokes are aggressive in content.

The first category of content aggression can be divided into six areas of aggression. The most obvious type of aggression is **physical violence.** This is shown in the joke by a 12-year-old English boy, also implying stupidity of the Irish.

> *Two Englishmen continually beat up an Irishman. The poor Irishman, in self-defense, learns Kung Fu, the art of self-defense, but unfortunately it takes the Irishman so long to say all the necessary words before he strikes, that the Englishmen still beat him up.*

In a second joke, with the additional feature of violence toward an object (the motorcycles):

> *Eight skinheads (or bubbleboys, similar to American Hell's Angels) beat up an innocent man eating his breakfast; the poor man does not try to defend himself at all. The man retaliates by running over their motorcycles with his car.*

Continuing in the same line is **sexual violence.**

> *Two nuns, out for a walk, get raped; one nun turns to the other and says, "What are we going to tell Mother Superior when we tell her we've been raped twice?" The second nun replies, "But we've only been raped once, haven't we?" Whereupon the first nun answers, "But we're going back again aren't we?"*

Two of the most popular jokes in both England and the United

States, "Johnnie Fuckerfaster," and "Shagarada," involve seduction; the first of a little girl, and the second of Shagarada by the milkman, who promises her lots of milk, if Shagarada will get into bed with him. In both jokes, sexual fun is ruined by the mother calling 'Shagarada' or 'Johnnie Fuckerfaster.'

> *Johnnie Fuckerfaster, named that by his mom, was under the house with a little girl, and his mom didn't know he was there with the girl. She calls, "Johnnie, come here." And Johnnie says to the little girl, "I guess I'll have to go," even though they were in the middle of it. And so his mother yells again, "Johnnie Fuckerfaster," and so he yells back, "I'm fucking her as fast as I can."*

Sexual aggression of a third type is associated with curiosity and the lack of answering questions with truthful answers.

> *A little girl asks her father what his penis is, and he replies it is either a snake or a teddy bear. The daughter sneaks in at night to play with it, and when it spits in her eye, she bites its head off.*

In an American joke by a 12-year-old girl,

> *A man goes to a motel and takes a room called the Three Holes. He is warned three different times by the bellboy to not put his penis into the three holes, and three times he disregards the warning. He finally discovers, as he is screaming in pain with his penis stuck in the third hole, that the first hole was a goat's butt, the second a lady's vagina, and the third is a cow's milking machine that won't let go until it gets 10 gallons.*

A less obvious area of aggression is **mental aggression**. This is portrayed in a joke about Hell.

> *A man who has been bad all his life is sent to Hell, and the Devil gives him the choice of two rooms to spend the rest of his time in. He chooses the room where the others are all drinking tea, instead of the room where all the men are standing on their heads in manure. On his fourth cup of tea, the Devil comes in and tells everyone, "Tea break's over, boys."*

Other jokes concerning lunatics in looney asylums also fit into this category of mental aggression, where both the listener and the teller fear being like the person in the joke, crazy, or going to Hell. In one lunatic joke:

> *The warden comes around to see what the fellows are doing and how they are spending their time. In the first two rooms he visits, the people are all doing crazy things, but in the third room he sees a man reading a book. He thinks this is great, so he goes in to talk*

to him. As he enters the room, he sees a second man hanging from the light fixture; and so he asks the first man what that fellow thinks he is. "He thinks he's a light bulb." So the warden says, "Well, I'm glad to see you're occupying your mind with a book, something decent," and he says, "Will you tell him to get down?" "Stop being daft, I won't be able to read."

The fourth area within the category of content aggression is **ethnic violence**. In England, the two main groups picked on are the Irish, and the Jews, while in California the Polish are the butt of the jokes. The Irish, through their alleged stupidity, usually lose out, such as in the previous one where the poor Irishman gets beat up by the two Englishmen, and

Six Irishmen drown while trying to bury their friend at sea.

The Jews, through their alleged greed and desire for money, also die.

How do you kill a Jew? Throw a ha'penny under the bus.

Another Jew jumps off the Eiffel Tower when he thinks he sees a 10p piece on the ground. Unfortunately he is wrong, and the newspapers report his death the next day as: A Jewish man jumps and lands in a dustbin.

The most violent jokes about Jews though take place in German concentration camps. The Jew is pitted against other ethnic groups, such as the English, Irish, and the Scottish, but in each case the Jew gets the worst treatment.

One day the German commandant says, "Today the English will climb the barracks wall, the Irish will climb the watertower, and the Jews will climb the electric fence."

In the United States, the Polish are ridiculed as being allegedly incredibly stupid and dirty, and these two traits lead to their downfall.

How do you break a Polack's neck? Shut the toilet seat.

How do you break a Polack's finger? Punch him in the nose.

Cruelty and aggression towards animals appears as **violence towards animals** by humans, and violence by one animal toward another. The dog is a favorite animal in the jokes.

A man who brags his dog will not do what someone else orders it to do, finds that there is one command the dog can't or won't disobey. A man picks up the dog, throws it in the fire, and tells the dog to get out.

A well-endowed bull that enjoys jumping over a fence every morning to greet the cows on the other side with, "Hiya, I'm Billy Bigballs" gets a nasty shock when the farmer puts barbed wire on top of the fence. He jumps over and says, "Hiya, I'm Billy."

An example of violence by one animal toward another:

A poor hyena gets continually beat up by a lion in the jungle, and when his friend the monkey promises to help him fight the lion, the hyena feels reassured. Unfortunately, when the lion attacks the hyena, the hyena laughs so much the monkey thinks the hyena is winning and fails to aid him.

A final area within this category of content aggression is **fantasy**. This is represented by the joke:

Two biscuits were walking down the road, and one got run over by a car, and the other one said,"Oh, crumbs!"

Various other jokes and riddles have violence and fighting and aggression in mild forms, most of it fantasy, such as in a limerick where a whacking machine breaks and hits the teacher instead. In a long involved joke:

A couple named Hill are killed by a "hideous old fellow" who throws the couple in a crypt, and starts to play the organ. But when the couple comes alive, the man starts to play, "The Hills are alive with the sound of music."

Almost all jokes can be seen as aggressive. The teller of the jokes displays his hostility towards the listener, even if it is just to make the listener feel like a fool because he doesn't know the answer to the joke or riddle. As Legman has stated in his Introduction to *The Rationale of the Dirty Joke* (Vol. 1, Panther Books, 1972, p. 9 [also Grove Press, 1968]),

Under the mask of humor, our society allows infinite aggressions, by everyone and against everyone. In the culminating laugh by the listener or observer—whose position is often really that of victim or butt—the teller of the joke betrays his hidden hostility and signals his victory by being, theoretically at least, the one person present *who does not laugh.*

Children, although possibly unaware of the aggressive content of their jokes, certainly enjoy telling jokes and riddles to which their audience does not know the answer. Parents and teachers are often selected as victims, the child attempting to catch their parents or teacher in a position where the child knows more than the adult. This is especially evident in a very popular riddle that has many different answers, the child changing the answer as the listener gives the answer he knows. *"What is black and white and red all over?"* Some of the many answers I collected are: *"A newspaper"*; *"An embarrassed zebra"*; *"A zebra with blood-shot eye-balls"*; *"A skunk with diaper rash"*; *"A sun-burned penguin"*; *"A penguin-burger with ketchup"*; and *"A penguin on a meat hook."* A slight variation on this riddle is: *"What is black and white, black and white, and black and white?"* - *"A nun falling down the stairs,"* or *"Three penguins rolling down a hill."* Or, *"What is black and white with red in the back?"* - *"A nun getting stabbed in the back."* Any one of these answers can be used, and the listener has no idea which answer the teller knows or wants. Some of them are quite aggressive in content, especially the nun getting stabbed in the back, and the penguin on a meat hook.

Tricks and catches are especially designed to make the listener feel like a fool. These jokes are mainly told by the older children, aged 11-14, in which the child needs to keep a straight face and not give the joke away, if he is going to fool the listener effectively and "catch" him. The older child is better able to do this than the younger child who is apt to laugh. A favorite trick, in both England and the United States, is to have the recipient of the trick take a coin, preferably a quarter which has a rough edge. He draws around it with a pencil on a piece of paper. Then the person must roll the coin on its edge down his forehead and nose, and let it drop on the paper, trying to make it fall in the circle he drew. The place where the coin drops is where he must draw a second circle, and he repeats the process of dropping the coin on the paper, trying to get it into one of the circles. What he is unaware of, is that each time he rolls the coin down his face, he is leaving a black mark from the residue of the pencil left on the coin. Usually the laughter of the audience, or his inability to drop the coin in the circle, makes him quit.

A third type of joke that makes the listener feel like a fool, along with riddles with multiple answers, and tricks and catches, is the shaggy dog story. Here the teller relates a very long story, with as many details as he can manufacture, and ends with a punchline that doesn't resolve the problem in the joke, and leaves the listener hanging. A favorite with the English children involved a yellow Ping-Pong ball, while in the United States and England I collected several versions of a story about a gorilla who wanted to play tag.

A final type of aggression of teller towards listener, is when the teller and some of his audience share the aggression felt or displayed towards a third party. In children's jokes this appears as two different types of jokes; jokes that make fun of adult authority figures, such as parents or teachers; and ethnic jokes that mock specific groups.

Adult authority figures are in a position to control and rule the child, and the child's only chance of striking back is to mock them within his jokes. I found six different adult authority figures that were made to look foolish and silly; parents, teachers, the police, the doctor, church officials, and those under a prison warden, either in a criminal prison, concentration camp, or lunatic asylum.

Some examples of adult authority figure jokes are:

There were three boys who were called Mind-your-own-business, Manners, and Trouble. One day Trouble got lost. A policeman found them trespassing and took them to the police station. Mind-your-own-business went inside and Manners stayed outside. The sergeant asked Mind-your-own-business his name, and he said, "Mind-your-own-business." Then the sergeant said, "Where are your manners?" "Outside." "Are you looking for trouble?" said the sergeant. "Yes."

"Doctor, doctor, I only have 59 seconds to live." "Wait a minute."

Teacher: "What would you have if you had 10 apples, and the boy next to you took 6 apples from you?" Boy: "A thump-up (fight), Miss."

Why did the vicar go to church walking on his hands? Because it was Palm Sunday.

There's a woman and her son in a big large store. And her son shouts, "Mom, I want to wee wee." So she goes, with a bright red face, "Sshh, son, everybody will hear ya." She says, "Next time say, mom, I want to whisper." So he says, "Alright." And then he's at home and he wants to go to toilet, so he says to his dad, "Dad, I want to whisper." So the father says, "Go on son, whisper in my ear."

Ethnic jokes are probably the most obvious aggressive jokes, the teller and part of his audience sharing in mocking and laughing at the stereotype of a group. The Irish stereotype in England is that of a stupid person, but lovable, and most of the jokes aren't very nasty in content or tone. The Irishman commits mistakes because of his stupidity, and when he is compared to the Englishman and Scottishman, he comes out on the bottom. In contrast, the Jewish stereotype in England is a more serious and nasty stereotype, especially the jokes that take place in Nazi concentration camps. The main characteristic of Jews that is used against them is their alleged desire for money, and their greed, no matter what the cost, and even risking death for a few pennies. In California, the Polish are similar in characteristics to the Irish, except that the Polish are shown as even dumber, dirty, and very inept, unable to do anything right. Plus, the Polish stereotype is much nastier than the Irish stereotype, and a Pole is compared to shit, and his house is identifiable because he swims in the cesspool out front.

In all, children's jokes can be seen as aggressive, but usually in only a mild degree. The jokes make the listener feel like a fool because he doesn't know the answer, but in a funny and amusing manner. Most children state that they tell jokes because they are funny and fun to tell, and they enjoy making their friends laugh. Their main purpose in telling jokes is to communicate with their friends and peers, and not to express hostility, although jokes can be a harmless outlet for aggression and hostility, especially towards adult authority figures who control so much of their lives. Jokes that are aggressive in content are a small part of the total number of jokes told by children, most being harmless riddles and funny stories. Aggression and hostility in children's jokes then can be seen as a latent or subconscious purpose to the jokes, and the children are only aware of the conscious, surface meaning and purpose of the jokes, to make their audience laugh.

NOTE

All the jokes included in this paper are from a collection of jokes from English and American school children aged 6-14. The jokes were collected in part for the requirements for a Master of Arts in Folklore at the University of Leeds, England. This whole collection of jokes is to be published in *A Joke for Every Occasion*. [*Editor's Note:* Announced date of publication: April, 1978. Heinrich Hanau Publications, 59 Old Compton Street, London W1V 5PN, England.]

Dirty Dinghy

Oh, die a dingy, dirgesome death
Of dingleberry tea,
For if you don't I'll have to put
My dinghy out to sea.

—Wesli Court

Seasoned Curse

Summer's summer,
Fall is fall,
And winter's winter,
Dammit all.

—Wesli Court

ANALYSIS OF A FOUR-LETTER WORD

Margaret Fleming

In Book III of *Gulliver's Travels*, Gulliver visits the Grand Academy of Lagado. Here is his description of one of the scientists at work there:

> The Projector of this Cell was the most ancient Student of the Academy. His Face and Beard were of a pale Yellow; his Hands and Cloaths dawbed over with Filth. When I was presented to him, he gave me a very close Embrace, (a Compliment I could well have excused.) His Employment from his first coming into the Academy, was an Operation to reduce human Excrement to its original Food, by separating the several parts, removing the Tincture which it receives from the Gall, making the Odour exhale, and scrumming off the Saliva.[1]

This passage illustrates both the devotion of the true scientist and the repugnance of the ordinary person to the study of shit. But to the pure all things are pure, and a devoted student of language may find the study of the word *shit* at least as fruitful as that of the substance.

Why study *shit*? Well, why not? *Shit* has not had its share of serious scholarly attention; but, like any other word, it has a history; it has grammatical characteristics; and it has a range of meanings wider than one might suppose. But also, because of its second-class citizenship in the English language, *shit* calls attention to itself and is thus easier than most words to isolate and to study. My feeling about analyzing it can be summed up this way: "I am a member of the human race, and nothing human can be alien to me."

It is not easy to be serious about studying *shit*. One is apt to find people either shocked or amused by it. And repugnance appears in unexpected places. I was much surprised when I showed a first draft of this article to a class of mine—all teachers or prospective teachers of English—to have one student, a retired military man, shove it away as abruptly as if I had given him the kind of embrace Gulliver received from the scientist. He said, "I can't forget what my old Sunday School teacher used to say: 'Cecil [not his real name], there is filth in the world, but you don't have to wallow in it.' " Could there be a clearer example of mistaking the word for the thing?

That's one extreme. The opposite is typified by Joe, the high school boy who first inspired this article by asking his teacher if he could do his research paper on four-letter words. She of course refused. While Cecil mistakenly attributed to *shit* the power to contaminate, Joe more accurately attributed to it the power to shock or annoy.

A third attitude that neither desires to shock nor is shocked by *shit* is that held by perhaps a majority of English speakers, who use this word as matter-of-factly as any other in their vocabularies. This attitude toward *shit* is best exemplified for me by my husband John (his real name—appropriate, isn't it, in this context?). In my own middle-class, suburban upbringing, *shit* was a taboo word, ranking high on the scale of objectionability. I was not accustomed—or even permitted—to use the word in its literal or any of its figurative meanings. John, however, grew up in the slums of New York City, and *shit* was—and still is—part of his everyday vocabulary. When I first knew him, I used to react with a start every time he said it, but soon my linguistic curiosity took over, and I began to notice the many uses he made of *shit*. Some of his expressions were already known to me; others were new, but have since been verified and added to by many interested and cooperative friends.

We are so accustomed to thinking of the "four-letter" words as ancient and unchanged that it may come as a surprise to learn that while *shit* is indeed ancient, it has not always been a four-letter word. TABLE I, based on *The Oxford English Dictionary* [OED], 1933, Vol. IX, shows that in earlier centuries there were different forms for the noun and the verb, including its past tense and past participle. Since the 19th century, however, the single form *shit* has been used interchangeably for all these functions. We see here a very common tendency in language change, simplification and reduction in number of forms.

The following anecdote, told of the Scottish poet, Robert Henryson, illustrates an early use of the modern spelling of *shit*:

> . . . being very old he dyed of a diarrhea or fluxe, of whome there goes this merry, though somewhat unsavory tale, that all phisitians having given him over & he lying drawing his last breath there came an old woman unto him, who was held a witch, & asked him whether he would be cured, to whom he sayed very willingly. then quod [said] she there is a whikey tree in the lower end of your orchard, & if you will goe and walke but thrice about it & thrice repeate theis words whikey tree whikey tree take away this fluxe from me you shall be presently cured, he told her that beside he was extreme faint & weake it was extreme frost & snowe & that it was impossible for him to go: She told him that unles he did so it was impossible he should recover. Mr Henderson then lifting up himselfe, & pointing to an Oken table that was in the roome, asked her & said gude dame I pray ye tell me, if it would not do as well if I repeated thrice theis words oken burd [board] oken burd garre [make] me shit a harde turde.[2]

The author of this narrative, Sir Francis Kinaston, published it in 1639. Henryson, who died about 1508, if he had written the story himself, would very probably have used the older spelling *shite*. This spelling is still given as an alternate form in the *OED*, published in 1933, but I have never heard it used. TABLE II illustrates some of the contexts in which *shit* was used from the 14th through the 18th centuries. The earliest examples, drawn from reputable texts in different fields, show no trace of "dirtiness" in the word. It is not until the 18th century that we begin to see a certain self-consciousness, manifested by such renditions as *s..te*, *sh-t*, and *sh—*, which become more frequent toward the close of the century. As Noel Perrin points out in *Dr. Bowdler's Legacy* (New York, 1971, p. 2), the age of delicacy and expurgation was in full flower by this time, which no doubt accounts for the disappearance of *shit* from respectable literature from about 1795—the latest entry for it in the *OED*—until the present century.

Shit is closely related to similar words in other Germanic languages and more distantly to the Greek *skatos*, which has given us the word *scatology*, literally "the science of shit." All these words have been traced back to Indo-European, the hypothetical parent of most modern European languages.

The conjectural Indo-European root *skei-* had the basic meaning of "to separate", and it has given us, in addition to *shit*, such widely differing words as *science* (from the Latin *scire*, "to know"—that is to *separate* one thing from another), *shin* (from *shinbone*, originally "a piece cut off"), *sheaf*, *scissors*, and *schizophrenia*, in all of which the notion of separation can be discerned.

It is easy to see the perception of the act involved in this root meaning of *shit*. TABLE III compares it with some of its synonyms, showing what other perceptions appear and thus how *shit* is distinctive. These are not all exact synonyms, of course. For example, *turd* is a countable, whereas *shit* and *crap* are collective, nouns. So you can *have shit* or *a pile of shit* or *a crock of shit* or even *the shits* (diarrhea), but not an exact number of *shits*, and although you can *not give a shit*, you can *take* any number of *shits*. On the other hand—or in it—you can *have* as many *turds* as you can hold.

There are differences in usage, too. *Dung* and *manure* are used almost exclusively of animals, whereas *shit* can be used for animals and humans both. *Stool* and *feces* are primarily medical terms. Of all the words, only *crap*, *ordure*, and *excrement* seem to be true synonyms for the noun *shit* and only *crap* and *defecate* for the verb. *Evacuate*, *excrete*, and *eliminate* are close in some of their senses, but all of them have much more general meanings as well.

Under synonyms we might also consider such euphemisms and baby-talk as *bowel movement, poop, poo-poo, grunt, caca, number two, business, big job*, and doubtless many others belonging to individual families or small dialect groups. Other euphemisms—*messes, piles, doo-doo, cow chips* (and *buffalo chips*), and *pancakes*—are most commonly used to refer to animal excrement. Many persons invent their own imaginative euphemisms, such as *make a deposit in the bank*. One of the most amusing I've seen is that of 17th-century William Byrd of Virginia, who enters in his diary every day, usually right after describing what he had for breakfast, the notation *I danced my dance.*[3]

Manure and *stool* both illustrate some interesting aspects of language change. *Manure*, a shortened form of *manoeuvre*, first meant "to work with the hands." Then it became specialized to mean "work the soil" or "cultivate." Then it became still further specialized to signify only that part of cultivation that involves fertilization. Then the verb became a noun and was transferred to the fertilizer commonly used, animal excrement, which is still its meaning today. *Stool*, originally—and still—a piece of furniture, was an early euphemism for *commode* (itself a euphemism), particularly in the compound *close-stool.* The first half of the compound was often dropped, in keeping with the common tendency of speakers to shorten words, and produced phrases like *at stool* and the verb *to stool.* Finally, by the process of transference, the word was applied to what the close-stool contained.[4]

Looking at all these words, we can see that they reflect various perceptions of the act of defecation and the product thereof: **separation** in *shit, turd, crap,* and *excrement*; **emptying out** in *evacuate* and *eliminate*; **value** (or lack of) in *feces* and possibly in *crap*; **appearance** in *ordure* and *dung* and in the euphemisms *chip, pile,* and *pancake*; **use** in *manure*; **container for receiving** in *stool* and possibly in *crap*; **place of origin** in *bowel movement*; **sound** in *grunt* and possibly in *poop*; **effect** in *mess*; and **desirable regularity** in *business.* Oddly enough, shit's most noticeable characteristic, odor, is not found in any of these terms.

Most of these root meanings are long since buried in *shit* and its synonyms. Today *shit* has one literal meaning, the same it has always had, but many figurative uses, as we shall see.

The connotations of *shit* range from strongly pejorative through slightly negative to occasionally positive, or at least neutral, uses. In its literal meaning of "excrement", *shit* can be completely neutral, as in *to take a shit.* Many figurative uses retain the sense of the literal meaning, as in *scared shit-*

less. One often hears *scared spitless,* possibly a euphemism, but the implications of the two expressions are not parallel. *Scared spitless* implies an inability to produce saliva because of fear. *Scared shitless* implies a lack of shit from having already lost it—another well-known physical reaction to fear.[5] *He almost shit in his pants* refers to the same reaction, although in use it as often connotes surprise or excitement as fear. The same goes for *have a shit fit,* which also illustrates the very prevalent tendency of slang to rhyme.

Such expressions as *shit on you, eat shit,* and *go shit in your hat,* often used as insults, are vivid enough, but less imaginative than the metaphorical *up shit creek without a paddle, then the shit hit the fan,* and *wish in one hand and shit in the other and see what you get first.* The Dictionary of American Slang[6] gives the expressions *shit green* (or *blue*), connoting fear, and *shit in high cotton,* meaning "to be better off than previously." Similar to the first is the World War II expression *shit little blue cookies,* also connoting some strong emotion such as fear. Other well-known expressions are *shovel shit,* which can be either literal or figurative, and *not know shit from Shinola,* both of which illustrate the alliterative tendency of slang.

The above examples emphasize the qualities of the noun *shit* or the circumstances surrounding the act, but in *the eagle shits* ("payday" in the military), and in *shit out of luck,* the verbal notion of squeezing out is suggested. The military description of creamed beef on toast as *shit on a shingle* may have something to do with its appearance or taste, but probably more to do with attitudes toward institutional cooking. *Shit* is nominal and passive in *beat the shit out of someone, knock the shit out of him, kick the shit out, stomp the shit out,* and so on. In these expressions it could be taken literally, but more often it seems to mean "insides" or "stuffing." Compare *knock the stuffing out of him* and *beat the tar out of him,* which are almost synonymous.

In many of its uses, *shit* has completely lost the sense of its literal meaning. For example, it is one of the current slang names for drugs. *The Dictionary of American Slang* (p. 703) cites references from 1956 through 1962 in which it means "heroin", but I have been told that it is also used to refer to marijuana. In other non-literal uses, *shit* means variously "stuff", as in *all that shit*; "anything" or "nothing", as in *he don't show me shit*; and "something worthless", as in *I don't give a shit*. In *get your shit together*, it means "stuff" or "belongings"—not only material objects, but attitudes; the connotation is "straighten out" or "shape up." *Shit* is almost neutral in expressions like these; any negative connotations are usually carried by the context or tone of voice.

In some non-literal expressions, however, *shit* is definitely negative. In *he's full of shit*, it means "wrong ideas", "pomposity", or "hypocrisy." It implies deliberate deception or misleading in such an assurance as *I wouldn't shit* (or *bullshit*) *you* and also in the incredulous interjection *no shit?*

When we consider compounds and epithets using *shit*, we can see that *shit-brindle* (a distinctively colored dog), *shit-kicker* (cowboy), *shithouse, shit paper*, and to some extent *shitpants* retain the literal meaning. But *shitpants*, as well as *shitface*, can sometimes be used affectionately, usually for children. *Shit-breech*, the 17th-century counterpart of *shit-pants*, was also sometimes used in this half-humorous sense. *Little shit* can also be used of animals or children this way, as in *look at that little shit climb the tree*, and *he's a cute little shit*. But the opposite, *big shit*, suggests someone or something trying to be impressive, as does *hot shit*. *Weak shit* is ineffective, and its opposite, *tough shit*, is "bad luck." *Shithead* is another common compound, but one that has nothing affectionate about it. If your boss is a *shithead*, and you get on his *shit-list*, it's *tough shit* for you.

Among the animal compounds, only *bullshit, horseshit*, and *chickenshit* have acquired commonplace figurative uses. There are a few others, less widespread in use. *The Anatomy of Dirty Words* (p. 37) gives *buzzard shit* as a military term for "roast beef hash." Other combinations I have heard are *pig shit, leaping bat shit, as tight as hen shit*, and *that's a rotten crock of sour owl shit*, and *lower than whaleshit—and that's at the bottom of the ocean*.

Bullshit, the most frequent of the animal compounds, usually connotes hypocrisy or downright lies, as in *what a bunch of bullshit!* but also trouble in general, particularly that caused by red tape, inconsideration, or stupidity, as in *why should I put up with all this bullshit?* To *bullshit* someone is to deceive or mislead him deliberately, but just *to bullshit* or *to bullshit with* him is to have a friendly conversation. The connotation is triviality or lack of seriousness, rather than deception or hypocrisy.

Horseshit, used as a noun, is similar to *bullshit*, but it is not used as a verb. So, although you can *bullshit* someone or *bullshit with* him, you cannot *horseshit* him or *horseshit with* him. *Horseshit*, however, has uses as adjective and adverb that *bullshit* doesn't have, as in *he did a horseshit job* (bad), and *the motor's running horseshit.*[7]

Chickenshit can be a noun, meaning "petty stuff", but it is more often used as an adjective meaning "trivial" or "meanly trivial", as in *that chickenshit bastard of a sergeant made me polish my shoelaces*, or, as John often says when tangled up in red tape, *what is all this chickenshit bullshit?*

Although *shit* and its compounds are still not universally found in print or in polite society, the taboos seem to be weakening fast. A few survivors persist, but the cult of delicacy that produced so much expurgation is just about dead, and our society seems to be gaining enough semantic sophistication to realize that a word is only a symbol and can in itself be neither dirty nor clean.

Shit has been around for a long time and looks like continuing. As long as it exists, it seems foolish to pretend that it doesn't. I hope that this detailed observation and analysis of it has served to direct attention away from its "dirtiness" and its shock value and toward its usefulness as an index of social and linguistic behavior. Like any detailed examination of language, this one shows certain attitudes and cultural backgrounds on the part of its speakers that are reflected in their use of the language. And analysis of this or any other word gives insight into the functions of language and the processes by which it changes as it shapes, and is shaped by, the way we live our daily lives.

Notes

[1] Jonathan Swift, *Gulliver's Travels* (New York, 1963), p. 135. The book was first published in 1726.

[2] Robert Henryson, *Poems and Fables*, ed. H. Harvey Wood (Edinburgh and London, 1933), pp. xii-xiii.

[3] *Colonial American Writing*, ed. Roy Harvey Pearce (New York, 1956), pp. 436-446. — [*Editor's Note*: Byrd's entry brings to mind the following graffito—the brightest jewel in Saul G.'s collection—commented upon as follows: "The handwriting was the purest Spencer, every curlicue exquisitely executed, each whorl placed exactly. This [graffito] was found on the left wall of a men's room stall in the now defunct restaurant called ROTH'S on Broadway and 47th Street, New York City, circa 1935, and I copied the legend in my little notebook so as to get it down exactly . . .

> *'On the night of June 25th, Colonel R. S. Henderson sat here, after eating a fine fish dinner, and deposited a soft, tan stool.*
>
> *(signed) COL. R. S. HENDERSON'*

I cannot remember whether or not I wept."]

[4] These changes in meaning can be traced from earliest to most recent in the *OED* and from most recent backward in *The American Heritage Dictionary of the English Language*, published first in 1969. Almost any word will yield unsuspected linguistic riches through this process.

[5] Edward Sagarin, in *The Anatomy of Dirty Words* (New York, 1969), p. 42, interprets *scared shitless* in the opposite way, "unable to produce shit because of fear." The reader can choose whichever interpretation seems more valid, based on personal experience.

[6] Harold Wentworth and Stuart Berg Flexner, *Dictionary of American Slang* (New York, 1967), pp. 467-468.

[7] [*Editor's Note*: In our correspondence, Prof. Fleming mentioned the following terms from Romanian, here given in translation: "I'm shitting in your mouth." — "Taking a shit all dressed up." — "May you take a shit in your mother's cunt!" and "He likes to be right there—at the curly top of the shit," comparable to the English "King Shit."

Several (uncommon) expressions formed with *bullshit* are listed in Henry Morgan's "The Cape Cod Reader," *Verbatim* III, No. 3 (1976), p. 16.— In the same publication, see also the excellent article on *shitepoke* (*shitsack*) by Steven R. Hicks, "That Dirty Bird," p. 1.]

TABLE I

NOUN FORMS

scite	Old English	*Past*	
scitte	Old English	scat	Old English
schit	13th century	schoot	14th cent.
schyt	14th cent.	schote	15th cent.
schit	16th cent.	shyt	14th cent.
sheitt	16th cent.	shote	15th cent.
scheitt	16th cent.	shit	19th cent.
sheitte	16th cent.		to present
scheitte	16th cent.		
shite	16th cent. to present	*Participle*	
		-scitan	Old English
shit	16th cent. to present	sciten	Old English
		i-schete	14th cent.
		schetun	14th cent.
VERB FORMS		shitten	14th-18th c.
Present (Infinitive)		shit	19th century to present
scitan	Old English		
schite	14th century		
schete	14th cent.		
schyte	15th cent.		
schyyte	15th cent.		
shyte	14th-16th c.		
shyt	16th cent.		
shite	14th-18th c.		
shit	17th century to present		

TABLE II

1385	Chaucer*	. . . a shiten shepherde and clene sheep.
1387	Trevisa (history)†	þey wolde . . . maken hem a pitte . . . whan þey wolde schite . . . ; and whanne þey hadde i-schete þey wolde fille þe pitte aȝen.
1400	Lanfranc (medicine)	If he may not schite oones a day, helpe him þerto . . . with clisterie.
1425	*Castle of Perserverance*	þey schul schytyn for fere.
1484	*Aesop's Fables*	The wulf . . . shote thryes by the waye for the grete fere that he had.
1527	Andrew (medicine)	An ounce for them that spetteth blode, pysseth blode, or shyteth blode.
1677	Buckingham	You're such a scurvy . . . Knight, That when you speak a Man wou'd swear you S—te.
1720	Gibson *Farrier's Guide*	I have known a hide-bound Horse shit often, and his excrement soft.
1730	*Round about the Coal-Fire*	He was taken with a sharp griping Pain, which made him sh-t Pins and Needles as he thought.
1787	Burns	Just sh-- in a kail-blade, and send it.

*"Prologue to the Canterbury Tales," *The Works of Geoffrey Chaucer*, ed. F.N. Robinson (Boston, 1957), p. 22, line 504.

†*The Oxford English Dictionary* (Oxford, 1933), Vol. IX, p. 715. The obsolete letter þ is equivalent to *th*, the ȝ to *g*. The following examples are all from the same source.

TABLE III

Noun	Derivation	Root	Meaning	Verb
Shit	Anglo-Saxon	SKEI-	cut, split, separate	to shit
Turd	Anglo-Saxon	DER-	split, peel, flay	—
Crap	Middle-Dutch?		tear off, cut off; husks of grain	to crap
Dung	Anglo-Saxon		kin to Old Norse "heap"	—
Manure	Latin	OP-	to work with the hands, maneuvre > cultivate > fertilize > fertilizer	to manure (archaic)
Stool	Anglo-Saxon	STA-	stand > standing seat > close-stool > contents of close-stool	to stool (archaic)
Feces	Latin	faex	dregs, waste	to defecate
Ordure	Latin	GHERS-	bristle (related to "horrid")	—
Excrement	Latin	SKERI-	cut, separate, sift	to excrete
—	Latin	EU-	empty out	to evacuate
—	Latin		out of the threshold	to eliminate

Information on this table is taken from *The American Heritage Dictionary of the English Language* (New York, 1969), and from the *OED*. One unique feature of the former is its appendix of Indo-European roots, shown on the chart in capitals.

PROSTITUTA IN MODERN ITALIAN
I. SUFFIXATION AND THE SEMANTIC FIELD

Edgar Radtke

The present analysis is meant to be a contribution to the linguistic treatment of marginal vocabulary.[1] Looking at current bibliographies, one will soon be convinced of how shamefully "erotology" is neglected in the field of lexicology. This paper therefore presents a linguistic analysis of sexual vocabulary, in the hope of stimulating further scientific investigations of the sphere of so-called "taboo language." The special rank held by sexual vocabulary serves to reveal linguistic structurizations that are typical of this segment of language. It is my intention to prove that suffixation may function as an indicator of special vocabulary; the object is to work out a descriptive analysis of how a linguistic pattern—in this case suffixation—determines marginal vocabulary: does suffixation function as an indicator of sexual vocabulary?

Not all suffixes used in word-formation have been considered here; only suffixes of a subjective approach.[2] Such nominal suffixes represent a new orientation toward the original lexeme, while the new, suffix-bound word assumes an augmentative, diminutive, pejorative, or endearing meaning.

The suffix-bound lexemes of the semantic field *prostituta* in 20th century Italian are:[3]

attricetta 1. *attrice* "actress" + *-etta*; 2. literary; 3. rarely used; 4. euphemism; periphrastic; 6. a prostitute of higher rank; 7. used most frequently in connection with the adjective *lussuosa* "luxurious, expensive"; often found in advertisements in newspapers.

bagascetta 1. *bagascia* "whore" + *-etta*; 2. colloquial; 3. frequently used; 5. mainly in northern Italy, especially Milan; 6. an old, slovenly prostitute; 7. from Vulgar Latin *bacassa*?

baldraccaccia 1. *baldracca* "whore" + *-accia*; 2. colloquial; 3. frequently used; 6. an old, slovenly prostitute.

baldraccona 1. *baldracca* "whore" + *-ona*; 2. low colloquial; 3. frequently used; 6. a low prostitute.

bardassone 1. *bardassa* "a young woman" + *-one*; 2. literary language; 3. less frequently used; 7. *bardassa* also means "a young homosexual man who prostitutes himself"; "an effeminate young man."

cagnaccia 1. *cagna* "bitch" + *-accia*; 2. low colloquial; 3. less frequently used; 4. animal metaphor; dysphemism; 7. Middle French *caigne*; Portuguese *cadelona*.

cavallona 1. *cavalla* "mare" + *-ona*; 2. low colloquial; 3. frequently used; 4. animal metaphor; dysphemism; 6. a low prostitute; a streetwalker; 7. in different contexts, *cavallona* also means "fat woman."

cortigianuzza 1. *cortigiana* "courtesan" + *-uzza*; 2. literary language; 3. less frequently used; 4. euphemism; 6. a prostitute of higher rank.

cravattona 1. *cravatta* "necktie" + *-ona*; 2. low colloquial; 3. rarely used; 4. metonymy; dysphemism; 6. a lesbian prostitute and pimp.

donnaccia 1. *donna* "woman" + *-accia*; 2. colloquial; 3. frequently used.

donnina (allegra) 1. *donna* "woman" + *-ina*; *allegra* "cheerful, merry"; 2. literary language; 3. frequently used; 4. euphemism; 7. Spanish *mujer alegre;* French *joyeuse.*

donnuccia 1. *donna* "woman" + *-uccia*; 2. colloquial; 3. less frequently used; 4. euphemism.

donnucciaccia same as **donnuccia**; *donna* + *-uccia* + *-accia.*

donnucciola same as **donnuccia**; *donna* + *-uccia* + *-ola.*

drondona 1. *dron-dron* "prostitute" + *-ona*; 2. *Furbesco* (criminals' slang of Rome); 3. rarely used; 4. blending; 5. slang of Rome.

femminaccia 1. *femmina* "woman" (vulgarism), "broad" + *-accia*; 2. colloquial; 3. less frequently used.

ficona / figona 1. *fica, figa* "fig"; "vulva" + *-ona*; 2. low colloquial; 3. less frequently used; 4. metonymy; dysphemism; 5. northern Italy: **figona**; 7. also means "sexy girl."

galletto 1. *galla* "gallnut" + *-etto*; 2. slang; 3. rarely used; 4. metonymy; *Camorra* (secret society of the Naples underworld); 6. a prostitute of higher rank.

gallinella 1. *gallina* "hen" + *-ella*; 2. colloquial; 3. less frequently used; 4. animal metaphor.

lolitina 1. *Lolita* (name) + *-ina*; 2. literary language; 3. less frequently used; 4. euphemism; 6. an underage prostitute; 7. from Vladimir Nabokov's novel *Lolita* (1955).

mignottaccia 1. *mignotta* "whore" + *-accia*; 2. low colloquial; 3. less frequently used; 5. originally a Roman term; 6. a low prostitute; 7. from French *mignotte*; from *mignon* "pretty, dainty, delicate, sweet."

ninfetta 1. *ninfa* "nymph" + *-etta*; 2. colloquial; 3. less frequently used; 6. an underage prostitute; 7. Spanish *ninfa*; French *nymphe*.

ninnella 1. *ninna* "sleep" + *-ella*; 2. slang; *Camorra* (see **galletto**); 3. rarely used; 5. Naples; 6. a young, pretty prostitute.

ninnola same as **ninnella**; *ninna* + *-ola*.

peciona 1. *peci* "female breasts" + *-ona*; 2. colloquial; 3. less frequently used; 4. metonymy; 5. Lago Maggiore; Milan.

porcella 1. *porca* "sow" + *-ella*; 2. low colloquial; 3. less frequently used; 4. animal metaphor; dysphemism; 5. Sicilian regionalism: **purcedda**.

porcellone same as **porcella**; *porca* + *-ella* + *-one*.

puttanaccia 1. *puttana* "whore" + *-accia*; 2. low colloquial; 3. less frequently used; 6. a low prostitute.

puttanella see **puttanaccia**; *puttana* + *-ella*.

puttanellaccia see **puttanaccia**; *puttana* + *-ella* + *-accia*.

puttanona see **puttanaccia**; *puttana* + *-ona*.

scopona 1. *scopare* "to sweep"; "to copulate" (vulgar), "to fuck" + *-ona*; 2. low colloquial; 3. frequently used; 6. a low prostitute.

scrofaccia 1. *scrofa* "sow" + *-accia*; 2. low colloquial; 3. less frequently used; 4. animal metaphor; dysphemism.

sgualdrinaccia 1. *sgualdrina* "prostitute" + -*accia*; 2. colloquial; 3. frequently used.
sgualdrinella see **sgualdrinaccia**; *sgualdrina* + -*ella*. Used less frequently than **sgualdrinaccia**.
troiaccia 1. *troia* "sow" + -*accia*; 2. low colloquial; 3. less frequently used; 4. animal metaphor; dysphemism; 6. a low prostitute.
troiona see **troiaccia**; *troia* + -*ona*.
vaccaccia 1. *vacca* "cow" + -*accia*; 2. low colloquial; 3. less frequently used; 4. animal metaphor; dysphemism; 6. a low prostitute; 7. French *vache*; Portuguese *vaca*; Romanian *vacă*.
vacchina see **vaccaccia**; *vacca* + -*ina*.
vaccona see **vaccaccia**; *vacca* + -*ona*.
vecchiaccia 1. *vecchia* "old woman" + -*accia*; 2. low colloquial; 3. less frequently used; 4. dysphemism; 6. an old prostitute; 7. also means "old slut."
zingarona 1. *zingara* "gypsy woman" + -*ona*; 2. low colloquial; 3. rarely used; 4. metonymy; 5. Umbria.

Limiting this study to a quantitative approach, let us examine the distribution of the words according to their stylistic level. With the exception of seven lexemes, all the terms belong to colloquial or low colloquial speech:

TABLE I
Distribution of Nominal Suffixes According to Stylistic Levels

Stylistic Level	Suffix-bound Lexemes	%	
Literary Language	3	7.14	
Colloquial	14	33.33	
Low Colloquial	21	50.00	83.33
Slang	4	9.53	

We mentioned earlier that suffixation implies a personal feeling of affection or contempt towards the object or person denoted. As the concentration of such formations in colloquial and low colloquial speech most obviously proves, these suffixes intensify the affective attitude towards the concept. Thus the scale reflects this basic quality of suffixation.

The occurrence of these suffixes divides the whole complex into two categories:

(i) Suffixes of frequent use:
  -accia 13 x   *-ella* 6 x   *-ona* 11 x
(ii) Suffixes used rarely, occupying a peripheral position only for interpretation:
  -etta/-etto 4 x   *-ina* 3 x   *-ola* 2 x
  -one 2 x   *-uccia* 2 x   *-uzza* 1 x

Discussion of Frequent Suffixes

Among suffixes of frequent use, *-accia* and *-ona* share the most important rank because of their definitely pejorative nuance:

-ONA: In *baldraccona, cavallona, cravattona, drondona, figona, peciona, puttanona, scopona, troiona, vaccona,* and *zingarona,* the suffix *-ona* adds a moral judgment which the original term did not have. The suffix indicates the pejorative function. That is why the lexemes, without exception, definitely are vulgarisms in popular speech.

-ACCIA: The same is true for *-accia,* where Tuscan and Sicilian influences confirm the pejorative character:[4] *baldraccaccia, cagnaccia, donnaccia, femminaccia, mignottaccia, puttanaccia, scrofaccia, sgualdrinaccia, troiaccia, vaccaccia,* and *vecchiaccia.* Especially the *-accia* series includes a great number of animal metaphors which illustrates the low social position that this suffix underlines.

-ELLA: The suffix *-ella* preserves its purely diminutive function to indicate "nice harmlessness": *gallinella, ninnella, porcella, puttanella, puttanellaccia,* and *sgualdrinella.* The speaker aims at a certain kind of minimization of prostitution by the use of this suffix.[5] The suffix partly conditions the endearing function of these lexemes. It arouses a feeling of pity or sentimentality.

Discussion of Less Frequent Suffixes

-INA: *donnina, lolitina, vacchina.*
In *donnina,* the suffix assumes a euphemistic function, mini-

mizing the sememe of "prostitution." In *lolitina*, the suffix intensifies the sememe "youth" and at the same time evokes a tone of affection and pity. It may be considered an ironic form of *Lolita* which appeared in Nabokov's novel. To a certain degree, *vacchina* reduces the vulgar element which predominates in *vacca*.

-ETTA/-ETTO: *attricetta, bagascetta, galletto, ninfetta*. *Attricetta* ironizes the aspect of profession and introduces an ambiguous nuance, including an aspect of endearment. *Ninfetta*, like *lolitina*, denotes above all the youth of the prostitute. *Bagascetta*, originally a term of endearment, is equally widespread in Milan where it has already suppressed *bagascia*. *Galletto* is a slang expression from the *Camorra* of Naples which creates some confusion. Rafael Corso, in his *Das Geschlechtsleben in Sitte, Brauch und Gewohnheitsrecht des italienischen Volkes* (Nicotera, 1914, p. 220), derives it from *gallo* "cock."[6] I reject this idea for a slang term, i. e., a sphere which makes use of metaphors in order to conceal the proper meaning of the term, and I link it with *galla* in the Roman criminals' slang (*Furbesco*) at the beginning of this century, as noted by Luigi Zanazzo in his *Usi, costumi e pregiudizi del popolo di Roma* (Turin, 1908, p. 460). The connection with "gallnut" seems at least more *gergo*-like than the *cock*-interpretation, the point of association being "lightness," i. e. moral frivolity.

-ONE: *bardassone, porcellone*.
In the first case, the augmentative suffix causes a crucial transformation of meaning, as *bardasso* "young" is quite common in southern Italian speech. The other lexeme, *porcellone*, takes on a "caractère augmentatif-hypocoristique, ce qui est une manifestation particulière de l'emploi euphémistique [*sic*] des formes disphémiques."[7]

-UZZA: *cortigianuzza* / -UCCIA: *donnuccia, donnucciuola*. The evaluation of these lexemes depends on the given contexts and admits several nuances: "The meaning of the suffix [-*uzzo*, -*uccio*] oscillates in the written language between a diminutive, pejorative and endearing value. In general, the word composed with -*uccio*/-*uzzo* includes more than one of these nuances."[8]

-OLA: *ninnola, donnucciuola.*
The suffix in *ninnola* in the *Camorra* slang of Naples has a diminutive function. At this point I question Kugler's interpretation: *ninnola* Spielzeug ("toy").[9] This lexeme surely is derived from *ninna* "young, beautiful prostitute" that produced the following derivations in the slang of Naples: *ninna da pampino* "a prostitute who engages in oral coitus," *ninna con spuzatella* "a busy prostitute," *ninnella* "a young, beautiful prostitute" and *ninnola.*[10] The same diminutive function is valid for *donnucciuola.*

Conclusions

In the field of semantics we see that morphemes enrich the number of lexemes. Suffixes most obviously contribute to the shading of the semantic field *prostituta.* These morphemes determine a dimension of their own that modern theories have not yet applied. In this sense I define suffixation as a dimension of subjective approach that tends to a structuralization of the whole semantic field, as our selected examples indicate (*see* TABLE II).

It is interesting that no lexeme absorbs more than two dimensions of subjective approach: this limit marks a degree of saturation. We see that suffixation contributes to fill up minimal linguistic gaps, thus granting an enlarged capacity of communication. Thus it represents a factor that modern word-field theories should consider as a structuralizing pattern, the importance of dimensions having so far been underestimated.[11]

If we include an extralinguistic approach, we see that the subjective attitude of society towards a sexual phenomenon, in our case prostitution, culminates in pejorative and deprecatory formulas. Language reflects an abnormal attitude towards a given social area. This very abnormality determines marginal or special vocabulary[12] and is a crucial aspect of its definition.

Returning to the problems presented at the beginning, I have documented that marginal or special vocabulary may be determined by morphological features such as suffixation. Furthermore, these pertinent characteristics have a function: to reflect social behavior.

TABLE II

Suffixation As a Dimension of Subjective Approach

BS = Basic Seme (*Archisem* in German)
D1 = Dimension of negative valuation
D2 = Dimension of positive valuation
D3 = Dimension of affection/pity (endearing function)
D4 = Dimension of irony
D5 = Dimension of minimizing intention (diminutive aspect)

	BS	D1	D2	D3	D4	D5
(1) Puttana						
puttana	+					
puttanella	+					+
puttanellaccia	+	+				+
puttanaccia	+	+				
puttanona	+	+				
(2) Slang lexemes						
drondona	+	+				
galletto	+		+		+	
ninnella	+		+		+	
ninnola	+		+		+	
(3) Animal metaphors						
cagnaccia	+	+				
cavallona	+	+				
gallinella	+			+	+	
porcella	+			+	+	
porcellone	+	+				+
scrofaccia	+	+				
troiaccia	+	+				
troiona	+	+				
vaccaccia	+	+				
vacchina	+	+			+	
vaccona	+	+				

Notes

[1] Those unfamiliar with marginal vocabulary are urged to consult the useful introduction by Gian Beccaria, "Linguaggi settoriali e lingua comune" in *I linguaggi settoriali in Italia*, ed. Gian Luigi Beccaria (Milan: Bompiani, 1973), 7-59.

[2] See Salvatore Battaglia and V. Pernicone, *La grammatica italiana* (Turin, 1957), 135-136: ". . . suffissi che imprimono nei nomi stessi i segni di giudizio che può riguardare la grandezza o la piccolezza..., oppure può esprimere un sentimento di affetuosa simpatia . . . o di disprezzo." [". . . suffixes that impose the signs of the speakers' judgment on the very names, a judgment that may concern the greatness or the smallness . . , or it may even express a feeling of affection . . . or of scorn."]

[3] The lexemes are taken from my analysis *Aspekte des erotisch-sexuellen Vokabulars des heutigen Italienisch mit besonderer Berücksichtigung der übrigen romanischen Sprachen am Beispiel des Wortfeldes "prostituta"* [Aspects of the erotic and sexual vocabulary in modern Italian, with special consideration of other Romance languages as shown by the semantic field "prostitute"], typescript, Mainz, 1974.

The numbers in the word list refer to the following available data:

1 = word-formation and translation
2 = stylistic level (literary, colloquial, low colloquial, slang)
3 = occurrence (frequent, less frequent, rare)
4 = lexicological patterns
5 = regional provenance
6 = semantic aspect: kind of prostitute/prostitution
7 = additional comments.

[4] In the rest of Italy, *-accia* with accretional function is still alive; the suffix then expresses, as it does in Provençal, a collective idea, e.g. *coltellaccio* "all the knives."

[5] Cf. modern French *fillette* "a young prostitute."

[6] *Gallo* denotes in modern Italian "a young man who flirts with women"; cf. the worldwide Italianism *pappagallo*. An analogous interpretation for the French *cocotte* is found in Leo Spitzer, *Über einige Wörter der Liebessprache* (Leipzig, 1918), 31-51.

[7] Stanisław Widłak, *Moyens euphémistiques* [sic] *en italien contemporain* (Krakow, 1970), Zeszty naukowe Uniwersitetu Jagiellón skiego: Filologia; Prace Językoznawcze Zeszyt 26, page 58.

A TAXONOMY OF THE PROVENANCE
OF METAPHORICAL TERMS OF ABUSE

Reinhold Aman

As is true of every other aspect of the new transdisciplinary science *Maledictology*, we also lack a system of classifying terms of abuse on the basis of their *provenance* or *literal meaning*. The present attempt to establish such a system, or taxonomy, is the result of twelve years of refining earlier systems needed while analyzing 2,500 abusive nouns and adjectives in the Bavarian dialect.

In the course of preparing my lexicon of Austro-Bavarian insults, a number of recurring classes of provenance presented themselves. Additional subclasses had to be established when material from other languages became available.

None of the classification systems for abusive terms used by other researchers—most of whom work(ed) in ignorance of similar research published as early as 1890—is as detailed as the system presented below. It is hoped that your critical review of this taxonomy will enable us to establish a universal taxonomy applicable to all languages and dialects.

A major benefit derived from presenting material by provenance (rather than alphabetically) is the grouping of single-word insults and derogatory phrases by metaphors and similes involved. The article by Warren and Brempong (page 141), using an earlier version of this taxonomy, illustrates its applicability to non-Indo-European languages. The researcher interested in *transfer of meaning* need not read a glossary from *A* to *Z* to find the desired data; instead, one simply consults the appropriate subclass to find all related material gathered.

Such a taxonomy, thus, is primarily intended to organize data according to the literal meaning, to make us aware of the semantic shifts (transfers of meaning), and to observe the predominance of, e.g., professions, animals, or objects used figuratively (metaphorically) to label human beings accused of having certain unpleasant characteristics and annoying physical, intellectual, or social shortcomings.

The *Activity* class is probably the most productive one because of the multitude of negatively valued verbs; because of the great amount of terms in this class, it ought to be broken down into several subclasses, perhaps by morphological elements (word-formation).

Not all terms of abuse can be classified readily, and others may have to be cross-listed. A compound noun should be classified according to its essential element; e.g., *shit-sack* under "Object" (sack), not "Excretion" (shit). The French *Jean-Foutre* belongs to the "First Name" class, not under "Activity" (*foutre* 'to fuck').

Kike, of which we do not know its provenance (but *see* Tamony's article, page 269), holds the record of silly if not stupid "explanations." It may have to be cross-listed under "Family Name" (*-sky*), "First Name" (*Isaac, Ike; Mike*), "Abstract" (*circle, kikel*), "Activity" (*to keek*), and "Profession" (*keeker, kiker* 'fashion spy'). However, it does not belong under "Religion."

Finally, how far back should one trace a word's meaning? We must not confuse its *literal* meaning with its *etymological* meaning. When classifying terms, we are not concerned with etymology but solely with denotation, the literal meaning. *Hamburger* 'fool; jerk; asshole' should be classified under "Food," not "Region/City" ('a native of Hamburg'); *Neanderthal man* 'primitive boor' is to be listed under "Prehistoric Creature," not "Region" ('valley of the Neander river'); and *hick* not under "Profession" ('farmer') or "Characteristics" but under "First Name" ('Richard'). Tracing the meaning back even further, such as to its "real" meaning contained in its (Indo-European) root would be absurd. And it suffices to show, for instance, that the Italian *paglietta* 'a devious, unscrupulous lawyer; a shyster' literally means "strawhat," not "little straw."

Listed below is the taxonomy, with samples from several languages. All literal meanings are shown in double quotation marks, while the transferred, figurative, or metaphorical use is indicated by single quotation marks.

TAXONOMY

1.0. HUMAN

1.1. Nationality/Ethnic Group: *Polack; Turk; Chinese;* German *Schlawiner* "Slovene":'cunning, deceitful man.' Spanish *Alarbe* "Arab" : 'uncouth, brutal person.'

1.2. Region/City: Yiddish *Litvak* "Lithuanian":'skeptic; shrewd businessman'; German *Abderit* "native of Abdera" (city in ancient Greece) : 'simpleton.'

1.3. Race: *Nigger* (as applied to other than Blacks, usually).

1.4. Religion: *Bigot* "by God": 'a person obstinately or intolerantly devoted to his/her opinion'; Yiddish *Goy* "gentile":'blockhead'; German (from Yiddish) *Schickse* "Christian *or* Jewish woman":'cheap broad; whore.' *Cretin* "Christian."

1.5. Political Affiliation: *Commie; Fascist; Nazi.*

1.6. Profession: *Butcher* 'unskilled surgeon'; *Slave driver* 'harsh, severely exacting supervisor'; Spanish *Flautista* "flutist":'penilinctor.'

1.7. Family: *Auntie* 'effeminate male homosexual'; *Cry-baby; Son-of-a-bitch;* Yiddish *Mamzer* "bastard":'nasty man' (etc.); German *Rotzbub* "snot-boy":'sassy youngster'; German *Warmer Bruder* "warm brother": 'male homosexual, queer.'

1.8.1. Last Name: *Dunce; Quisling; Weisenheimer;* German *Kraftmeier* "strength-Meier":'man who shows off, or brags about, his strength.'

1.8.2.1. First Name, Female: *Ginger* 'prostitute who robs her clients'; French *Marie-Salope* "Mary Slut":'slut; miserable, pitiable wretch'; Bavarian *Gretl* "Margaret": 'silly, simpleminded woman'; *Xanthippe.*

1.8.2.2. First Name, Male: *Hick* "Richard"; *John* 'prostitute's client'; *Hillbilly; Smart-alec* "Alexander"; German *August* 'fool; jerk'; French *Jean-Foutre* "John Fuck": 'troublemaker; ungrateful man; hypocrite'; Spanish *Juan Zoquete* "John Chump":'blockhead.'

2.0. BODY PART

2.1. Human: *Asshole; Prick; Cunt; Tits; Twat-face.*

2.2. Animal: *Chicken-brain; Amoeba-brain; Pig-head; Rat-face;* Yiddish *Khazer-fisl* "pig-foot":'one who acts holier-than-thou but has conspicuous defects'; Austrian *Katzn-Nabl* "cat-navel":'silly, stupid person'; German *Hundsfott* "dog-cunt":'scoundrel, knave.'

2.3. Plant: *Banana-head; Cabbage-head; Pickle-puss; Pea-head.*

2.4. Object: *Egg-head; Shit-head; Fat-ass; Addle-pate* "liquid manure head/brain"; *Butter-fingers; Motor-mouth: Pimple-face;* Quechua *Aka-siki* "shit-arse":'jerk; fool.'

2.5. Miscellany: *Red-neck;Yellow-belly; Fuck-face; Sour-puss;* German *Geizhals* "avarice-neck":'stingy man';Yiddish *Lehakhes-ponem* "spite-face":'pigheaded, spiteful, obstinate troublemaker.'

3.0. EXCRETION
Shit; Turd; Fart; Snot; Crud "dried semen"; Spanish *Mocoso* "nasal mucus":'snot-nose; impudent brat; inexperienced youth.'

4.0. ACTIVITY
Mother-fucker; Cunt-licker; Muff-diver; Cock-sucker; Fish-eater 'Catholic'; *Lick-spittle (Spit-licker);* German *Speichellecker* "spit-licker":'servile flatterer, toady'; French *Lèche-cul* "lick-arse, ass-licker":'flatterer'; Spanish *Antropófago* "man-eater":'primitive brute' (Costa Rica); *Whiner; Blabberer; Bluffer; Clod-hopper; Hog-humper* "one who copulates with hogs":'native of Iowa'; *Show-off; Fuck-off;* German *Spinatstecher* "spinach-piercer":'male homosexual who engages in anal intercourse' (*Spinat* 'feces'); *Hanger-on; Gadabout;* Yiddish *Tsitsis-bayser* "one who bites [fervently kisses] *tsitsis*" (fringes of prayer shawl):'overly devout, holier-than-thou, religious show-off'; Austrian *Kirzlschlicker* "candle-swallower":'overly religious show-off'; Christian counterpart of the Jewish *Tsitsis-bayser.*

5.0. CHARACTERISTICS
Dummy; Fool; Nobody; Moron; Imbecile; Nitwit; Shorty; Bony; German *Bockbeiniger* "billy-goat-legged one":'obstinate pighead.'

6.0. CREATURE

6.1.1. Prehistoric, Human: *Caveman; Troglodyte.*

6.1.2. Prehistoric, Animal: (no examples known).

6.2.1. Mythological, Human: *Witch; Monster; Zombie; Ghost.*

6.2.2. Mythological, Animal: *Mooncalf* 'simpleton'; German *Drachen* "dragon":'shrew; nagging woman.'

6.3. Miscellany: *Freak; Yahoo.*

7.0. ANIMAL

7.1. Mammal: *Cow; Pig; Monkey; Copy-cat;* German *Bibelhengst* "Bible-stallion":'bigot; religious zealot'; *Dog-in-the-manger* 'one who selfishly withholds from others that which is useless to him'; German *Neidhammel* "avarice-wether":'envious man; dog-in-the-manger.'

7.2. Bird: *Goose; Jay; Turkey; Vulture.*

7.3. Reptile: *Crocodile* 'one who hypocritically affects sorrow'; *Snake; Snake-in-the-grass; Reptile.*

7.4. Amphibian: *Frog; Toad;* German *Kröte* "toad":'sassy young woman.'

7.5. Fish: *Shark; Loan-shark.*

7.6. Mollusk: *Clam.*

7.7. Crustacean: *Crab; Shrimp.*

7.8. Insect: *Gadfly;* Bavarian *Weps* "wasp":'restless person, one who never sits still.'

7.9. Miscellany: *Animal; Beast; Parasite; Vermin; Worm.*
Note: Further subdivisions are possible in each class: Domesticated vs. Wild; Native vs. Exotic; Edible vs. Nonedible (taboo, etc.).

8.0. PLANT

8.1. Tree, Wood: *Chump;* German *Klotz* "wooden block, log, chump":'blockhead'; *Son-of-a-birch/beech* (hum.).

8.2. Grass, Grain: *Hayseed.*

8.3. Flower: *Wallflower;* German *Mauerblümchen* "wallflower":'girl rarely asked to dance.'

8.4. Fruit: *Fruit* 'male homosexual'; German *Pflaume* "plum" :'foolish person.'

8.5. Vegetable: *Vegetable;* Bavarian *Erdapfl* "earth-apple, potato":'uncouth, boorish, crude man; peasant.'
Note: Further subdivisions: Native vs. Exotic; Edible vs. Nonedible (e.g. taboo, poisonous).

9.0. OBJECT

9.1. **Tool, Utensil:** *Tool; Hobnail; Dumbbell; Douche-bag; Yo-yo* (a toy, even though a name in the Philippines); *Knob; Crack-pot; Wind-bag;* German *Stöpsel* "cork, plug":'runt'; Bavarian *Kruzifix* "crucifix":'a very annoying, nasty, rotten man; troublemaker'; Yiddish *Farshtoybte mezuze* "dusty mezuzah":'old spinster'; German *Flegel* "flail":'churl; uncouth youth.'

9.2. **Musical Instrument:** Spanish *pandero* "large tambourine" :'silly person; prattler'; German *Flöte* "flute":'silly person'; Bavarian *Schoasdrumme* "fart-drum":'an old woman.'

9.3. **Clothes:** *Wet blanket; Stuffed shirt; Smarty-pants; Slyboots;* German *Lump* "rag":'scoundrel;bum';*Saboteur* (French *sabot* 'wooden shoe').

9.4. **Food:** *Creampuff; Fruitcake; Hotdog; Meatball; Hamburger; Dumpling; Wiener; Kraut.*

9.5. **Animal Product:** Quechua *Maqllu* "unfertilized egg": 'male homosexual.'

9.6. **Plant Product:** *Sap; Stick-in-the-mud.*

9.7. **Miscellany:** *Dung-heap; Slime; Scum; Clod; Drip.*

10.0. SOUND
Dingaling; Ding-dong; Spanish (Navarra) *renrén* 'fool.'

11.0. ABSTRACT
Pain; Pain-in-the-ass/neck; Cube; Square; Zero; Fraud; Pest; Spanish *Náusea* 'disgusting person'; German *Ekel* "nausea":'nasty, disgusting person'; German *Hundertfünfundsiebziger* or *175er* "hundred-seventy-fiver": 'male homosexual' (based on former section §175 of the Criminal Code); *Vierhundertfünfundsiebziger* or *475er* "four-hundred-seventy-fiver":'very rich homosexual' (humorous: a *175er* who owns a Mercedes *300*).

12.0. MISCELLANEOUS
Namby-pamby; Fuddy-duddy; Nincompoop; Has-been; Nerd; Twerp; Snarf (humorous: 'one who gets sexually aroused by smelling girls' bicycle seats').

COMMON PATIENT-DIRECTED PEJORATIVES
USED BY MEDICAL PERSONNEL

C. J. Scheiner

All professions have a slang which serves to convey a large amount of information or an entire situation in a shorthand form. Negative feelings or situations can be expressed verbally, and often very colorfully, through the use of pejoratives which, if they are incorporated into a professional slang, become part of a semi-secret vocabulary that reinforces a sense of solidarity and separation from others not of the particular profession.

Two conditions anger physicians and medical personnel in particular: *(1)* patients who do not follow medical advice, and *(2)* patients who do not respond as expected to medical therapy. The former may be considered a defiance of authority, while the latter is a reminder of the limitations of the medical practitioner.

The following is a short list of commonly encountered pejoratives directed against patients, collected from oral use in a large hospital in New York, from 1976 to 1978. The list does not include terms as commonly used by non-medical personnel, for example *stupid* or *creep*, nor does it include pejoratives that simply incorporate medically related terms, e.g. *spineless* or *shithead*. This study is not in any way exhaustive, and does not include many terms used possibly in various specialty areas of this particular hospital, and certainly not all the terms used in various hospitals in or outside of New York.

Botanist see **Veterinarian**

Crock   a patient who medically abuses himself, often with alcohol. Either short for "crock of shit" or from "crocked" = drunk.

Dispo   a patient admitted to the hospital with no real medical problem other than being unable to care for himself/herself in his/her present circumstances. Short for "**dis**position **pro**blem."

Ethanolic   an alcoholic.

F.O.S.   abbreviation for "full of shit." 1: a severely constipated patient, often impacted with months of unpassed feces. 2: a patient who lies to gain medically unnecessary drugs.

Fruit Salad   a group of stroke patients, all totally unable to care for themselves. See **Vegetable**.

Geologist see **Veterinarian**

Gork   a mentally deficient patient, either congenitally, secondary to chronic drug or alcohol abuse, or following a cerebral contusion or bleed. Also, "to heavily sedate."

Gorked Out   semi-comatose.

Gun and Rifle Club   a trauma ward to which stabbing and gunshot victims are admitted.

Hotdog   a flamboyant or bizarre patient, usually with psychiatric problems.

H.Y.S.   abbreviation for "**hys**terical."

International House of Pancakes   a neurology ward occupied by patients, often stroke victims, all of whom babble in a different language.

Loxed   a decreased state of consciousness, usually following a cardiac or respiratory arrest. Contraction for "lack of oxygen." Also, "loxed out."

No Squash   a condition of irreparable brain damage, most often from trauma, intracranial hemorrhage, drug abuse, or prolonged anoxia; see **Vegetable Garden**.

O.D.   abbreviation for "overdose." A particularly despised patient, as the cause of this malady is self-induced.

Pits the medical screening area of a hospital, particularly hated by physicians because of the enormous amounts of insignificant medical maladies that must be treated there in a hospital setting. Also known as the **Screaming Area**.

P.M.D. abbreviation for "private medical doctor." A physician who refers his apparently ill patients to the hospital Emergency Room rather than diagnose and treat them himself. This is one of the few pejoratives directed at a member of the professional group.

P.O.S. abbreviation for "piece of shit." A general term for patients medically ill because of their own failure to care for themselves (most often alcoholics).

Potato Patch see **Vegetable Garden**

P.P. abbreviation for "professional patient." A person who appears regularly, either daily or weekly, at the Emergency Room for trivial complaints such as the refill of innocuous medicines or the treatment of chronic symptoms that are never present at the time of examination.

P.P.P. abbreviation for "piss poor protoplasm." A debilitated patient, often requiring surgery, who needs extensive medical treatment, including transfusions, before he is able to undergo definitive therapy.

Quack a patient who fakes symptoms to gain unnecessary hospitalization or drugs.

Rose Garden see **Vegetable Garden**

Saturday Night Special a patient, usually an alcoholic, who has spent his money, and comes to the hospital on the weekend looking for a meal and a place to stay.

Schizo short for "**schizo**phrenic." Any mentally abnormal patient.

Screamer a hysterical patient.

Screaming Area see **Pits**

Scut menial medical procedures that must be carried out, usually relegated to the least senior member of the medical team. Also, any patient held in extremely low esteem.

SHPOS acronym for "sub-human piece of shit." A chronic **P.O.S.** A critically ill patient who, after intensive medical care and rehabilitation, fails to follow medical instructions, and is readmitted to the hospital in his previous critical condition.

Stage Mother an adult who coaches younger patients as to their alleged symptoms, and generally states what medical tests and procedures are necessary.

THE COCKNEY'S HORN BOOK
THE SEXUAL SIDE OF RHYMING SLANG

Leonard R. N. Ashley

Slang as a word came into English (from slang itself) before 1756, when it was first recorded. As a lively linguistic phenomenon, slang has been with us much longer, as the *Dictionary of the Canting Crew* and *A New Canting Dictionary* (both in the first half of the Eighteenth Century) testify. With Grose's *Dictionary of the Vulgar Tongue* (first published in 1785 and frequently reprinted), slang came into its own and in our century has attracted such experts as the redoubtable Eric Partridge. Dr. Johnson ponderously pontificated that "of the laborious and mercantile part of the people the diction is in great measure casual and mutable," but it is in their slang that they show their genius.

I have written extensively on British slang for food and drink and money and now wish to offer a brief article on another necessity, sex. Other articles on British sexual slang will follow, but here I shall limit myself to rhyming slang. I do not mean *claptrap, sure cure,* and *hot shot* (though sexual meanings attach to *AC/DC, rough stuff,* and so on) but the Cockney rhyming slang that involves *apples* (*apples and pears* = 'stairs') and *Bristols* (*Bristol City* = 'tittie'). Use your *loaf* ('head').

In "Rhyme and Reason: The Methods and Meanings of Cockney Rhyming Slang, Illustrated with Some Proper Names and Some Improper Phrases" (*Names* XXV, No. 3, September 1977, 124-154) I examined chiefly those examples which derive from proper names. These included some sexual slang:

> A comedy in the vulgar, popular "Carry On" series was called *Carry On Up the Khyber*, hinting to the informed who recognize that *Khyber Pass* (famous from the days of the British *raj* in India) rhymes with *ass*. . . . No use objecting that the Cockney says *arse* and that it does not rhyme; how do you think he pronounces *pass*? (A Spanish teacher telling an East London class to "roll your r's" is asking for trouble. . . .)

* * *

On BBC television on October 29, 1975 they [the comedy team of Morecambe and Wise] gave us this little exchange:

> *I grew spices for a man in India.*
> *Ginger?*
> *No, he was married.*

Got it? No? Well, *ginger beer* = 'queer.'

* * *

But who can cope with *trolley* = 'copulate' (from *trolley and truck*, in a country where our truck is a van!) . . . .

* * *

> Oh, my sister's name is Tilly,
> She's a whore in Picadilly,
> And my mother is another in The Strand.
> And my brother peddles arsehole
> At the Elephant and Castle.
> We're the finest f——ing family in the land.

The fact that the slang contains other meanings for *elephant*, or that *au fond* there are plenty of terms for 'bottom'—*bottle* (and glass), *North Pole* ('hole'), and *Khyber* (as we have said)—deters no one. The peculiar Cockney pronunciation of *castle* (carsole) is to be found also in rhyming slang such as *Crimea* ('beer'), *Balaclava*, *chaver*. . . .

Then I had to explain that *chaver* = 'sexual intercourse', perhaps derived from the French *chauffer* ("to heat up") or the Romany *charvo* ("to fool around"). These foreign tongues are rather complicated!

The concentration in that article on proper names produced theatrical names (*J. Knowles* = 'holes'; *Tommy Dodd* = 'sod', as in sodomy and *sod off* = 'fuck off'; *Beattie & Babs* = 'crabs', including the word as used for body lice; and *Mae West* = 'breast'), play titles (as *Colleen Bawn* = 'horn', that is 'erection', also *Marquis of Lorne*) and people's titles (*Duke of Kent* = 'bent', which is the equivalent of the American *twisted* sexually but not as queer as *kinky*), etc. Place-names turned up (*Burton* [on Trent] = *rent*, 'a male hustler'; *Hampton Wick* = 'prick', with "He gets on my wick" for the US "He bugs me"; and *Niagara* [Falls] = 'balls', but in the sense of UK *rubbish* and US *bullshit*, not 'testicles'—those are *bollocks*, *fun and frolics*, and *cobblers* [awls]—the latter serving for both *bollocks* and *bullshit*). Also in evidence were department stores in London such as *C & A* = 'gay' (homosexual)—with "Cocksucker and Arsehole" explaining the initials—and *Barker's* = *starkers* ('nude', US *stark naked*). Literature provided *Friar Tuck* = 'fuck', and horses both *Berkeley Hunt* = 'cunt' (in the sense of "you stupid cunt," not a synonym for *vagina*—often "you stupid *berk*") and *Harry Wragg* = 'fag', after a once-famous jockey, but *fag* in the sense of cigarette, not US faggot—for which the UK is *pouf* or *poufter*, *nancy*, *fairy*, etc. *Beggar boy's* [ass] is not sexual: it means Bass (ale). More examples are *Pat and Mick* = 'prick', *Rory O'More* = 'whore' (also *scrubber*, *slag*, etc.), and *Alphonse* = *ponce* ('pimp'). The article went into detail about linguistic and historical matters and attempted to demonstrate that in Cockney Rhyming slang's onomastic aspects we have one more example of the "richness, good sense, and terse convenience" for which Jakob Grimm praised the English language.

There are other, more general if less modern and correct, studies of Cockney rhyming slang, though they tend to skirt *Tom Tit* ('shit'), *rattle* [and hiss] ('piss'), *you and me* ('pee') and *me and you* ('screw', which in England often means *pay packet* or *wages* but has come to mean, as in the US, 'fuck', *stuff*, even *bugger*). To Julian Franklyn's standard book *The Cockney* have been added an anonymous *Dictionary of Rhyming Slang* (published by John Langdon, London, 1941) and little books such as Bob Aylwin's *A Load of Cockney Cobblers* (1973) and the even smaller *Rhyming Cockney Slang* (1971, edited by Jack Jones). From these we may garner some rhyming slang on sexual matters not covered in my onomastics article.

Mr. Aylwin has a two-page section on "Vulgarity." Too brief, and he occasionally is unreliable: *elephant* [and castle] is not "arse" but the rhyming "arsehole." To *Berkeley Hunt*, however, he is able to add these other words for *cunt*, though he mixes up the terms used to describe female anatomy and those used only as insults (stupid *berk*): *gasp & grunt, growl & grunt, Joe Hunt, sharp & blunt*. He misses the acting duo of *The Lunts* and *junta* = *cunter* 'playboy', *ass-bandit*, formerly *molrower* (now obsolete, like so many other vivid sex terms: *swive, Athenian, ell*, etc. — Partridge has a charming book on *Shakespeare's Bawdy*). He gives us several terms for tits/titties (*Bristol Cities, cat and kitties, Tale of Two Cities*) and balls (*coffee stalls, orchestra stalls*, and *flowers and frolics*, as he has it for *bollocks*) and also lists:

All forlorn Horn	*Giggle Stick* Prick	*Levy & Frank* Wank
Bang & Biff Syph[ilis]	*Gypsy's Kiss* Piss	*Mad Mick* Prick
Beattie & Babs Crabs	*Hampton Wick* Prick	*Manchester Cities* [Titties
Bottle & Glass Arse	*Hanson Cabs* Crabs	*Marquis of Lorne* Horn
Coachman on the Box Pox	*Hit & Miss* Piss	*Pat & Mick* Prick
Colleen Bawn Horn	*Jodrell Bank* Wank	*Threepenny Bits* Tits
Cream Crackers Knackers [balls]		*Khyber Pass* Arse

Some problems: *Bang* usually means 'fuck' (often 'fuck hard', which in UK is *fuck rotten*), so one would always have to add the & *Biff*, while some of the other expressions (he does not indicate which) omit the rhyming word; *horn* requires the explanation we have given above; and some of the expressions require notes (Jodrell Bank is an astronomical observatory, though Aylwin marks it "R.H.A."—Royal Horse Artillery?). It has to make *eighteen pence* ('sense') to non-native speakers.

Elsewhere Aylwin lists a few more "Vulgarities": *Samuel Hall* ('ball'), words for breasts (*brace and bits, east and west, Jersey City, thousand pities, towns and cities, fainting fits*), whore (*boat and oar*), queer (*Brighton Pier*, though often in the sense of "peculiar" rather than what Aylwin calls a "puff", *collar and cuff*), pimp (*fish and shrimp*), love (*heavens above*), kiss (*hit or miss* again), geezer (*ice cream freezer*, a *geezer* being an old man in common parlance but a *client* to a *rent boy*), spunk (*Maria Monk, spunk* meaning courage as in US "full of spunk" but equivalent to sperm or *cum* in some British circles), bitch (*Miss Fitch*, the opposite of masculine *butch* in *camp* homosexual slang), *nancy* (*tickle your fancy*, a *homo*), and others which are *two thirty* ('dirty'). He gives both *two by four* and *six to four* for 'whore.'

Jack Jones adds *band in the box* (*pox*), *fife and drum* (*bum*, as in posterior, an example of the nursery lingo which gives us *ta* = thank you and *pee* = piss), *iron hoof* ('pouf'), *Nervo and Knox* ('pox', from part of the old Crazy Gang vaudeville team), etc. His *oily rag* ('fag') is a cigarette.

Since "Ducange Anglicus" and his *The Vulgar Tongue* (1857), which noted some still current examples (such as *barnet* = 'hair', from *Barnet Fair*), rhyming slang has been of interest to the general public in England. (Even in America we have picked up examples you may not have noticed as such: *brass tacks* = facts in "let's get down to brass tacks" and *sorry* [and sad] = bad in "what a sorry sight.") In Britain there are fairly frequent journalistic articles on rhyming slang. We may cite "Slang It to Me in Rhyme" in the *Daily Telegraph* (December 17, 1971). There "vulgarities" are restrained but we find: *Alan Whickers* = 'knickers' (women's panties), the Barrow Boy's donkey *barrey moke* = *poke* ('fuck'), *Bristol Cities* = 'breasts' (titties, of course), *Brahms 'n' Liszt* = "inebriated" (*pissed*), *fainting fits* = 'the bosom', *ginger beer* = 'queer' (not as in peculiar), *oily rag* = 'fag' (apparently unaware of the non-smoking variety), and *padlock* = "anatomy again" ('cock', penis). *Tale of Two Cities* is glossed as "a literary approach to the human form divine this time" and *Tom Thumb* (*bum*) as "also, but the rear as opposed to the front projections." *Brahms* can also mean 'urinated' as well as 'drunk' (*pissed as a newt* or *harry flakers*, which is 'half drunk'). Whickers is known for a BBC–TV travelogue of recent vintage (though *Errol Flynn* = 'chin', *Vera Lynn* = 'gin', and murderer *Dr. Crippen* = 'dripping', as in cookery rather than in the clap, have stayed in the language though they have passed out of the news). The *Telegraph* author's shyness (or his editor's) seems to prevent him from speaking more to our purpose. He also finds it convenient to deny much familiarity with things *yank*: *Mutt and Jeff* = 'deaf' he says is "popular, but oddly enough based on an American [comic] strip cartoon (I think)," while he doesn't seem to recognize the American origin of *George Raft* ('draught'), *Mickey Mouse* ('house'), *Raquel Welch* ('belch'), and so on.

This pose is at least as old as Capt. Francis Grose's Preface to his dictionary of 1785 in which he stresses that the author,

> when an indelicate or immodest word has obtruded itself for explanation, . . . has endeavoured to get rid of it in the most delicate manner possible; and none has been admitted but such as could not be left out without rendering the work incomplete, or in some manner compensate by their wit for the trespass committed on decorum.

The result has been too much neglect of the often witty slanguage of the Cockneys (and others) and in rhyming slang false modesty about words that simply look as if they might be sexual: *cock* [linnet] = 'minute', not to mention expressions such as *old cock* (buddy, *mate*), *standing peter* (we say "standing pat"), *peter that* ('shut up'), or even *pissing down with rain* ('raining cats and dogs'). One rejoices in *Maledicta*'s frank interest in words that are a vital part of our linguistic heritage. "Who else will tell you these things?" I, for one, propose to continue my onomastic and other linguistic studies in British and American sexual slang and hope to fill more of these pages in *Maledicta* in the future with articles on the difference between US and UK "low" vocabularies, "Kinky English" (British terms for sexual perversions), "Get you, Mary" (the use of proper names in *camp* slang), and studies of *poufs* and *dykes* and *aunties* and *chickens* and *flashers* and *leather queens* and other denizens of the sexual subcultures. The next installment may possibly deal with the salty language of *scrubbers, rent, drag queens,* and the ladies who advertise in London corner shops "Chest For Sale" and "Miss Fifi Gives French Lessons." If you see me in low dives—"I'm writing a book."

HOW TO HATE THY NEIGHBOR
A GUIDE TO RACIST MALEDICTA

Merritt Clifton

In his old age, philosopher Martin Buber wrote, "I have come to
the conclusion that there are only two sorts of people. There
are those who are for humanity, and those who are against us."
Jesus held similar views: "He who is not with me is against
me" (Luke 11:23, Matthew 12:30). "There's us an' there's
them," the man on the street might put it, "an' they're all
alike." Less refined in his language, but equally self-certain,
self-righteous, and emphatic, he might then evoke any word
or phrase below. From great teachers to the first great ape
who learned to talk, thereby distinguishing himself in his own
eyes from 'inferior' primates, "There's us an' there's them"
stands as cornerstone of all great institutions and great civili-
zations. Only the identity of "them" changes, to protect the
guilty.

Terms used to label "them" can be categorized in as many
ways as we categorize ourselves. There are **sexual** "thems":
*cunts, twats, queers, queens, cocksuckers, fags, mama's boys,
Teddy-boys, Apaches,* and enough others to fill a glossary as
long as this one. There are **social** "thems": *twits, bums, creeps,
fops,* and many terms with enough racial or ethnic overtones
to be included here. Most commonly, however, "them" is them
of **another color, another language, another background**:
strangers, to be held at arm's length. Every society mixes men
and women, at least in the bedchamber. Rich and poor are
always with us. Outsiders, foreigners, are not. In extremely
isolated societies, like China during the Great Wall era, or

Japan before Commodore Perry, the single phrase "foreign devils" might cover all external threats to the familiar, "civilized" status quo. In highly transient, unstable societies, however, such as Western and Eastern Europe both since the Middle Ages, with almost ceaseless warfare, international commerce, and boundary shifts, the number of different types of foreigner requires invention of numerous different terms, to make sure all are properly identified. Identification is necessary because knowing who and what a stranger is reduces his threat; one can expect certain behavior and be prepared for it. Thus the most quarreled-over regions of Europe, from the Balkans to Basque country, the Alsace-Lorraine to Ireland, have spawned racial and ethnic maledicta with a vigor and virulence equal to that of flint and gunpowder. As refugees from those lands arrived in the United States, Canada, Australia, and New Zealand, they transferred their invective from European to domestic targets; competing with blacks for jobs, they made *nigger* common speech, and with other immigrants, similarly established *mick* and *polack*. As the Melting Pot mixed and mingled all, tensions became dissipated through humor, so that *niggers, micks,* and *polacks* appear most often today in jokes, not serious speech. Especially since radio, television, and mass circulation books and newspapers, racist and ethnic maledicta have lost their punch; we know each other now. But the words remain alive. So do the attitudes, only now "them" more often refers to **abstract belief** than to external characteristics: *Christers. Commies. Pigs.*

Because serious, dedicated racists have so declined in numbers as to leave the language and diction of racism somewhat obscured, the following strives to give exact meanings and origins, as opposed to commonly known general meanings. Not all, but a sound majority or the terms below derive from one or another of three common sources. The first is not external appearance, as one might suppose, but diet, and in particular to dietary taboos for one group of people that another violates. The second is habitual or traditional occupations, including social practices violating other taboos. The third is external appearance. A fourth, less offensive group of terms are simply diminutives, indicating excessive familiarity or inferiority on the part of the person thus addressed. These last are the terms most often used today, and those most often reflecting unconscious racism rather than deliberate, self-cognizant racial hatred.

Arky Any person from Arkansas. Sometimes extended to mean anyone from the Ozarks. Primarily applied to "white trash," or poor white sharecroppers; very rarely applied to blacks and Indians.

Aussie Anyone from Australia, other than aborigenes.

Ayrab Anyone from an Arab country, or of Islam religion excepting Black Muslims, or of Arab ancestry. Sometimes applied to Sephardic Jews by Jews of [East] European descent, as a gesture of extreme contempt, indicating the European Jewish attitude that Jews having adopted some Arab customs are not true Jews at all. Popularized by singer Ray Stevens in "Ahab The Ayrab"; now chiefly humorous.

Bean, Bean-eater, Beaner, Beano Any Chicano, Mexican, Latin American, or other brown-skinned person for whom beans are a dietary staple. Still a fighting insult, but less so since the movie "Freebie & The Bean," with a Chicano narcotics agent as co-hero.

Belgie Anyone from Belgium. Not commonly used in North America, but common in England and particularly in Agatha Christie mystery novels.

Bible-belter Anyone from the so-called Bible Belt, covering the American South and Midwest. Applied chiefly to poor whites of the sort attending revival meetings; implies ignorance, gullibility, and backwardness. Sometimes also applied to blacks, especially black Baptists.

Black The preferred term for referring to dark-skinned people of African ancestry today, but a fighting insult a generation ago. Terms such as "blackmail," "blackguard," and "blackhearted" today fall from favor because of black's racial implications, though race had little to do with coining those terms originally, most of them dating back to times when blacks and whites had little contact, hence little friction.

Blackie Diminutive applied to any black person.

Blood A black ghetto term for any black person, but most often applied to young men. Possible derivation: "blood brother," related to "soul brother."

Bogger, Bog-rat, Bog-hopper Irish countryfolk in Ireland itself; anyone of Irish descent elsewhere. From the peat-bogs of Ireland, chief source of fuel and fertilizer for Irish peasants.

Bohemian Legitimate term for anyone from Bohemia, a region now incorporated into Czechoslovakia. Toward the end of the Middle Ages, *Bohemian* became a derogatory name for refugee soldiers-of-fortune; Sir Walter Scott speaks of Bohemians of this sort in his novel, *Quentin Durward*. Such soldiers-of-fortune usually were rude, ill-dressed, and unkempt, and gradually the *Bohemian* label shifted from them to anyone of similar appearance and habits. By the late 19th century, career students, poor artists and writers, and their associates were all considered *Bohemians*, regardless of dress, cleanliness, and mannerisms. When following World War I the Dada movement emerged in art and literature from Eastern Europe, *Bohemian* once again became associated with genuine Bohemians. However, as the Beatniks and others adopted tenets from Dada, Bohemianism again came to refer to a manner of living: long hair, dismal quarters, and intellectual expatriatism, in particular. Now largely fallen from usage.

Bohunk Applied to legitimate Bohemians, orginally; literally describes ancestral link between Czechoslovakians and Hungarians through the Huns and the Magyars. Subsequently, anyone called a *Bohemian* has also been called a *Bohunk*, especially if large, clumsy, dull-witted, or loutish.

Boss Any overbearing or racist white person, used by blacks in mockery of the slave's mandatory "Yowsah, Boss," to any order or request. Step'n Fechit always exaggerated his pronunciation of "Yassuh" to "Yowser."

Boy According to time-honored Deep South usage, any black person *younger* than a white speaker. Also applied sometimes to other non-whites, and used in ironic retaliation by blacks. See **Uncle**.

Brother Shortened form of "soul-brother." See **Blood**.

Buck, Buckwheat Initially, a *buck* meant any young Indian male, after the traditional buckskin loincloth. Later the term was applied to young black males as well. Buckwheat was simply the wild wheat bucks ate, a darker, coarser wheat than that cultivated for white people. In time, however, *Buckwheat* became a general term applied to all blacks, whether bucks or not. Still later, *Buckwheat* became adopted by urban blacks as a form of familiar greeting: "Hey, Buckwheat! Wha's happenin'?" Subsequently, during the sixties, some urban whites adopted the greeting, unaware of its origins and implications, so that whites too may be called *Buckwheat* on occasion. A false but popular etymology has *Buckwheat* coming from "Aunt Jemima," the black woman pictured on the trademarked Buckwheat pancake mix. Actually, "Aunt Jemima" made the pancake mix box because blacks had been associated with buckwheat for fully three centuries before her.

Burrhead, Burry-headed Either blacks or South Sea Islanders, whose hair grows in kinks resembling grass burrs.

Cajun Originally applied strictly to Acadians, the French settlers in New Brunswick, who after a prolonged, bitter, and bloody war with English settlers were driven from Canada into the Mississippi River basin. Gradually they migrated south, mixed extensively with Indians and other immigrant whites, and retained only some semblance of the French language from the Acadian culture. Today a *Cajun* is almost anyone from Louisiana, particularly rural dwellers; anyone in the Mississippi River region, north or south, who bears a French name or speaks with a French accent; anyone from that region of mixed white and Indian ancestry who isn't definitely something else; any black trying to pass as white or Indian; and especially anyone claiming descent from the original Acadians.

Californicator Loosely, anyone from California or advocating Californian ways of life and urban sprawl. Popularized by the Oregon anti-development and anti-litter signs and bumper-stickers: DON'T CALIFORNICATE OREGON. Directed at

Californian tourists and businessmen, these signs caught on like wildfire circa 1970 and now may be seen throughout the American West.

Canajun Any Canadian, but especially a French-Canadian. Related to *Cajun*; perhaps a blend of *Cana*dian + *Cajun*.

Canuck Any Canadian, probably after 'Johnny Canuck,' an 18th- and 19th-century cartoon character similar to Yankee Doodle and John Bull. Many dictionaries say "chiefly French-Canadian," but this isn't supported by observation of usage in Canada.

Carpetbagger Orginally, *carpetbaggers* were northern fortune-seekers who flocked into the beaten South after the American Civil War, attempting to marry into land-owning families, seizing political power because former Confederate soldiers could neither hold office nor vote, and generally looting, raping, and otherwise making themselves obnoxious. They were named after their cheap suitcases, stitched together from carpeting material. Gradually, a *carpetbagger* came to be any outsider who entered the South to effect change, regardless of what that change might be. The term also spread to other regions, acquiring a meaning in labor relations similar to *scab*: an imported laborer. A *carpetbagger* in labor, however, more often works in management than on production lines.

Chico A familiar diminutive applied to males of Spanish-American descent, especially in professional sports: Chico Cardenas, Chico Fernandez, and Chico Salmon, for instance, all Latin-American major-league infielders, and Chico Ruiz, a Chicano infielder. Since the sixties, "Chico" is dropping out of usage: Cardenas, for one, eventually refused to answer to it, and no player has been called "Chico" on the big-league level since 1973.

Chile Bean See **Bean**.

Chinaman Accurately, any person of Chinese ancestry. Commonly applied to all Asians in the American Midwest.

Chink Any Chinese person, or person of Chinese ancestry.

Chocolate Any black person, but especially a woman or homosexual. Used as often as an endearment as for derogatory purposes, by both blacks and whites. Literally, a black person one would like to eat, unless used as just a euphemism for *nigger.* See **High Yaller.**

Clod-hopper Any rural person, especially a farmer. Refers more often to independent, land-owning farmers than to "white trash," and is very rarely used with reference to non-whites. Also applies to a farmer's boots or overshoes.

Colored Formerly the favored term for dark-skinned people, especially of African descent. Still used in the South, but almost obsolete elsewhere.

Coolie Anyone of Oriental descent; any Oriental, but especially one of lower caste, working in the fields.

Coon Any black person, especially black males. This dates back not much farther than the 1880s, most probably, and could be still more recent. After Ku Klux Klan lynchings began to attract widespread criticism circa 1886, night riders began euphemistically calling their raids "coon-hunts," after genuine raccoon-hunting, a rural Southern pastime somewhat similar to fox-hunting, conducted on horseback, with dogs, but by night rather than by day because raccoons are nocturnal. The object of a "coon-hunt" of course had to be a "coon." (Folklore: What sort of dog is best for coon-hunting? A bloodhound. — See definition of **Blood.**)

Corkney Pun on the Cockney accent and traditional Cockney alcoholism.

Corn-husker Any Nebraskan, after Nebraska's main crop and dietary staple. Originally derogatory, since corn-husking is a dull, tedious task, but made respectable by the University of Nebraska Corn-Husker football and basketball teams.

Cowboy In the derogatory sense, anyone who affects "cowboy" mannerisms. A dude. Used as a regional slur against any resident of cattle-country; implies latent homosexuality, bestiality, swaggering bravado without real courage, and general obnoxiousness.

Dago Any Italian, Spaniard, or Portuguese person, or person of Italian, Spanish or Portuguese descent. Derived from the first name, *Diego.* (Folklore: Why does time fly in Italy? Because every time you turn around, you see a *day go.*)

Darkie Diminutive, patronizing term for any black person, but especially Southern blacks. Stephen Foster's songs have fallen into academic disfavor over frequent mentions of *darkies*: "You can hear them darkies singin', you can hear their banjos ringin'. . . ."

Desert rat Any rural American Southwesterner, used with pride by *desert rats* themselves.

Dink Literally, any physically small person, from *dinky*. Used in England, Canada and Australia as a synonym for "stupid," somewhat inaccurately. During the Vietnam War, *dink* became especially strongly identified with Southeast Asians, both physically small and considered stupid, or at least backward, by most American soldiers. Accepted usage among U.S. soldiers confines *dinks* to Vietnam, Cambodia, Thailand, and Laos. Common usage elsewhere includes any Oriental, Italians, Pakistanis, Indians, and sometimes even Irishmen.

Dutch, Dutchman, Dutchie Anyone from the Netherlands, Germany, or other countries speaking German and German dialects. From *Deutsch*, name of the common language. Also anyone descended from those speaking *Deutsch*.

English Yelled by French-Canadians at descendents of Irish and Scots who speak English and have in the French view surrendered their cultural identity to the English. This gains sting because even third- and fourth-generation Irish and Scots Canadians still resent British invasions of their *auld sod*.

Eskimo Victorian euphemism for anything vulgar or indelicate, from such customs as eating whale blubber and lending visitors a daughter to sleep with.

Esky Diminutive for *Eskimo*, applied chiefly to Eskimo people and customs, rather than as a euphemism. Also used as euphemism, however; see above.

Frito Any Chicano or Mexican, after the "Frito Bandito" advertisement featuring a "Mexican Bandit" who stole corn-chips.

Frog Anyone French, speaking French, or of French ancestry. Shortened from "frog-leg eater," after a former staple of French peasant diets. French revolutionary Louise Michel came to anarcho-socialism by way of her determination to save dumb frogs from brutal death through enabling poor peasants to buy beef and eggs. All her life she remained haunted by the sight of legless frogs miserably eyeing her while they buried their hindquarters in mud and bled to death.

Fudgsicle A black person who behaves white: "Black on the outside, white on the inside." Actually, the trademarked Fudgsicle is all chocolate-colored, unlike the vanilla ice cream bar coated with chocolate. See **Oreo**.

Golliwog Any non-white, also sometimes including dark-skinned Italians, Spaniards, and Portuguese. Chiefly British. Possibly related to *polliwog*.

Gook Any Oriental person, or person of Oriental descent. The term has at least two possible origins. One is that Oriental languages sound to Western ears like "gobbledygook." The other stems from use of *gook* to mean a "disgusting mess." *Nuoc mam,* the fish paste mixed with rice to provide most Japanese, Koreans, Chinese, and Southeast Asians with their principal source of protein, is undeniably "gook" to Western eyes and palates, since it includes literally every part of almost every kind of fish, snail, slug, and grub available. *Gooks* in World War II were almost exclusively Japanese. *Gooks* before and after, however, have been much more broadly defined, including allies as well as enemies of the soldiers most using the word. See Tom Suddick's discussion of "our gooks" versus "their gooks" in his Vietnam War novel, *A Few Good Men.*

Goy Yiddish term for any non-Jew. Variant, diminutive, is *Goy-Boy,* mostly used with reference to a non-Jew dating a Jewish girl, or having married into a Jewish family.

Grape-stomper Applied indiscriminately to those of European Latin extraction—French, Spanish, Portuguese, Italians, and Romanians. Refers to stomping grapes to make wine, a practice considered unsanitary by the English. Usually directed at males, but not always.

Greaser, Greaseball Anyone of Latin extraction. In particular, Chicanos, Mexicans, Puerto Ricans, and Puerto Rican immigrants to the United States. Stems either from Latin cookery, which uses a great deal of olive oil, or "grease," or from slicked-back, greasy hairstyles worn by Latin men. Recently both terms have been expanded in popular usage to cover non-Latins wearing greasy hairstyles as well. "The Fonz," for instance, is a *greaser* even though his Italian last name is almost never mentioned in the "Happy Days" TV series, and even though he makes no reference whatever to traditional Italian culture or values.

The Greek Way Anal intercourse, sodomy. So-called because homosexuality was the prevalent sexual norm in ancient Athens, though "The Greek Way" today may be heterosexual as well. Note the contrast between this and **The Irish Way**, below.

Gringo Any foreigner in Mexico or Latin America in general, especially American tourists.

Gypsy Short form of "Egyptian," whence the European gypsies are supposed to have come. While *gypsy* is not offensive to gypsies themselves, it is offensive when applied to Jews, Czechoslovakians, Hungarians, and others of dark skin and Eastern European origins, all of whom have been traditionally called *gypsies* by those of Nordic descent. Hitler's equation of Jews and Slavs with gypsies, and subsequent efforts to kill them all, are by no means unique in European history. See *The Painted Bird*, by Jerzy Kosinski, for a succinct description of attitudes throughout Eastern Europe.

Habitante, Hab Any French-Canadian, especially rural dwellers. Literally, a *habitante* is an "inhabitant"; figuratively, it means a tenant-farmer or share-cropper on a great estate, such as were operated in Québec by French nobility and the Catholic Church until into this century. The shortened form of *habitante* was adopted by the Montréal Canadiens hockey team as a nickname some years ago, and eventually incorporated into the official team name. Thus headlines call the Canadiens "The Habs." At one time, that might have been like calling the Milwaukee Brewers the "Milwaukee Krauts." Today it means no more than when Brooklyn fans called the Dodgers "dem bums."

Half-breed Anyone of mixed racial or ethnic ancestry, especially those mixing white and Indian blood. Reference: Cher Bono's hit song, "Half-Breed." She herself is one.

Hassid Shortened, usually derisive form of *Hassidim*, the orthodox Jewish sect most responsible for creating Israel, but now resented by more liberal Jews who view Judaism as a cultural rather than religious identity, and do not believe in literal interpretation of the Torah. — Also, a black condom with a white tip is called a *Hassid*, after traditional Hassidim dress.

Head Nigger in Charge Akin to **Kingshit Nigger**, but implies belonging to the governmental bureaucracy, as opposed to organized crime. Popularized by the sixties hit play, "Big-Time Buck White," derisively called "Big-Time Buckwheat" in some circles. For reasons unknown, the name and character of "Head Nigger In Charge" were excised from the Watts performance version and the mass-market paperback taken from that version. They did appear, however, in the guerrilla theatre and Harlem versions.

Heeb, Hebe Any Jew, but especially educated and moderately well-to-do Jews. *Heeb* and *Yid* may occasionally be interchangeable. In general, however, they apply to distinctly different social classes, and a *Heeb* is apt to be liberal, while a *Yid* is generally a fundamentalist. From Hebrew, the formal language of the Jews.

Hick Anyone of rural background, especially poor whites. Implies ignorance, backwardness, and gullibility; "hicks from the sticks."

High Yaller A black person, usually female, of light complexion, usually through some white ancestry. Means literally that the person's skin tone is highly yellowish, as opposed to simply dark brown. In whorehouse slang, *high yallers* and *chocolates* are the two standard "flavors" of black prostitute.

Hillbilly Literally, anyone living in hill country, or from the hill country, anywhere in the United States or Canada. Most often used as synonym for *Bible-Belter, Hick*, and sometimes *Clodhopper*. Dictionaries usually associate the term with the rural South, incorrectly, since in Québec hillbillies are residents of the Lost Nation region of the Eastern Townships, just above Vermont and New Hampshire.

Honky Any white person, in black ghetto slang, but especially one espousing liberal causes, integration in particular. The implication may be that such people honk their horns a lot, i.e. make noise, but don't actually do much about what they profess to believe. In short, a *honky* is a hypocrite. The *honky* derivation from *hunkie* is dead wrong. A professor at Berkeley, California presented the *hunkie* → *honky* theory about ten years ago in an assembly on racial awareness at Berkeley High. The 2,000 black kids present just about laughed him off the stage. They knew the clear and distinct difference between *honkies* & *hunkies* whether or not he did. The "horn-honking" explanation may well be wrong, but I got it from various black militants I used to know. Blacks in the South and later in Northern ghettoes had little or no contact with Eastern European immigrants, who settled mainly in the northern Midwest. If a particular term applied to some whites were to become indiscriminately applied to almost all whites, it would more likely have been *mick, Mac,* or *kraut,* or one or another of the strictly regional terms used in the South & southern Midwest. A further note: I have never heard *honky* applied to any white professing right-wing views, except occasionally by suburban **oreos** trying to join the soul movement. George Wallace, for instance, is almost always called something much, much stronger, like "motherfucker." See **Hunkie.**

Hop-head Usually, a beer-drunk. Sometimes applied indiscriminately to persons of German background, referring to the German fondness for beer.

Hunkie Unrelated to **honky,** above, despite erroneous popular etymology. Actually, *hunkies* are Hungarians and others of Eastern European descent. The term is closely related to *bohunk* and *hun.*

Hun Anyone descended from the Huns, who were the scourge of Europe after the collapse of the Roman Empire. During World War I, the term *hun* became almost exclusively identified with the Germans, whose alleged barbarity compared with other soldiers was chief subject of British War Ministry propaganda. Otherwise, *huns* usually include Austrians, Czechoslovakians, and anyone else with a Germanic surname.

Ike Familiar, derisive name for any Jewish male, from the common name, *Isaac.*

Indian giver One who makes a gift, then reclaims it. Indians, according to white settlers, were notorious for breaking treaties and promises sealed with gifts. Actually, the Indians seldom understood the agreements to mean what the whites said they did.

Injun Derogatory name for any Native American person.

The Irish Way Heterosexual anal intercourse. Traditionally, Irish wives would roll over on their stomachs when their husbands became amorous, allowing them only anal entry to prevent pregnancy. This particular form of sodomy carried no social stigma, and is described by J. P. Donleavy with some gusto in *The Ginger Man.*

Jap Any Japanese, or person of Japanese descent.

Jay-hawker Any Kansan. During the Civil War and Reconstruction era, raiders from Kansas often attacked suspected rebel sympathizers in Missouri, raping, robbing, and plundering. On one such raid, Jesse James' father was hanged, though he had always supported the Union and opposed slavery. This inspired young Jesse to join Quantrill's rebel guerrillas, with whom he participated in the infamous Lawrence and Fort Pillow massacres. In the former, civilian men, women, and children were bloodily slain; in the latter, several hundred black soldiers were mutilated, tortured, and burned. All of this, however, only returned a few *Jay-Hawker* favors with moderate interest. *Jay-Hawkers* were so named because Missourians thought their behavior resembled that of thieving and bullying blue-jays, a concept doing the birds injustice.

Jew-Boy Diminutive for male Jews; a reversal of **Goy-Boy.**

Jigaboo, Jig, Jigger Any black person in contemporary usage, but properly these mean only rural, Southern blacks. *Jig* could be shortened from *Jigaboo*, or could refer to *jigging*, the most popular form of dancing among rural blacks. *Jigger* specifically means "one who jigs."

Johnny Reb Any Southerner today. Originally meant anyone fighting for the South in the Civil War.

Junglebunny A rural, barely civilized black person; in earlier usage, a newly imported slave. Today, a synonym for *nigger*.

Kike Yiddish word, derisive, for any Jew. Stems from traditional Jewish self-hatred; when persecuted by everyone else, many Jews found even liking themselves difficult.

Kingshit Nigger Anyone atop the ghetto heap, after "The Kingfish" on the "Amos 'n Andy" program. *Kingshit* means literally "King of Shit"; boss over inferior businesses and personnel.

Kraut Specifically, a German or one of German ancestry. Can also refer to anyone with any kind of Germanic background. From *Sauerkraut*, a traditional German dish despised by the British as a hell of a way to treat a cabbage that could be boiled with potatoes.

Lemon-eaters, Lemon-suckers Same origin and meaning as *Limey*.

Limey Any Britisher, but especially sailors, from Admiral Nelson's custom of giving his crews citrus fruits to prevent scurvy during the War of 1812.

Mac Any Scotsman or Irishman, or person of Scots or Irish ancestry. From the prefix *Mc-* or *Mac-* attached to many Scottish and Irish surnames, meaning originally "son of," like the Scandinavian suffix *-son* or *-sen* and the Welsh prefix *Ab-* or simply *A-*, sometimes also spelled "Abe."

The Man White people, in black ghetto slang. Specifically, white bosses, landlords, law enforcement people, and political decision-makers. Example: the television program "Chico & The Man."

Marblehead Any Greek, or person of Grecian ancestry. Refers to the marble statuaries for which ancient Greece was famous. Richard Henry Dana used the term as if it were perfectly polite and proper in *Two Years Before The Mast*, telling us something about even liberal attitudes toward immigrants among the 19th-century intelligentsia.

Mexican, Mex *Mexican* applied to a Mexican national is not offensive. Applied to a *Chicano*, however, who holds U.S. citizenship, it is a fighting insult, since it implies that the *Chicano* has no right to live north of the Rio Grande. In fact, many *Chicanos*, if not most, can trace their ancestry back to *Californios*, part Spanish but mostly Indian, who occupied the southwestern states long before *Anglos* settled among them. *Mex* is a derogatory shortening of *Mexican*.

Mick Variant of *Mac*, above. Applied chiefly to Irish and those of Irish descent; only rarely to Scots. This is probably because *Mick* is also a nickname derived from the Catholic name *Michael*: Mick Jagger. Or, familiarly, *Mickey*, as in Mickey Cochrane and Mickey Mantle.

Mister Charley Black ghetto term synonymous with *The Man*, now largely fallen from usage, and always more common in Harlem than anywhere else. James Baldwin briefly popularized the term with his essay, *Blues For Mister Charley*, a middle-sixties best-seller.

Murphy Any person of Irish descent, from the common Irish surname. Common in the 19th century, but now remembered mainly as part of *Murphy Bed*, a kind of bed that folds out of a closet, generally found in tenements such as Irish immigrants inhabited.

Negro Any black person, from the Spanish and Latin word for "black." Formerly the "polite" term for blacks, but now considered racist and euphemistic.

Newfie Anyone from Newfoundland. Newfie jokes are in Canada what Polack jokes are in the United States, since Newfoundlanders are considered notoriously stupid and backward due to their isolation from urban centers. The world's slowest railroad, serving Newfoundland for over a century, was nicknamed "The Newfie Bullet."

New Yawker Derisive term for any current or former resident of New York City, especially Manhattan. Implies affectations and a narrow view of the rest of the country. From a New Yorker's pronunciation of New York: *New Yawk*.

Nigerian Euphemism for *Nigger*, below. Not insulting when actually applied to Nigerian nationals, but otherwise a fighting insult.

Nigger, Nig, Nigra The most common of racial slurs, *Nigger* applies to anyone with dark skin or black ancestry, regardless of national origin, place of residence, and other characteristics. A *Nigger* can in fact be nine-tenths white, with a lighter complexion than most whites. He can also be a dark-skinned Slav, with no black ancestors, who is merely suspected of having some. He could even be an obviously and genetically "pure" white person who allegedly "behaves like a nigger." *Nigger* comes from *Negro,* listed above. **Nig** is a shortened form used primarily as a racist nickname: Nig Clarke, a black catcher who played big-league ball before blacks were driven from "white" leagues. **Nigra** is an affectedly polite variant of *Nigger* used primarily by "white trash" and others mocking liberal racial attitudes. *Niggers* are generally divided into three classifications: **Bush Niggers, Field Niggers,** and **House Niggers,** from the three types most commonly found on slave-owning plantations before the U.S. Civil War. A *Bush Nigger* is one "straight from the bush," newly domesticated, if at all. He also may remain free, in the bush-country, not yet captured and "civilized." A *Bush Nigger* accordingly is unrestrained, loud, obnoxious, and often violent, by stereotype. He is looked down upon by *Field Niggers,* who are slightly domesticated, but who remain essentially clumsy, ignorant, backward bumpkins in the sight of *House Niggers.* While the *Bush Nigger* may be free already, and while the *Field Nigger* may become a nominally free sharecropper, the *House Nigger* always remains a white person's slave in cultural attitudes, if not by law. He is an *Uncle Tom,* an *Oreo,* or a *Fudgsicle,* bowing and scraping, never asserting himself, usually collaborating with *The Man* or *Mister Charley* to keep other blacks down. These three grades of *Nigger* are used more commonly by blacks themselves today than by whites. Moreover, in all-black company, *Nigger* has become a generic synonym for "human being"; the author was once warned by a black gang-leader that "them Chinese niggers is the worst kind." *Nigger!* may also be screamed by blacks at whites, on the theory that the last thing any white would want to be is a black person.

Nigger heaven Any mundane or inferior concept of perfect happiness, such as having a fresh watermelon, a keg of malt-liquor, a box of fried chicken, and a whore to screw. [*Editor's Note*: According to former U.S. Secretary of Agriculture Earl Butz, "Coloreds" want only three things: a tight pussy, loose shoes, and a warm place to shit.] — Also, a slum or tenement chiefly occupied by blacks.

Nigger logic Any inferior, erroneous, overly simplistic or absurdly convoluted form of reasoning.

Nigger-lover Any white person sympathetic to black people. Implies that the person in question has sex with blacks in a manner violating taboos against interracial mingling; if a woman, that she copulates with black men; and if a man, that black men have anal intercourse with him. No taboos oppose white men copulating with black women, or sodomizing black men as a means of asserting sexual and social superiority.

Niggerology "Black Studies," as discussed among white faculty members in a college lunchroom.

Niggertown A style of garishly covered, overstuffed furniture often preferred by uneducated urban blacks, from the part of a town blacks live in.

Work like a Nigger To do any especially hard, brutal work, or any kind of work in great amounts, under difficult conditions.

Nip Any Japanese person, or person of Japanese ancestry; from *Nippon*, the formal name for Japan.

Ofay Any white person in black slang. Now largely obsolete. Origin uncertain.

Okie Strictly speaking, a refugee from the Oklahoma Dust Bowl of the Great Depression era. Also, any current or former resident of Oklahoma. By extension, *Okie* includes other Dust Bowl refugees, from Kansas, Nebraska, and Texas. In California, *Okie* also includes descendents of *Okies*, if they retain rural lifestyles and mannerisms associated with the original refugees. Since the original *Okies* competed with *Chicanos* for migrant farmworking jobs, *Chicanos* began using *Okie* as a general insult aimed at anything and anyone. Even today, an earwig is an *Okie* in the barrio. Poet Lorna Dee Cervantes remembers innocently asking a white exterminator, as a child, if he'd ever killed any "okies," thereby discovering in a hurry what the word really meant when he took offense. Other derivations include **Okie Camp**, referring to any untidy dwelling, especially one occupied by many people and surrounded by a junkyard, and **Okie Trick**, meaning any dirty trick or underhanded deal, or any shortcut in performing a difficult or time-consuming job; while *Okies* were generally regarded as domestic gypsies, they were also widely, often secretly, admired for resourcefulness in keeping old cars running, brewing moonshine, and getting the best of every bargain.

Orangeman A Northern Irish Protestant, after his traditional holiday colors, the opposite of a Catholic Irishman's green. The colors in turn stem from the reign of William of Orange, under whom the British conquered Ireland.

Oreo Same definition and derivation as **Fudgsicle**; black on the outside, white on the inside, like the trademarked *Oreo* chocolate cookie. An *Uncle Tom*, or *House Nigger*.

P.R. A Puerto Rican, or person of Puerto Rican ancestry. Literary reference: Leonard Bernstein's "West Side Story." Abbreviation for **Puerto Rico**.

Paddy Any male Irishman, or man of Irish descent, especially if rural. From the Celtic name *Padraic* "Patrick."

Paki A Pakistani, especially Pakistani immigrants to Canada following the Bangla Desh civil war.

Paleface Any white person, in movie and television depictions of Indian-talk. Actually, contemporary Native Americans seldom if ever use the word.

Panhandler Many dictionaries claim beggars came to be called *Panhandlers* from extending an old pan by the handle when seeking alms. Actually, the term was originally akin to *Okie*, and meant a refugee from the Oklahoma and Texas panhandles, where the Dust Bowl was worst. *Panhandler* came to mean "beggar" because so many ex-Panhandlers were forced to beg for their sustenance. Used as a verb, *to panhandle*.

Peanut Any black person, but especially one making pretensions to learning, and even more particularly, one claiming scientific knowledge. From George Washington Carver's famous work with peanuts, long a black dietary staple before becoming a snack-time favorite of people everywhere. "Mr. Peanut" is a caricature of Carver, surprisingly ignored by black militants, who have violently protested against "Aunt Jemima." See **Buck**.

Pea-souper Any French-Canadian or Quebecker, after the Québec dietary staple.

Peat-bogger, Peat-digger Any rural Irish person specifically. More generally, anyone from Ireland, or of Irish descent, after the peat bogs providing most rural Irish with their fuel and fertilizer. See **Bogger**.

Pedro Any Spanish-speaking person, used primarily in New York City, mostly in reference to Puerto Rican immigrants. From the common first name, akin to "Peter."

Peon Means "peasant" in Spanish, and has no more negative connotations there than "peasant" usually does. In English, however, the pronunciation is "pee on," and the word is accordingly given a sneering twist implying that the person labeled may be peed on with impunity. Applied primarily to *Chicanos*, but also occasionally to "white trash" living in the American Southwest.

Pepsi Any modern French-Canadian, especially a Quebecker, after Pepsi-Cola, the favorite beverage of young French-Canadians. Digs at the traditional French sweet-tooth, and at the sexual prowess of young men who drink a soft-drink instead of a "man's drink"—beer or hard liquor.

Pickaninny Any young black person, usually one under ten, usually from a rural background, but not always. Derivation perhaps from Portuguese *pequenino* "very little."

Piss-ant Literally, a *piss-ant* is a pismire, a common household pest. Figuratively, *Piss-ants* are "peasants"; insignificant people, usually blacks or "white trash."

Polack Anyone from Poland, with a Polish surname, or of Polish ancestry.

Portagee Anyone from Portugal, or of Portuguese descent.

Potato Anyone from New Brunswick, a potato-growing province. Implies stupidity.

Potato-eater Anyone from Ireland, or of Irish descent, after the Irish dietary staple.

Reb Same as **Johnny Reb.**

Redcoat Originally this meant a British soldier or Hessian mercenary employed by British soldiers. By extension, it came to mean any soldier or police official in the former British empire, and still does, though since red uniforms have been abandoned by all but the Royal Canadian Mounted Police and the Buckingham Palace Guard, the term is dropping from usage.

Redneck Any white rural Southerner, or any rural person if white, especially if male; also working-class whites, especially males, with Southern roots, origins, or political and social attitudes formerly identified with the South. In particular, *Rednecks* are racists and support the death penalty. From the sunburned necks white Southerners acquired while working in the fields. The sixties brought *Redneck* into popularity, though it goes back at least into the 19th century in limited usage.

Redskin Any Native American, after the red warpaint they traditionally wore when attacking white settlers. Formerly insulting, now seldom used except in connection with the Washington Redskins football team. Also, **Redman**, used mainly in the South, now remembered as a brand of chewing tobacco favored by *Rednecks.*

Rube Any rural person, but usually applied to Easterners and Upper Midwesterners, rather than to "white trash," who have enough other names. Formerly used often as an affectionate nickname: Rube Goldberg, Rube Waddell, Rube Marquard, and Rube Benton.

Rusky Any Russian, person of Russian descent, or with a Russian surname. Less commonly, a **Rooshkin.** Both are semi-synonymous with "Communist" among right-wingers.

Sambo Any black person, from the children's story "Little Black Sambo."

Saucer-lip Any black, but especially a black woman, most often a native African. From the Ubangi tribe's custom of extending lower lips by inserting wooden semi-circles into them. A long lower lip is considered a sign of beauty and distinction.

Scalawag A native white Southerner who collaborated with *Carpetbaggers* during the Reconstruction period. Extended to include native white Southern *Nigger-lovers* in general.

Scot-free During the English subjugation of Ireland, Scots mercenaries could kill, rape, and rob the Irish without fear of legal penalties. Thus anyone getting away with murder, rape, robbery, or other flagrant crime is said to go off *scot-free*: "free as a Scotsman."

Sheik Anyone of Arab descent or living in the Arab nations, when used in the collective sense. When applied to an individual, male, of the upper class, this can be a correct title, and is insulting only when it isn't.

Shine Any black, but especially an urban black male, after the black shoeshine "boys" who formerly were found in all train and bus depots.

Shylock, Shyster A Jewish professional, lawyers and merchants especially, after William Shakespeare's character Shylock in *The Merchant of Venice.*

Simon Legree Any "slave-driving" boss, especially a white man supervising blacks, after the character by that name in Harriet Beecher Stowe's *Uncle Tom's Cabin.* See **Uncle Tom.**

Slant Any Oriental person, or person of Oriental ancestry, after his or her "slanted" eyes.

Slob, Slobovian Anyone of Slavic background, including Czechs, Yugoslavs, and Russians; as well as Romanians and Hungarians. Also some Poles. Originally derived from the name for the Slavic peoples and Slavonic languages, *Slob* came to be applied to anyone who dressed like a Slav, in a bulky fur overcoat secured by rope. Gradually it grew to mean any sloppy dresser, and by extension, any sloppy housekeeper and any fat person who looked as if he ought to wear a bulky overcoat to conceal his physical condition. *Slobovian* is a derivation of *Slob* used by cartoonist Al Capp in *'Lil Abner*, to designate residents of his fictitious but obviously Slavic region, *Lower Slobovia*.

Slope Same origin and meaning as **Slant**. (Folklore: Why is there good skiing in China? Because they have six billion slopes.)

Slum-monkey Chiefly British, chiefly applied to Cockneys but gradually used to mean blacks as well, as England's black population increases. Refers to any slum-dwellers, but especially children, and suggests the poor represent an inferior order of humanity.

Soul brother Any black man, but young men in particular. A corresponding term for women is **Soul sister**. Refers to sharing a common cultural background, including *soul food*, which originally meant food white people would not eat, such as buckwheat, ham-hocks, chitlins, collard greens, okra, and watermelon. Used as early as the twenties, but became popular during the sixties.

Spade Any black person, but especially black males. Also, a black card-sharp. Probable origin is the expression, "Black as the ace of spades." The association with *Field Niggers* may be mere coincidence, as dark blacks were usually kept in the fields, while those with lighter skins were allowed to become *House Niggers*. See **Nigger**.

Spaghetti, Spaghetti-eater Any Italian, or person of Italian ancestry, after the Italian dietary staple.

Spaniard Slang term for a louse or flea, most commonly used among Frenchmen and French Canadians.

Speak White! A command uttered by Anglophone Canadians to Francophones, implying that French ancestry is not racially "pure."

Speedy Gonzalez A young male *Chicano* or Mexican, after a legendary Latin lover who was notoriously quick to ejaculate. The Hanna-Barbera cartoon mouse "Speedy Gonzalez" is a take-off on the original. Former major league outfielder Tony Gonzalez was nicknamed "Speedy" early in his career, but refused to answer to it, and it was eventually abandoned. (Folklore: Speedy Gonzalez seducing a virgin: "Now, this won't hurt a bit, now did it?")

Spic Anyone from any Latin nation, or of Latin ancestry, from the Latin pronunciation of the English word "speak."

Spiv, Splive Same meaning as *Spic*, origin uncertain; chiefly Canadian usage.

Spook Any black person, because blacks are difficult to see in the dark.

Squarehead In most common usage, a Scandinavian, especially a Swede. Popular misconception: Nordic heads are square-shaped. — In Québec, an Anglophone. The origin of this term as applied to the English in Québec seems to be a reference to Westmount Square, where the most prominent English financiers and shipping magnates traditionally live. The French idea is that while Québec City is the capital of the province, to the English it might as well be this "Little England" in the middle of Montréal, whose denizens could travel from there to Victoria Square daily and never hear or speak a word of French, or be conscious of a French presence. The stereotype is accurate with regard to the upperclass English, but actually the vast majority of English in Québec are and always have been Scots-Irish dirt & dairy farmers.

Squid, Squidjigger Squidjigging is a common method of fishing for squid, involving jiggling a baited hook. By extension, all fishermen are *Squids* and *Squidjiggers*. By further extension, this includes all sailors and then all residents of nautical communities. In Canada, a *Squidjigger* is any resident of the Maritime provinces.

Strine Specifically, the Australian dialect, after pronunciation of the word "Australian." By extension, means about the same as **Aussie**.

Stubble-jumper The Canadian equivalent of **Okies**, the *Stubble-jumpers* fled poor dirt-farms during the Great Depression and migrated westward. Their descendents are still called *Stubble-jumpers* today, as are dirt-farmers in general.

Swamp rat Usually, but not always, the same as **Cajun**. Specifically, anyone living in or coming from the great Southern swamps. Like *Desert rat*, this isn't really derogatory.

Taco-eater Same as **Bean, Bean-eater**.

Tarheel Anyone from the Carolinas, where producing hemp tar was a major industry in colonial and post-revolutionary days. Formerly derisive, but adopted as a general nickname like "Hoosier" for people from Indiana.

Texican While Texas remained a part of Mexico, Anglo settlers there called themselves *Texicans* to distinguish themselves from Spanish-speaking Mexicans. The term remains in use among Texans attempting to preserve their regional heritage. Now, however, it recalls various affinities with Mexico, rather than with the United States.

Tex-Mex The half-Spanish, half-English dialect spoken by *Chicanos* throughout the American Southwest, as labeled by *Anglos*. By extension, all *Chicanos* are *Tex-Mexicans*.

Tom Short form of **Uncle Tom**.

Trash Short form of **White trash**.

Turk Any male who behaves as Turks allegedly do—copulating indiscriminately, usually violently, without discernible preference for female vaginas or other males' anuses.

Uncle Any black man *older* than the person speaking. For instance, Joel Chandler Harris' *Uncle Remus*. See **Boy**.

Uncle Tom The old black slave who cooperates with Simon Legree in recapturing refugee slaves in Stowe's *Uncle Tom's Cabin*. By extension, any black who accepts white values and sides with whites against blacks in any sort of racial squabble.

Vanilla Mildly derisive term for whites, used by urban blacks. Usually applied to females, often half-affectionately.

WASP Any White Anglo-Saxon Protestant, or person accepting *WASP* values.

White-eyes The usual Native American term for whites, used by militants; see e.g. *Akwesasne Notes*.

White trash Poor rural whites, chiefly Southerners but also including *Okies* and others who were originally Southerners, hillbillies, etc., before moving elsewhere. The implication is that *White trash* are the dregs of the white race, an attitude *White trash* themselves accept and perpetuate with continual self-denigration and struggle to escape the label.

Whitey Black slang for any white person.

Wild Indian As in "running around like wild Indians." Means violent, seemingly chaotic behavior; tribal dances appeared formless to uninitiated white observers.

Wog Probably short for "polliwog," a species not quite up to full frogdom. (Actually not a species at all, but a stage of growth.) Thus anyone rating lower than a *Frog* in an Englishman's eyes is a *Wog*. This includes all dark-skinned peoples, regardless of actual race and national origin.

Wop Any Italian, or person of Italian ancestry today. Originally from the abbreviation for **Without Passport**, *W.O.P.*, frequently applied to illegal Italian immigrants after the first quotas were instituted after World War I. Proof: Photographs exist of Italian and other illegal immigrants herded behind a sign on Ellis Island that says in big letters: **W.O.P.**, meaning *With Out Passport* in typically bad bureaucratic English.

Yank, Yankee, Yankee Doodle, Yankee Doodle Dandy Any American, outside the United States. Within the United States, any resident of the original thirteen American colonies, including Vermont, then just a territory belonging to New Hampshire. Origin is widely disputed, but the term became popular shortly before the American Revolution, through the song "Yankee Doodle." Derivations include *Connecticut Yankee,* meaning any shrewd, practical wheeler-and-dealer, and *Yankee ingenuity,* meaning inventiveness and resourcefulness. Both refer to qualities claimed by *Yankees* for themselves, as opposed to qualities attributed to them by others.

Yaller Same as **High Yaller.**

Yellow hordes The large Oriental populations constituting the *Yellow peril.*

Yellow peril The Japanese, in World War II and before. The Chinese during the Korean War. Generally, any Oriental threat to Western security and stability.

Yid A European Jew, especially Eastern European who speaks Yiddish. A *Yid* is usually an uneducated working-class Jew, whereas *Heebs* are of the professional class and have enough schooling to speak and read Hebrew. By extension, *Yid* is often applied to any Jew, anywhere. See **Heeb.**

Yid-kid Same as **Jew-boy.**

Zebra A black with some white ancestry, especially with one white parent. Used mostly by Northern, non-ghetto black separatists.

Zulu Any black person, especially African blacks, after the Zulu tribe. Not offensive when applied to an actual Zulu.

[*Editor's Note*: Also see Sterling Eisiminger, "A Glossary of Ethnic Biases in American English," *Maledicta*, Vol. III (1979), which complements Abraham Roback's *A Dictionary of International Slurs* (1944), reprinted 1979 by Maledicta Press.]

ENTOMOLOGY

Merritt Clifton

For Scott Mace,
Editor, *Bug Tar*

Flies is the niggers of the insect world—
    they filthy, they stink, they loud, they black,
    they eat shit off the white man's dogs.

Dungbeetles is the spics—
    they filthy, they stink, they fat, quiet, and brown,
    they eat shit on the white man's farms.

Bees is the honkies—
    they buzz, buzz, buzz, go straight 'cept the queens,
    work hard, drop dead, & the boss-man gets the honey.

Wasps is scabs—
    sting the honkies, chase the niggers,
    keep the spics low, & live in mud huts.

Ants is the union—
    equal, together, & none with brains.

Grasshoppers is artists—
    fiddle the diddle, bounce around,
    & spit on everybody.

NELSON ROCKEFELLER
AND
MORT DOUCE

Lois Monteiro

Remember the old man who married the young woman, and after the honeymoon it took the undertaker three days to wipe the smile off his face? The belief that men die of heart attacks during sexual intercourse is deeply ingrained in folklore. The French have a phrase, *mort douce* ("sweet death"), to describe such a demise,[1] and popular English phrases include, "He died with his boots on" and "What a way to go!" Coroners have been known to label it "D.I.S.," *death in the saddle*.[2] But such an event is unlikely according to research on the physiology of the sex act. The energy requirement for coitus is about the same as that needed to climb two flights of stairs. Nevertheless, cardiac patients often express fear of the dangers of sexual activity, and worry that they will literally die at orgasm.[3]

The media have implied that Nelson Rockefeller's sudden death, late in the evening away from home in a townhouse apartment accompanied by his 25-year-old aide, occurred as a result of (illicit) sexual activity. The New York *Times*, the Associated Press, and the United Press International have reported that a mysterious woman in a black evening gown was not only with him when he died, but that for some unexplained reason this woman delayed reporting the attack for one hour (post-coitus triste?).[4] The first "official," family-released report of the death said that he died at 11:30 p.m. in his Rockefeller Center office, while the later, sex-linked stories reported that the death occurred at 10:30 p.m. in his West 54th Street townhouse, and that the woman with him apparently panicked and delayed calling for medical help until 11:30, a full hour later. The fact that there was no autopsy before the body was cremated serves only to increase the sense of mystery about the death.

The medical literature on sudden, heart-attack death shows that a demise "in the saddle" is very unlikely. In one study of 5,559 sudden deaths, it was discovered that 34 took place in sexually compromising situations. Of these deaths, 18 were caused by cardiac disease.[5] The chances of Rockefeller's death occurring under such circumstances are statistically slim if possible. Two members of his immediate family, a son and grandson, have requested further investigation to get at the truth that will rule out the possibility of "scandal."[6] It may of course be important to Rockefeller's future biographers to ascertain whether or not the circumstances surrounding his death did have sexual overtones; the important aspect of the press report for us, however, is that the media have chosen to emphasize those possible aspects of the case that reinforce the belief that (illicit) sexual activity, especially for a 70-year-old man, can be fatal to the heart. By implication and innuendo the presentation of the story in the media taps this commonly held belief rather than reflecting medical probability. The folklore about the Rockefeller family that includes stories of John D. Rockefeller's living on mother's milk when he was in his nineties is further enlarged with the newest myth: Nelson's dying in the saddle while his close friend and political colleague, Henry Kissinger, was a guest at his home, with Happy Rockefeller. Careful husband that he was of his reputation over the three score and ten years of his measured life, Nelson Rockefeller was at the last destined to fulfill a Jamesian fate; for, as one of Henry James's characters in *The Portrait of a Lady* decides, "the worst of dying was. . .that it exposed one to be taken advantage of."[7]

REFERENCES

[1] G. Legman, *Rationale of the Dirty Joke* (n.p.: Castle Books, 1968), p. 272.

[2] Edward Massie, "Sudden Death During Coition — Fact or Fiction," *Medical Aspects of Human Sexuality* 3 (June, 1969), pp. 22-26.

[3] Thomas P. Hackett, and Ned H. Cassam, "Psychological Intervention in Myocardial Infarction." In W. Doyle Gentry (ed.), *Psychological Aspects of Myocardial Infarction and Coronary Care* (St. Louis: C.V. Mosby, 1975), pp. 137-149, esp. 144. — See also Lois Monteiro, *Cardiac Patient Rehabilitation* (New York: Springer, 1979), pp. 129-136.

[4] U.P.I., February 8, 1979, "Rockefeller's Aide Remains Silent on Missing Hour"; A.P., February 9, 1979, "Paper: Rockefeller Aide Never Phoned."

[5] Masahiko Uneo, "The So-Called Coition Death," *Japanese Journal of Legal Medicine* 17 (1963), pp. 330-332.

[6] Providence (R.I.) *Journal Bulletin*, February 13, 1979, p. 1.

[7] Henry James, *The Portrait of a Lady. The Novels and Tales of Henry James*, IV [New York edition], (New York: Scribners, 1908), p. 422.

[*Editor's Note*: Our interests are strictly linguistic and medical, not moralistic.

Do other languages have terms for *mort douce*? If so, are they loan translations from the French? In German, for instance, there exists not even a loan translation for this concept (*der süße Tod*).

The English expressions, "death in the saddle" and "he died with his boots on," most likely are from Old West/Pioneer lingo, describing a common occurrence in those days; their original meaning, "to die unexpectedly (and violently), before one had a chance to straighten out one's affairs," was extended to include this similar situation, viz. dying unexpectedly while "riding a woman."

If Rocky indeed died while getting his rockies off—as a depraved wit might pun—it surely was not as embarrassing as the *mort douce* that happened to a French Catholic bishop about five years ago: he died in a Parisian whorehouse.]

PROTESTANT MARRIAGE VOWS REVISED

John Hughes

WILT THOU, JOHN, have this woman to be thy wedded wife? To live together after God's ordinance in the holy state of matrimony? Wilt thou comfort and keep her in sickness and in health? Wilt thou provide her with credit cards and a four-bedroom, two-and-a-half-bath home with central air and professional decorating, a Mercedes, two weeks in the Bahamas every spring, and a week at Aspen just after Christmas so that she might regain her composure after the holidays? Wilt thou paint the house every two years, clean the gutters each and every spring, and see that the lawn is cared for? Wilt thou *try* to remember the little things that mean so much, like flowers on her anniversary, kind words when she's had a rough day or a bad tennis match, and an occasional, "Gee, honey, you look pretty today." Wilt thou be understanding when she is tired, headachy, or upset about something, when she has her period, when she is pregnant, when she feels "ugly," or when she has a big pimple on her chin? Wilt thou come home from work on time or at least call when you're going to be late? Wilt thou caulk the windows in the kid's room, clean out the attic, adjust the TV roof attenae, fix the faucet in the kitchen, throw out all those old shirts in your closet, call the vet, go to the drugstore and pick up prescriptions and Tampax, run the bath water for her while you're upstairs, zip her dress, carry in the groceries, help with the 2:00 A.M. feeding? Wilt thou *not* watch football all weekend and drink beer all night? Wilt thou not be such a pig when you shave and shower? Wilt thou listen patiently to long and boring stories about kids' colds, friends' cancerous aunts, girl friends' husbands' misdeeds, periods, yeast infections, schools, houses, furniture, drapes, kitchen tile, clothes, shoes, makeup, hair, sore feet, Jesus Christ, and decorator checkbook covers?

WILT THOU, JANE, have this man to be thy wedded husband? To live together after God's ordinance in the holy state of matrimony? Wilt thou honor him, comfort and keep him in sickness and in health? Wilt thou do all the dirtier things around the house, like clean the bathrooms, change the diapers, empty the kitty litter, scoop up the dog poop, clean vomit, clean the oven and under the kitchen sink? Wilt thou balance the checkbook and pay the bills? Wilt thou pick out the carpeting, drapes, wallpaper, sheets, bedspreads, kid's clothes, appliances, and Christmas cards? Wilt thou do the shopping, drop the shirts off at the laundry and remember to pick them up, refrain from cleaning out his drawers and organizing his wallet? Wilt thou try not to get *too* fat after the first child, do chest exercises to keep your breasts from sagging, and pay attention to other parts of your body so that it will not get really gross? Wilt thou have some patience on the occasions when he cannot perform? Wilt thou not nag and pester or ask stupid questions or accuse him of misconduct when he comes home drunk? Wilt thou not call him at the office and ask stupid things like, "Do you love me?" or "What do you want for dinner?" Wilt thou put up with his loud and rude friends, make him sandwiches late at night, remember his mother's birthday, admire his muscles, laugh at his jokes? Wilt thou wear your clothes for two or three seasons, go easy on his money, avoid using his razor on your legs, keep all your facial junk off the sink, and give him the good side of the bed?

FOR AS MUCH AS JOHN AND JANE have consented together in holy wedlock and have witnessed the same before God and this company, by the joining of hands and the giving and exchanging of rings, I pronounce that they are husband and wife in the name of the Father, the Son and the Holy Ghost. You may now kiss the bride, but don't mess up her face or hair because she still has to have her picture taken.

[Reprinted from the Editorial, *National Lampoon* Magazine (February 1979), by permission of John Hughes and *National Lampoon*. Copyright © 1979 by *National Lampoon*.]

ELEMENTARY RUSSIAN OBSCENITY

*Boris Sukitch Razvratnikov

This article will concern itself with the pedagogical problems encountered in attempting to introduce the basic concepts of Russian obscenity (*mat*) to English-speaking first-year students at the college level. The essential problem is the fact that Russian obscenity is primarily derivational while English (i.e., in this context, American) obscenity is analytic. Thus when Russians wish to express themselves obscenely they will derive the necessary words on the basis of obscene stems, usually *xuj-* 'prick', *pizd-* 'cunt', or *eb-* 'fuck.' Americans, however, will insert an obscene word functioning virtually as a particle, usually *fuck* or *fucking*, but also sometimes *shit* as well as the milder *hell* and *damn*. Compare the following examples:

(1) **Ja nixujá ne znáju.** *I don't know a fucking thing.* Or, *I don't know shit.*
(2) **On egó spízdil.** *He fucking stole it.*
(3) **Zakrój ebálo!** *Shut the fuck up! Shut your fucking mouth!*
(4) **Otpízdit' / otxujárit'** *To beat the shit out of.*

In example (1), the obscenity in Russian is carried by *nixujá* 'nothing', which is derived from *xuj* 'prick', while in English the insertion of *fucking* before *thing* renders the sentence obscene. The same general explanation applies to the remaining examples.

Related to this difficulty is the fact that when English does employ derivational processes in the production of obscenity, the stems used generally differ from those used in Russian; cf. the alternative translation of (1):

(5) **Xujnjá / pizdëž** Bullshit
(6) **Pizdovátyj** Fucked up, in the sense of "strange, weird."
(7) **Xujevátyj** Sort of crappy.

A third aspect of the lack of isomorphism between the two approaches to obscenity consists of the fact that the derivational nature of Russian obscenity permits the creation of obscene lexical items which cannot be translated into English without additional contextual explanation:

(8) **Ebál'nik** Face, nose; cf. mug, snout, also the epithet cuntmouth.
(9) **Pizdobrátija** A group of buddies; cf. a fine bunch of fuckers.
(10) **Naxujárit'sja** To drink too much; cf. to get fucked up.

A conceptually related phenomenon in English is the insertion of fucking immediately before the stressed syllable in polysyllabic words, e.g. fan-fucking-tastic, il-fucking-literate, etc.

Thus the first difficulty to be faced in the teaching of Russian obscenity to American students is the fact that the two languages rely on significantly different processes for the rendition of obscenity, and the resultant lack of isomorphism is not readily grasped by the elementary student without a great deal of explanation.

The second problem which must be taken into account is that of active vs. passive mastery. In general, first-year Russian students are significantly more concerned with developing their own ability to express themselves obscenely in Russian than with learning to understand Russians expressing themselves obscenely. Thus while it is possible to explain the complexities of Russian obscene usage vis-à-vis English to such students, these explanations are of far less interest to them than basic equivalencies which do not require additional elucidation, e.g. pososí xuj 'suck (my) cock.'

One other factor which must be noted is the need for more adequate dictionaries of Russian obscenity. It is unfortunate that the dictionaries currently available do not differentiate among archaisms (cf. Eng. *swive, jazz* 'fuck'), regionalisms (cf. Eng. *stump-sucker* 'faggot', *juke* 'fuck'), uncommon forms (cf. Eng. *tube steak* 'cock', *furburger* 'cunt'), double entendres (cf. Eng. *pole* 'prick', *box* 'cunt'), expressions which are possible but not fixed (cf. Eng. *Go take a flying fuck at a rolling doughnut!*), and standard, common usage (cf. Eng. *prick, cunt, fuck you, eat shit*). Admittedly, such a task is an extremely difficult one, especially due to the difficulty in obtaining concurring judgments from native speakers. Although the efforts which have been published to date are quite important, the beginning Russian student, and even the more advanced student, would have difficulties in attempting to use the currently available dictionaries for any but passive purposes.

The following annotated list, thematically organized, is intended to serve as the basis for a single introductory lecture on Russian obscenity. In view of the various problems elucidated above, it is primarily limited to those expressions which are relatively common in Russian while still being relatively isomorphic with their English equivalents. Certain phrases and proverbial expressions which do require more clarification than mere translation comprise a notable exception to this principle. They are included because they were quite popular with students. The current list has been tested repeatedly in the classroom and is intended to fill a single fifty-minute class period. While this list will certainly appear somewhat random and incomplete to native speakers of Russian, and while there may be some disagreement regarding translations, given the intent and limitations of the list, i.e. the introduction of Russian obscenity to American students with only one year of Russian in a single class period, it is hoped that it will prove useful in the advancement of knowledge. In a lecture based on this list, it is suggested that the instructor combine an attitude of dry pedantry with one of light-hearted prurience, as this has proven to be most effective in communicating the material to students.

THE LIST

I. Body Parts

Xúj *Prick*
Naxújnik *Rubber*
Pososí xuj! *Suck (my) cock!*
Xuesós *Cocksucker.* Used to mean "idiot."
Xuj na kolësax! *Prick on wheels!* An abusive vocative.
Xuj moržóvyj! *Walrus-prick!* An abusive vocative for a dirty old man.
Xuj tebé v glaz / rot! *A prick in your eye / mouth!* Note dative pronoun and accusative of motion.
Xuë-moë! An exclamation. Cf. Eng. "Fuck-a-duck!"
Ploxómu xúju i volósiki mešájut. *Even the short hairs get in the way of a bad prick.* Cf. Eng. "The poor workman blames his tools."(!)
Xúem grúši okoláčivaju. *I'm whacking pears with my prick.* Used to mean "I'm not doing a fucking thing" or "I'm doing something useless."
Sto xúev v žópu — ne tésno? *A hundred pricks up the ass — isn't it a bit tight?* : "Aren't you overdoing it?"
Jajcó (nom. pl. *jájca*, gen. pl. *jaíc*) *Balls.* Lit. 'eggs'; cf. also Eng. "nuts."
Emú tol'ko slónu jájca kačat'. *All he's good for is swinging an elephant's balls.* Cf. Eng. "He's only fit for shoveling shit." *Idí!* 'Go!' can be substituted for *emú tol'ko* to give the expression a meaning like "Fuck off!"
Pizdá *Cunt*
Pizdënka *Pussy*
Pizdostradánie *Horniness*
Idí v pizdú! *Go up a cunt!* : "Fuck off!"
Pizdá vonjúčaja! *Stinking cunt!* An abusive vocative.
Pizdá mókraja *Wet / juicy cunt* : "hot, horny."
Pizdá s ušámi *A cunt with ears* : something ridiculous.
K pizdé rukáv *A sleeve for a cunt* : something unnecessary; cf. "Coals to Newcastle."
Mandavóška *Crab louse.* From *mandá* 'cunt' and *voš'* 'louse.'
Tít'ka *Tit*

Žópa *Ass*
 Žopolíz *Ass-licker*
 Žóp(oč)nik *Buttfucker*
 Idí v žópu! *Go up my ass!* Used to mean "Kiss my ass!"

II. Bodily Functions
1. Excretory

(Na)bzdét' (3 pl. *bzdjat*) *To fart silently.* Cf. *S*(ilent) *B*(ut) *D*(eadly).
Perdét' (3 pl. *perdját*; pf. *përdnut'*) *To fart with a noise*
 On ljápnul, kak v lúžu përdnul. *He blurted it out as if he'd farted in a puddle.* Used to mean "He stuck his foot in his mouth." Note that the *d* in *përdnul* is not pronounced.
(Na)srát' (3 pl. *srut/serút/sérjut*) *To shit*
 Srányj *Shitty*
 Sráka *Asshole* : "shitchute." No longer common except in the expression *Pocelúj menjá v sráku!* "Kiss my ass!"
 Čto ja v boršč nasrál, čto li? *What did I do, shit in the soup or something?* Used when someone is extremely angry at the speaker.
Govnó *Shit*
 Govënnyj *Shitty, full of shit*
 Govnjuk' *Shithead*
 On nastojáščee govnó. *He's a real shit.*
 Èto stoprocéntnoe govnó. *That's 100% shit.*
 Svoë govnó ne vonjáet. *He thinks his shit doesn't stink.* Used of critical people unaware of their own faults.
 On (inženér) kak iz govná púlja. *He's an (engineer) like a bullet made of shit.* Used of anyone who is bad at his/her job, the appropriate profession being inserted where there are parentheses.
 Govnó sobáč'e *Dog shit.* Used in a public statement by N. S. Khrushchev; it can be an abusive vocative as well as a descriptive term.
(Po)scát' (3 pl. *scat*; the letters *sc* are pronounced *ss*) *To piss*
 Prótiv vétra ne sci. *Don't piss into the wind.*
 Scat' ja na negó xotél. *Piss on him.* Lit. 'I would piss on

him.' Note that in both these expressions the key word may be spelled with a double *ss*, viz. *ssy* and *ssat'*.

Písat' (3 pl. *písajut*) *To pee.* This verb is especially useful in demonstrating the importance of stress and conjugation, since those are the only two factors differentiating this verb from *pisát'* (3 pl. *píšut*) 'write.'

Núžnik *Can, crapper.* Cf. *núžnyj* 'necessary.'

Pipí; Káka *Wee-wee* and *doo-doo* (*poo-poo*), respectively. While not, strictly speaking, obscene, they do serve as the functional equivalent in nursery language. *Pipí* appears to have been borrowed from French.

2. Sexual

Dróčít' (3 pl. *dróčát*) *To jack off*

Dročíla An epicoenal noun; when masc., it means "a jack-off"; when fem., it means "a prick-teaser."

Káždyj dróčit ⟩ *Everyone jacks off as he pleases* :
Kak on xóčet "Different strokes for different folks."

Minét *Blow job.* From the French *faire minette* "to eat pussy."

(S)délat' komú-to minét *To give someone a blow job*

Ebát' *Fuck.* The older forms of the infinitive are *etí* and *et'*. The 3 pl. is *ebút*. The past tense is *ëb, eblá* or *ebál, ebála*. The perfective can be formed with a wide variety of prefixes, such as the common *vy-* and *ot"-*.

Ebát' rákom *To fuck dog-fashion.* Lit. 'crab fashion.'

Raz"ebát' *To fuck over*

Eblívyj *Hot, horny*

Ebúčij Same as *eblívyj* but stronger. Note that this is an old native (as opposed to Church Slavic) present active participle.

Ëbannyj *Fucked / fucking.* Similar to idiomatic English.

Idí k ëbannoj / ebënoj / ebéne máteri! *Go to your fucked mother!* A functional equivalent of "Go fuck your mother!"

Ëb tvojú mat'! *Fuck your mother!* Lit. 'Fucked (masc.) your mother.' This is the most popular of all Russian obscenities. In Polish and Ukrainian it is referred to as "the Russian curse," while in Yiddish, with char-

acteristic irony, it is known as "a Russian blessing."
In the modern language, it is generally assumed that
the subject is the speaker, but Isačenko has cogently
argued that in earlier times the subject was *pës* 'a dog.'
It can also be used as an interjection as in *Peredáj, ëb
tvojú mat', sol'!* 'Pass, fuck your mother, the salt!':
"Pass the fucking salt!"

Ebí tja v rot! *Fuck you in the mouth!*

Èj ty ëbanaja v rot bljad'! *Hey you fucked-in-the-mouth
whore!* Note that the noun and participial phrase can
be inverted for a heightened effect.

Končát' (3 pl. *končájut*; pf. *kónčit'*, 3 pl. *kónčat*) *To come.*
Lit. 'to finish.'

III. Social Institutions and Other Expressions

Kúrva *Whore.* This word is not as common as the following
word, but it has been borrowed into so many East
European languages that it is now understood by most
people from Estonia to Albania. The Russian form
was evidently borrowed from Polish.

Bljád' *Whore.* Also used as an interjection. It is frequently
used to refer to a man or woman who cooperates with
the Soviet system.

Bljadun' *Whoremonger; pimp*

Bardak' *Whorehouse*

Požár v bardaké vo vrémja zemletresénija. *A fire in a whorehouse during an earthquake.* A description of utter
chaos.

Súka *Bitch.* Also used as an interjection.

Súkin syn *Son of a bitch*

Svóloč' This word is extremely difficult to translate, but is so
abusive that it is worth including. The verb *svolóč'*
means 'to drag.' The noun *svóloč'* implies someone
who has been dragged through something extremely
unpleasant, e.g. feces. One attempted definition runs
"Lower than a duck's feet."

U negó stoít. *He has a hard-on.* Lit. 'By him it stands', or 'he
has one that stands.'

V rot brat' *To take it in the mouth*
Sjad' na moj, da poezžáj domój! *Sit on mine, and ride home!*
Idí k čórtu! *Go to the devil!*
Idí v ad! *Go to hell!*
Prokljátyj *Damned.* Used as an interjection and adjective.

SOURCES

It would be impossible for the author to thank each of the numerous relatives and friends who have helped him in this and related endeavors over the past twenty years, but he wishes to acknowledge a special debt of gratitude to his father, who taught him his first abusive words in Russian, and to Professor Victor Raskin, who was most generous with his help and advice. The following works were consulted in the course of the preparation of this article and provided much of the material in it.

Carey, Claude. 1972. *Les proverbes érotiques russes.* The Hague: Mouton.
A Dictionary of Russian Obscenities. 1971. Cambridge. (Other data not supplied. This work appears to have been through a number of versions, but the author is not in a position to commit himself by specifying or speculating on details.)
Drummond, D.A. and G. Perkins. 1973. *A Short Dictionary of Russian Obscenities* (2nd edition). Berkeley: Berkeley Slavic Specialties.
Flegon, A. 1973. *Za peredelami russkix slovarej.* London: Flegon Press.
Galler, Meyer and Harlan E. Marquess. 1972. *Soviet Prison Camp Speech: A Survivor's Glossary.* Madison: University of Wisconsin Press.
Isačenko, A.V. 1964. "Un juron russe du XVIᵉ siècle." *Lingua Viget: Commentationes Slavicae in Honorem V. Kiparsky.* Helsinki. 68-70.
Raskin, Victor. 1978. "On Some Peculiarities of the Russian Lexicon." *Papers from the Parasession on the Lexicon.* Chicago: Chicago Linguistic Society. 312-325.

† † †

How about buying your own copies of *Maledicta*, Cheapo!?
May Shostakovich play a concerto grosso on your tympanum!

VERBAL AGGRESSION IN MEXICO CITY

Robert W. Tierney

Often in a society, the hostile, and usually pornographic, banter that certain sections indulge in, serves not only the useful purpose of releasing tension, but can be used as a thermometer to measure the direction that the society may be taking.

The valley of Mexico City is a prime example of this verbal playing and fencing. It is impossible to spend any time in the monumental traffic snarls of this metropolis without hearing some prime examples of this art.

As in most languages, there are social conventions regulating the vocabulary for excretions, genitals, and sexual intercourse. In descriptive terms, *huevos* ("balls") can be put to a variety of uses. One who is heavy in this part of the anatomy (*huevón*) is lazy, but one who is well-endowed (*tiene los huevos bien puestos*) has intrinsic valor. A large sucker (*mamón*) is a jerk, but one who is sucked (*mamado*) is well-built. A big fuck (*chingón*) is one who can do, but if fucked (*chingado*), it is much the same as in English. The "Machine Gun" (*más chingón*) is the most capable.

Verbally, the inhabitants of the valley don't do much in the way of urination or excretion as would be common in English, German or French; but they make up for this lack when they talk about anyone's mother and sister. On television, a psychologist described Mexico as a country "with little father, lots of mother and a whole parcel of brothers and sisters running around."

To understand, and be intellectually stimulated by the

banter of the valley of Mexico, one must understand the processes of *alburreando* and *apodando*. *Albures* are a system of double-meaning double-talk, not really "punning," as someone translated it into English; examples often sound like puns in translation or simple double-meaning jests; however, *albures* are more systemized than any such use in English. The *apodo* is a nickname or alias; there is not one public school in Mexico without *apodos* for the teachers bestowed upon them by the students.

The whole process is irreverent and as stimulating as a good game of chess. Once I commented to a Government Ambulance driver that "You fellows hang *apodos* on anyone; even Jesus Christ ain't safe." He answered with a routine about *Chucho el chiflis*—which sounded like the "Crazy George" routine that Bob Newhart did about George Washington. (*Chucho* is the nickname given people by the name of Jesús, and *chiflis* is "nutty.")

Which sections of the population in Mexico indulge in this sort of banter? It is not, as stated, reserved for the "lower" classes; the professionals, and the students at the National University, enjoy their verbal saber matches, too. With the changing social mores, the banter is no longer exclusively masculine, though "nasty" words do tend to be frowned upon by older members of the society when they sprout from the allegedly weaker sex.

The valley of Mexico is the only place where I have heard someone say, *Le mando a él una calurosa, afectuosa y fuerte chinga a su madre de mi parte* — "Please send him from me a warm, loving and vigorous **fuck your mother**." And really, being the reaction to an outrageous request, the statement is within good social context.

† † †

Still reading your friend's *Maledicta*?

May Truman Capote be attracted to your gluteus maximus!

ΠΥΓΜΉ–ΦΑΛΛΌΣ
FIST–PHALLUS

Elias Petropoulos

Two related gestures are used in modern Greece by way of insult: the *fist-phallus* and the *finger-phallus*. The finger-phallus gesture is known colloquially as *kōlodakhtylo* (literally, "the finger for the ass"), which refers more to the action of "goosing" than to the mere gesture. The slang expression, *Tha sou valō kōlodakhtylo* ("I will put the finger in your ass") means metaphorically: I will punish you, I will make things hard for you. The finger-phallus gesture is simple. To form or express it, one has only to bend the middle finger downward, while moving the hand up and down, *or* wiggling the finger at the same time (but not both the hand and finger together), and looking straight into the eyes of the person to whom the insulting gesture is directed. (See Figure 4.)

The finger-phallus (δάχτυλος-φαλλός) or *kōlodakhtylo* gesture has an impressive history, since it is known at least from the time of Socrates (5th century B.C.). The fist-phallus gesture (πυγμή-φαλλός), which does not seem to have any popular name, is almost equally old. The German literary historian, Ernst Theodor Echtermeyer, in 1833, pointed out a passage in the Latin poet Ovid (1st century B.C.) where the gesture of

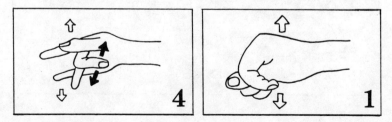

the fist-phallus is described, and eighty years later the Greek folklorist N. Politis corroborated Echtermeyer's interpretation of Ovid, but without adding anything more on the subject. I will try to fill this gap here.

The fist-phallus gesture is very common in Greece, especially among members of the underworld. The gesture is performed by passing or thrusting the thumb between the index and middle fingers, and then pointing this phallic fist at the person to be insulted. Three variations of the fist-phallus gesture can be distinguished, according to the intensity of the insult intended.

Variation No. I: The insulter shows the fist-phallus and pushes it at the insulted person's snout, shaking the fist-phallus up and down four or five times. The fist is kept in horizontal position, the fingers downward and the back of the hand up. This gesture is often accompanied on the part of the insulter with the typical phrase: *Na! (H)arpa!* ("There! Take it!") This gesture, in Variation No. I, presumably expresses the simple showing of the penis in the direction of the insulted person. Modern Greeks are quite conscious of this symbolism. (See Figure 1.)

Variation No. II: When the insulter is not satisfied merely by Variation No. I (Fig. 1), he attempts to test and upset the insulted person's calm by means of Variation No. II. In this, both hands move simultaneously and in one *violent* motion. Before engaging in this violent movement, the insulter spits into the palm of his left hand; then, with angry emotion, he beats on the open and moistened palm of his left hand, with the wrist of the right hand which has already assumed the form of phallic fist. (See Fig. 2.) The insulter displays this interlacement of the two hands to the insulted, simultaneously moving

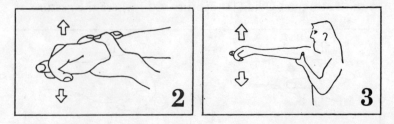

the phallic fist up and down several times. This violent gesture is usually accompanied by the standard expression: *Arpa, pousti!* ("Grab that, fag!"), to which the insulted replies or counters at once, with the equally standard phrase: *Ston kōlo sou, malaka!* ("Up your own ass, you jackoff/cunt!") Essentially, Variation No. II depicts an act of rectal coition which the insulted must support in imagination, or one that it is presumed he has the ambition to support in reality. The left hand of the insulter represents the anus (moistened, as aforesaid), and the right hand represents the penis.

Variation No. III: This is the final and most furious form of the fist-phallus gesture. The insulter's right hand being already in the shape of the fist-phallus, he stretches this arm in the direction of the insulted, meanwhile clapping his left palm up into his right armpit. (See Fig. 3.) Variation No. III is tantamount to the insulter threatening the insulted: *Tha ston khōsō etsi olon ton poutso!* ("Thus I will shove my whole prick into you!")

The gesture of the fist-phallus is well known among many peoples outside of Greece. Russians often use Variation No. I, and the French are fond of a gesture similar to Variation No. II. [Italians use a form of Variation No. III, in which the left palm strikes not in the right armpit, but on the right biceps, several times, while the right hand's vertical fist-phallus moves up and down, and gyrates with a reaming motion as it rises and falls. This is a whole pedicatory scenario. The finger displayed as penis in this gesture in Latin countries is not always the thumb, but may be the center finger: the ancient Roman *digitus impudicus* gesture, now known as "the finger" in English. Latin peoples also do not always identify the outthrust thumb in this gesture as the penis. Some pretend it represents the insulted's *nose*, which has been plucked off by the two fingers and is being "shown to him." More seriously it is considered to represent the *clitoris*, and is therefore a deathly insult when directed at a woman. According to Rabelais it represents a *fig* in a donkey's anus, which the insulted is being invited to seize with his teeth! This gesture appears as the opening action of Shakespeare's *Romeo and Juliet*, in 1596, where the Montagu and Capulet Italian servants insult each other in this way, under the name of "biting the thumb": the thumbnail of the Italian-ate fist-phallus being snapped contemptuously at the insulted under the upper front teeth. A derivative of this gesture is still very much alive in Germanic and English-speaking cultures under the name of "nose-thumbing," or in German "the long nose." In its most recent form, whether with one hand, or both —in the latter case the baby-finger of the first hand, and thumb of the second are linked—the element of the outthrust thumb or finger is modified, and all the fingers are spread wide and even waggled to "increase" the insult. The gesture in this form approaches another modern Greek gesture of insult or admonition: the *moudza* (μοῦντζα) or spread-open upraised hand —the older *Vade retro Satanas!* and modern *STOP!* handsign— which can be proffered in five different intensities, shown in a delightful Greek cartoon as the climax of the illustrated section on "Insult Signals" in Desmond Morris's *Manwatching*, 1977, pages 186-93. —*Translator's note.*]

As understood by modern Greek people, the fist-phallus is an indirect or symbolized exposure of the insulter's penis, an exposure intended to humiliate or terrify the insulted. Modern Greeks also have another gesture in which they point almost directly at their genitals. This is known to polite Athenians simply as *the vertical gesture*, and apparently has no other name. The vertical gesture is very simple: *A* says something to *B*, and *B* wishes to express his disdain of what has been said, or his contempt for *A*. To do so, *B* holds the palm of his hand stretched out vertically before him, and brings it down

suddenly, from the level of his face to that of his genitals. (See Fig. 5.) At the same time he shouts: *St'arkhidhia mou!* ("To my balls!") Very rarely, a woman "of loose morals" will perform this vertical gesture, with the appropriate and fatal phrase expressed as: *Sto mouni mou!* ("To my cunt!")

Finally, I would mention in passing, another form of gestural insult used in Greece. When two underworld characters are conversing intensely, sometimes one of them, with a glance downward at his genitals, will say: *Akous, Apostoli?* ("Are you listening to me, Apostolis?") This is a comic personification of the insulter's penis, who or which is being asked if it has heard what the insulter has said. (Implying again that the insulted is being threatened with pedication.) It should be observed that the name *Apostolis*, here given to the penis, is considered humorous in Greek. This little ceremony or byplay, of the question addressed to the speaker's own penis (which remains prudently silent) is considered, in Greece, to be particularly insulting.

(English version: G. Legman)

"May you get fucked by a donkey! May your wife get fucked by a donkey! May your child fuck your wife!"

Legal Curse, Egypt, circa 950 B.C.
[See *Maledicta* I/1, page 7]

PORTUGUESE NICKNAMES

Reinhold Aman *and* George Monteiro

In 1961, Professor George Monteiro published his article on Portuguese nicknames, "*Alcunhas* among the Portuguese in Southern New England," in *Western Folklore* 20/2 (April, 1961), 103-107.

Among these nicknames (*alcunhas*) are **Cabeça de Pau** "Blockhead," **Cabreiro** "Goatherd" (because of the man's habitually gruff, curt manners), **Maria da Cela** "Basement Mary" (she lived in a cellar and sold liquor upstairs), **Ratado** "Pockmarked," **Gago** "Stutterer," **Segueta** "Blindlike," **Perna de Pau** "Wooden Leg," **Torto** "Cockeye," **Pisco** "Squinter," **Garganta** "Gullet" (the name given to this woman by her husband), **Franco Mentiroso** "Frank the Liar," **Pinguinha** "Little Drop" (he has a predilection for liquor), **Areia** "Gravel" (he has a mind like sand, no brain), and **Facadas** "Knife-thrusts" (his father is said to have stabbed his wife seven times in an argument *during* their courtship).

Animal names used as nicknames include **Pardal** "Sparrow," **Vaca Amarela** "Yellow Cow," **Andorinha** "Swallow" (who, like this bird, flits from place to place, stopping nowhere for long but busily trying to account for everything), and **Bicho Feio** "Ugly Worm."

As Professor Monteiro states in footnote 7 of his article, he did not include nicknames whose provenience lies in off-color incidents or scatological associations. In 1978, however, he kindly checked his surviving notes, and now presents such nicknames for their "corrective" value of the original article bowdlerized eighteen years ago:

One maidenly lady, who went around each year selling admission tickets to her own birthday party, was widely known as **Rosa Borrada** "Shitty Rose," and two gentlemen were known as **Piça Pequena** "Little Prick" and **Piça Fria** "Cold Prick." One of their contemporaries was called **Pouca Tripa** "Very Small Guts," while another was called, simply, **Bolas** "Balls." For some unknown reason one woman was best known as **Maria dos Dois Cus** "Two-assed Mary." And one elderly gentleman lived with the burden of being known as **O Pai-Avô** "The Father-Grandfather," a reference to a mystery of kinship and possible incest.

☆ ☆ ☆

The following nicknames, collected recently, are from the New Bedford, Massachusetts area: Two big-talkers are known as **Caga-Farelos** "Trifle-Shitter," and **Caga-Lume** "Fire-Shitter"; while another talker is known as **Bacharel** "Chatterbox." A fellow noted for scratching his arse is **Ovo do Cu** "Egg from the Ass." **O Bexiga** "The Bladder" is so known because he used to clean out pig's bladders by blowing into them. Less dramatic is **Boca Grande** "Big Mouth," a talkative gossip. Among the women are **Burrinha** "Little Donkey," so named for her penchant for carrying abnormally heavy objects, and **Frangalha** "'Loose' Chicken," noted for her reputation for promiscuity. Incidentally, **Frangalha** is also known in the English-speaking community as "Fish Mary" because in earlier days she was wont to hang around the wharves with sailors and fishermen. A fisherman who sold morey eels in the streets and who boasted that his eels were the tastiest because they were the darkest was called **O Negras** "The Blacks." **Cigarrinha** "Little Locust" was famous for his hopping around, and **O Grilo** "The Cricket" was known for his constant singing. A dark-skinned white man was called **Melro Preto** "Black Merle." Another, known for his nastiness and meanness, was called **Faquinhas** "Little Knives." A rather proud and pompous man was called **Janota** "Fop." **O Estrela** "The Star" always had his head in the stars, counting them; while **Volta** "Change" would invariably predict that "the weather is about to change." One exceedingly religious family was sneered at as **Os Piedades** "The Pious Ones." A minor confidence man was known simply as **Chavecas** "Swindler," and a goat-skinner who made wine-skins and apparently used one or two of them himself was called **O Borracho** "Drunkard."

"I WANNA HOT DOG FOR MY ROLL"
SUGGESTIVE SONG TITLES

Laurence Urdang

In "You Know What," Allen Walker Read treated the subject
of "veiled language" and discussed the substitution formulas
You know what, You know who, You know where, etc.[1] Although language can be explicit, its suggestive nature yields
some interesting observations; we must continually deal with
metaphor and allusion. *You know what* and its variants are
broad examples of this genre; a more subtle example is *it*,
which serves as a suggestive substitute for sexual intercourse
and for various parts of the male and female anatomy. As a
corpus for examination, I have selected song titles chosen
from a major (but not exhaustive) reference work on the subject.[2] Song titles and song lyrics are before us a good deal of
the time. Some titles, e.g., *Indian Love Call, Song of India*,
etc., have little to do with their lyrics; in fact, some have no
lyrics at all. But a great number of popular songs composed
in the period 1892-1942 have titles derived from the lyrics.
In this study, however, I have ignored the lyrics entirely to concentrate on the titles. Thus, it may be found that in many cases
the titles are suggestive but the lyrics are relatively straight-
forward. Also, I have not resorted to any tampering with the
titles as one might be tempted to do, for example, by inserting a comma in *What Is This Thing Called, Love?*

I

It, being a pronoun, can scarcely be termed a "substitution
formula"; yet it does serve the same function as *You know
what* — often more explicitly — depending on the imagination

of the listener (or reader). Thus, it may stand for 'sexual intercourse' in titles like these:

> Can I Get It Now?*
> Do It Again
> Do It A Long Time, Papa
> Do It, Baby
> Do It If You Wanna
> Do It, Mr. So-and-So
> Everybody Does It In Hawaii
> Everybody Does It Now
> Get It Southern Style*
> He Wouldn't Stop Doing It
> How Do They/You Do It That Way?
> I Ain't Gonna Do It No More
> I Am Going To Have It Now*
> I Don't Want It Now*
> If It's Good Enough For The Birds and Bees
> If You Don't Do It Like I Want It Done
>   (I'll Get Somebody Else)
> If You Don't Give Me What I Want
>   (I'm Gonna Get It Somewhere Else)*
> I Got To Have It, Daddy*
> I Know How To Do It
> I Like The Way He Does It
> I Like What I Like Like I Like It*
> I Must Have It*
> I Wanna Get It*
> Mama Like To Do It
> That's The Way She Likes It*
> When I Can Get It*
> Why Can't You Do It Now?
> Woncha Do It For Me?
> You Can't Do It
> You Can't Get It Now*
> You Can't Guess How Good It Is*
> You Don't Like It—Not Much*

*Items so marked appear in Sections I and II, for they can be ambiguously interpreted as a sexual organ.

*You Make Me Like It, Baby**
You've Got To Learn To Do It
*You've Got To Sell It**

II

Titles in which *it* substitutes for a sexual organ are:
Bring It Back, Daddy
Bring It On Down To My House
Bring It On Home
Bring It On Home To Grandma
Bring It With You When You Come
*Can I Get It Now?**
Daddy, Let Me Lay It On You
Don't Give It Away
Don't Lose It [virginity?]
Don't Name It
Don't Wear It Out[3]
Ease It To Me
Give It To Him
Give It To Me Good
Give It To Me Right Away
Givin' It Away
He Took It Away From Me [virginity?]
How Can I Get It (When You Keep
Snatching It Back)?
How Do I Know It's Real?
*I Am Going To Have It Now**
*I Don't Want It Now**
If That's What You Want, Here It Is
If You Don't Give Me What I Want
*(I'm Gonna Get It Somewhere Else)**
I Got It, You'll Get It
*I Got To Have It, Daddy**
*I Like What I Like Like I Like It**
I'll Keep Sittin' On It (If I Can't Sell It)
I'm Sorry I Ain't Got It You Could Have
Had It If I Had It Blues
*I Must Have It**

It Must Be Hard
It Must Be Jelly
It's Right Here For You (If You Don't
Get It— 'Tain't No Fault Of Mine)
It's The Talk Of The Town
It's Tight Like That
It Won't Be Long
I've Got What It Takes (But It Breaks
My Heart To Give It Away)
I Wanna Get It *
I Want Every Bit Of It (I Don't Like It
Second Hand)
Nobody's Using It Now
Put It Right Here (Or Keep It
Right Out Of There)
Put It Where I Can Get It
Take It, 'Cause It's All Yours
Take It, Daddy, It's All Yours
Take It Right Back ('Cause I Don't
Want It In Here)
Take Your Finger(s) Off It
Take Your Hands Off It
That's The Way She Likes It *
Throw It In The Creek (Don't Want
Your Lovin' No More)
When I Can Get It *
Who'll Get It When I'm Gone?
Who Said, "It's Tight Like That"?
Wobble It A Little, Daddy
Won't You Get Off It, Please?
You Can't Get It Now *
You Can't Guess How Good It Is *
You Can't Have It All
You Can't Have It Unless I Give It To You
You Don't Like It—Not Much *
You Got To Wet It
You Make Me Like It, Baby *
You've Got To Sell It *

III

There are other suggestive terms which, in the present context, look quite explicit:

Blow, Gabriel, Blow
Blow, Katy, Blow
Blow My Blues Away
Blow That Horn
Climax Rag
Come, Josephine, In My Flying Machine
Comin' Thro' The Rye
Everybody Wants To See My Black Bottom
Fast-Fadin' Papa
Feeling My Way
For Sale (Hannah Johnson's Big Jackass)
Get Me Out Of That Crack
Holding My Own
Hot and Ready
Hot Nuts (Get 'Em From The Peanut Man)
I Ain't Givin' Nobody None
I Ain't Givin' Nothin' Away
I Ain't Gonna Sell You None
I Ain't Gonna Give Nobody None
  O' This Jelly-roll
I Ain't Gonna Let You See My Santa Claus
I Ain't Got Much, But What I Got, Oh, My!
I Can't Do That
I Go For That
I Just Want Your Stingaree
I'm Going To Show You My Black Bottom
I Needs A Plenty Of Grease In My Frying Pan
I Wanna Hot Dog For My Roll
Someone's Been Ridin' My Black Gal
Take Your Black Bottom Outside
Who'll Chop Your Suey When I'm Gone?
Who Played Poker [Poke 'er?] With Pocahontas?
Yes Flo (The Girl Who Never Says No)
You Ain't Gonna Feed In My Pasture Now

You Can Dip Your Bread In My Gravy,
  But You Can't Have None Of My Chops
You Can't Get To Heaven That Way
You Done Tore Your Pants With Me
You Go To My Head
You'll Never Miss Your Jelly Till
  Your Jelly Roller's Gone

IV

Thing serves almost as broad a purpose as *it*:
Daddy, Don't Put That Thing On Me Blues
Daddy, You've Done Put That Thing On Me
Do That Thing
I Can't Use That Thing
I Kept On Rubbing That Thing
I Like That Thing
I Love That Thing
What Is This Thing Called, Love? [with liberties]
You've Got That Thing
You've Got To Save That Thing
You Wonderful Thing

V

Finally, there are the somewhat more obscure canting ambiguities:
Back Water Blues [also known as
  "Retromingent Blues"?]
Ballin' The Jack
Daddy, You've Been A Mother To Me
Everybody Wants My Tootelum
My Old Daddy's Got A Brand New Way To Love

Of course, there are many others, particularly those that employ the words *jazz* and *jive*, which have (or once had) entirely different referents in Black English from those in White English.

Suggestive songs (like *She Said No*, in which the coyly risqué banter between a man and a woman is finally revealed as relating entirely to his attempts at selling her a subscription to *Liberty* magazine) and suggestive popular records (like *John and Marsha*, in which a man and woman utter one another's names in tones of increasingly feverish passion) depend on the fertility (and lubricity) of the listener's imagination. It may be interesting to explore whether such records have ever been banned from record shops or radio the way current censors ban books and magazines whose offensiveness rests in the minds of their readers. Such explicit (or assumed as explicit) recordings as one rendition of *The Old Oaken Bucket*, rumored to have contained specific obscenities, are rare.

FOOTNOTES

1. Originally presented at the Ninth Annual Conference of Linguistics, sponsored by the Linguistic Circle of New York, on March 14, 1964. First published in *Language*, April 1964; reprinted in *ETC.*, September 1964; reprinted, in a slightly modified version, in *VERBATIM*, Volume II, Number 3, December 1975, and in *VERBATIM: Volumes I & II*, Essex, Conn., 1978.

2. Brian Rust. *Jazz Records.* New Rochelle: Arlington House, 1978; 2 volumes, xic + 1966 pp.

3. This may be in the same category as, "It looked so nice out this morning that I decided to leave it out all day."

Editor's Notes

• As for *Hot Nuts,* above, for the past 26 years, Doug Clark's "Hot Nuts" band has enchanted fraternity parties throughout the U.S.A. Described by David Zucchino (in the Detroit *Free Press* magazine, 22 July 1979, pp. 19-25) as "titillating, vile, insipid, lascivious, juvenile, vulgar, trashy and foul," the "Hot Nuts" have been charming their college audiences with suggestive songs like "The Gay Caballero," "Milk the Cow," "My Ding-A-Ling," and lyrics such as "Roses are red and ready for plucking, girls out of high school are ready for . . . college." (Information supplied by Marie Helfrich.)

● Found in G. Legman's *The Limerick*, p. 456:

Girl (to music-store clerk): "Have you got 'Hot Lips' on a 10-inch Decca?"

Clerk: "No, but I've got hot nuts on a 9-inch pecker."

Girl: "Is that a record?"

Clerk: "Well, it's better than average."

● Also, related to *thing*, above: in a sketch of the "Benny Hill Show," there hangs a poster on the wall announcing a science fiction movie: THE THING WITHOUT A THING.

A RECIPE FOR THE FESTIVE SEASON
TURKEY WITH POPCORN DRESSING
(Serves 12)

One 15-lb. Turkey	*2 Cups Bread Crumbs*
Seasonings	*2 Diced Onions*
1 Can Bouillon	*3 Cups Popcorn*
½ Cup Diced Celery	

Method: Stuff turkey and bake at 325° about five hours, or until the popcorn blows the turkey's ass clear across the room.

A RECIPE FOR ALL SEASONS
BANANA BREAD
(Serves 2)

4 Laughing Eyes	*2 Milk Containers*
4 Loving Arms	*1 Fur-lined Mixing Bowl*
2 Well-shaped Legs	*1 Banana and 2 Nuts*

Method: Looking into laughing eyes, spread well-shaped legs slowly. Squeeze and massage milk containers very gently, until fur-lined mixing bowl is well greased. Check frequently with middle finger. Add banana and gently work in and out until well creamed. Cover with nuts and sigh with relief. Bread is done when banana becomes soft. Be sure to wash mixing utensils, and don't lick the bowl.

Note: If bread rises, leave town.

SIGMA EPSILON XI
SEX IN THE TYPICAL UNIVERSITY CLASSROOM

Don L. F. Nilsen

If you are wondering where to find sex in the typical American university, you need only look as far as the classroom desks. There you will find it in all its lurid detail, carved neatly into the woodwork. For the past three years now my university students and I have been reading our desks as well as our texts. And we have collected an amazingly large and diverse sample of creative graffiti. We were expecting sex to be one of the important preoccupations, but we did not realize the extent of its significance until we counted and found that approximately one out of every five pieces of graffiti related in some way to sex.

Most of what we have collected is going into a textbook showing how creativity works in language, but that which is sex-related is so entertaining that we were afraid people would concentrate on the content instead of the language processes. Besides with censors being what they are, a textbook containing such choice tidbits would probably never make it into the classroom. But believing in what the National Council of Teachers of English calls, "The student's right to his own language," we did not want to see all of this creativity disappear as the new formica-top desks replace the old wood ones. Therefore all the sex-related graffiti are being brought together in this article and what follows are uncensored samples of classroom graffiti, written but not signed, by various university students. The collection is a testament not only to college students' interest in sex but also to their ingenuity and their creativity.

To illustrate the innovative aspect of university graffiti, consider those sex-related graffiti where a word is broken in the wrong place, as in **It is better to have loved a short man, than never to have loved a tall** or **I like ass bestus**, where in the first case the *t* which belongs to the first word (*at all*) is placed on the second word instead (*a tall*), and in the second case the single word (*asbestos*) is divided in an unexpected way (*ass bestus*), which does not reflect the true make-up of the word.

Not only is there creativity at the word (or morphemic) level, but there is also great creativity at the sentence (or syntactic) level, as in **Use erogenous zone numbers**, where an expression is expanded by the addition of another word (*erogenous*), or as in **Have fun kids; it's later on you'll think**, where the expression "It's later than you think" is altered to give the new expression an entirely different effect. A graffiti dialogue goes:

> HE: *How do you like Kipling?*
> SHE: *I don't know, you naughty boy, I've never kippled!*

In this example the play on words is based on the *-ing* of Kipling's name. This has the same form as the *-ing* which marks a present participle, and therein lies the punning potential of Kipling's name. It is also possible to change the part of speech of a word without adding an ending at all. Everybody knows that in *meat loaf* the first word, *meat*, is a modifier of the noun *loaf*, but by changing the sentence, it is possible to make *meat* into a noun subject with *loaf* being the verb, as in **Don't let your meat loaf!**

Good graffiti writers are very careful in their word choices, with these choices more often than not being made on the basis of shock value. In such graffiti as **One man's queen is another man's sweathog** and **I did it in the privacy of my own crysalis while in metastasis**, the graffiti writer begins with set expressions and makes lexical substitutions into these expressions to change the tone, but in this case not the subject, of the expressions. This jarring relationship between particular words and the rest of the sentence can also be seen in **Let's be lewd** and in **Lassie is a bitch**.

One of the most common techniques of graffiti writers is the word play, or pun. Sometimes the word play is based on words which sound the same but are spelled differently, as in **Masseurs are people who knead people**, **Report obscene male — to obscene female** or **Go Hawaiian: Give your guy a lai**, where the play is based on the *need/knead*, *male/mail*, and *lay/lai* relationship. At other times the pun is based on a word which has two senses even though it has only a single spelling, as in **To go together is blessed; to come together is divine**, **It's all right to love a nun sometimes; just don't get into the habit**, **Coed dorms promote campus unrest** or **Raise the wages of sin**. One of the most common puns among graffiti writers is based on the multiple meanings of *screw* and related ideas as the following examples illustrate: **Alimony: The screwing you get for the screwing you got.** — **If Nixon would do to his wife what he's doing to the country, she'd be a lot happier.** — **Life is like a dick; when it's soft you can't beat it, and when it's hard you're getting fucked.** — **The earth is a whore and the human race is fornicating on her.** — **If you want a good screw, go to the local hardware store.** — **There are no virgins left; society has screwed us all.**

Sometimes the graffiti writer tries to force the reader into an indiscretion rather than writing the indiscretion himself. No one can read **Smuck fog** without being aware of the impending danger. There is even more potential for misreading something like **I am not the fig plucker but the fig plucker's son, and I can pluck figs until the fig plucker comes.** And the choice of the last word in **Nixon is a Cox sacker** was certainly as much on phonological as on semantic grounds. I am beginning to wonder if even such a harmless term as **Huck Finn** when written on a desk might have been written there in the hope that someone would mispronounce it.

University graffiti are not only full of lexical and phonological innovations, but logical innovations as well. Especially in the area of sex-related graffiti implication is common. What does the *it* refer to in **Motorcycles do it in the dirt?** Why would anyone want a person to **Vote for horizontal phone booths?** Just what kind of experience is being referred to in **I'm just an inexperienced little thing—looking for experience?** How

would the graffiti reader know that the answer to the question
What goes in hard and comes out soft and sticky? is "Bubble-
gum"? What high-frequency word has been omitted from
**Yuck rhymes with: muck, duck, luck, buck, cluck, stuck,
truck, tuck, etc.**? It is interesting that this same high-frequency word has also been omitted from *Webster's Third New International (Unabridged) Dictionary*. And exactly what is
implied by the very slight alteration of the last word in **A jug
of wine, a waterbed, and WOW!**? What is meant by the *something* of the following formula?

$$\male = 0$$
$$\male - \female = 0$$
$$\female - \male = 0$$
$$\female + \female = 0$$
$$\male + \male = 0$$
$$\female + \male = something$$

And finally, consider the implications of the following three-
fourths of a poem:

I told him how to do it, how to hold his lips just so.
I told him to be ready when I gave the signal go.
He tried his best to please me, and he did as he was told.

The graffiti reader at this point is not sure exactly what is being implied, but he certainly assumes that it has something to
do with sex, and is therefore surprised to read the last line:

But it's hard to learn to whistle, when you're
only three years old.

What impressed us most about university sex-related graffiti was the number of subjects treated. They run the gamut
from the perfectly acceptable topics of marriage, family life,
dirty old men, and beauty through the controversial issues
like birth control, overpopulation, and women's lib, and even
extend into taboo areas like fetishes, sex-related diseases, homosexuality, incest, masturbation, prostitution, swinging,
rape, and oral sex. These subjects will be treated in pretty much
this same climactic order so that the reader can adjust gradually to the tone and wording, which in some cases may be
shocking.

Marriage is a fairly frequent subject and puns are a frequent device, as in **Women without horse sense become nags** **and Statistics show great increases in marriages. Life seems to** **be just a marry chase.** Other statements are based on unusual logic that ranges from tautology, as in **Marriage is the prime** **cause of divorce**, to incongruity, as in **Stamp out first marriages.** In between there are all kinds of logical strangenesses like **A wife who can't cook and won't is better than one who** **can't cook and will, Don't marry for money: you can borrow** **it cheaper**, or **The marriage ceremony is a knot which is tied** **by your tongue, but which cannot be untied by your teeth.** Most of the marriage statements have a negative tone to them, as in **Let our priests marry; it will give them a working de-** **scription of hell.**

To graffiti writers, the family is not an institution above criticism, as can be seen in **He who is henpecked may lend ear** **to other chicks, Richard Nixon can't stand pat,** or **Night Stu-** **dent, where is your wife now?** But in their usual technique of semantic inversion (putting good words in bad environments and bad words in good environments), writers reverse some of the old stereotypes, as in **I'm not a dirty old man, I'm just** **a sexy senior citizen** and **Bridge the generation gap. Turn an** **old man on.** The subject of beauty is also susceptible to semantic inversion, as in **Donna shaves her legs with a chain saw,** **You were never lovelier—and I think it's a shame!** and **Figures** **show that the average woman spends 75% of her time sitting** **down.**

We now come to the controversial issues like birth control. Some of the graffiti are in support of having children, as illustrated by **Support National Motherhood Week: Make one** **today!** or **May all your hang-ups be drip-dry** and **May all your** **consequences be little ones.** But most graffiti about having children are about not having them, as the following examples indicate: **Birth control is a high fly. — Make love, not chil-** **dren. — Orange juice for birth control; not before or after,** **but instead of. — Support planned parenthood now — before** **Mary has another lamb. — Tiny Tim wears a chastity belt. —** **Beware of Greeks bearing Trojans. — Nixon, pull out like your** **father should have. — The trouble with Nixon is that when he** withdraws, he only sticks it in again someplace else. — True planned parenthood is kidnapping. — Pope Paul leads a rhythm band. — Accidents cause people. — Familiarity breeds contempt — and children.

Much of the graffiti supporting birth control make special reference to "that pill," "the pill," or "a pill," which need not be further identified, as in: Gather ye rosebuds while ye may, but take that little pill each day. — Pop the pill for pleasure. — Pope Paul pops the pill. — The pill: a gadget to be used in any conceivable circumstance. — A pill in time saves nine... months. — A pill a day keeps the stork away.

When the unwanted pregnancy occurs, graffiti writers advise Look homeward pregnant angel. They ask Would you be more careful if it were you who got pregnant? And on the subject of overpopulation they write Overpopulation begins in the home, Overpopulation is everybody's baby, and Children should be seen and not had. But even though university students seem to be for birth control (or at least planned parenthood), and are against overpopulation, most of them seem also to be against abortion, as shown by Abortion is hard on little babies. — Abortion: Legalized murder. — Abortion is murder. — Abortion: Pick on somebody your own size! and Aren't you glad you weren't aborted?

College students are as confused as everyone else is about the feminist movement, as shown by the question Are the women in this country really revolting? The male chauvinist point of view is apparent in Women's lib is okay—I just wouldn't want my sister to marry one, There's only two ways to handle women, and no one knows either one of them, Join Male Chauvinism!, Rise up sisters!—Rather difficult for a sister, isn't it?, and UNI women read books. One example refers to the movement itself in Women's Lib is a Msleading organization. Compare this to the graffito representing the women's viewpoint Women's Lib is NOW. Other graffiti representing the female viewpoint include Pray to God and SHE will help you, A Woman's work is never done—or recognized, or paid for, or honored, or commended..., Beware chauvinists! Today's pig is tomorrow's bacon and You'll never be the man your mother was. Perhaps these last examples were not written by advocates of women's rights because they are rather flippant in tone, and it seems that most feminists are more serious. But at any rate, the male chauvinists and the women's libbers would probably both rally to the single graffito **Ban the bra!** but for entirely different reasons.

The bra is not the only article of clothing that appears in university graffiti. Some clothing goes up, as in **Up with skirts** and **Up the mini.** Other clothing goes down, as in **Down with pants!**, **Down with fig leaves**, **Down with zippers**, and **Hemlines are coming down; expect to hear some thighs of relief**, with this last graffito obviously having been written from the female point of view. And there are still other references to clothes, as in **Mickey Mouse loves the Minnie**, and **Sigmund's wife wore Freudian slips.** There are also graffiti that refer to no clothing at all, as in **Shame on the naked truth**, and **Those who sleep in the raw are in for a nude awakening.**

Various types of fetishes are also represented in graffiti. Clothing is mentioned in such graffiti as **George Washington wore ribbons in his wig**, and **Barry Goldwater wears pink underwear.** A shoe fetishist is defined as **A man who looks downward when he hears, "Gee, what a pair!"** There are also graffiti representing fetishes for various parts of the body. For knees there is **I'm in love with your knees!**; for thighs there is **Is the thigh the limit?** and **Able Mable Thunderthighs**; for the lips there is **Pat is a frog, cuz that is how he kisses**; for the derrière there is **Lady Godiva's ride made her cheeks rosy**, and **Anal erotics are behind us all the way.** It will probably surprise no one that the part of the anatomy most referred to, directly or indirectly, is the breasts. The following are representative: **Mother Earth is not flat.** — **Eva Gabor wears a training bra.** — **I don't care if your name *is* Napoleon, get your hand out of my blouse.** — **Raquel Welch wears falsies.** — **Aunt Jemima is stacked.** — **Raquel Welch is a stuffed shirt.** — **Hugh Hefner keeps abreast of the times.** —⚥ **Two men walking abreast.**

Hair is also an important topic for graffiti writers. Referring to the type that grows on the top of the head there is

Brunettes forever, Redheads are for everyone, and The average Blonde has an I.Q. equaling that of a medium-sized radish
—from experiments conducted at the University of Michigan.
The other type of hair is referred to in Puberty is a hair-rais-
ing experience, Richard Nixon is a pubic hair in the teeth of
America, and Lower the age of puberty. And since we are in
that region of the body, we will add two rather astute observations: It takes leather balls to play rugby and Santa Claus
has pop-corn balls.

It is as if Santa had a disease of some sort — and indeed
there are sex-related diseases that appear in the writings of
graffitists: VD is God's perfect punishment for promiscuity,
VD: The gift that keeps on giving, and VD is nothing to clap
about. In the graffiti there is also reference to The girl from
Emphysema, and it is rumored that Books give you syphilis.
But there is a positive side as well, as when you are admonished
to Hire the morally handicapped, or when you are told that
Mononucleosis can be fun. It is heart-warming to know that
Moby Dick and Grape Nuts are not social diseases. Probably
the sex-related illness that affects the most university students is menstruation. Kotex is defined as Carpeting in the
playroom, and Tampax as Manhole covers.

Men's sexuality received a small amount of desk space, as
in Zap! You're sterile, and as when the three stages of man
are listed in chronological order as Tri-weekly, Try weekly,
and Try weakly! We were surprised to find no graffiti men-
tioning frigidity. Perhaps it has something to do with the age
of the writers that they were more concerned with virginity,
as the following illustrate: Chaste makes waste. — Virtue is
its own punishment. — Have you heard about Joe and his girl
friend? He called her Virge for short, but not for long.— Olive
Oil is not a virgin—Sweet Pea is popeye's kid. — To the virgins: Thanks for nothing. — Virginity can be cured. Pledge
yourself now. Give until it hurts. — Virginity is like a bubble
on the ocean—one prick and it's gone forever. — Virginity is
not incurable. — Fighting for peace is like screwing for chastity. — Mrs. Robert Kennedy is a virgin. — Impatient virgins
never die. They just lose their cherry pie.

This last example is a play on the expression, "Old soldiers never die, they just fade away," but the graffiti writer has taken so many liberties with the expression that it is difficult to see the relationship to the original. Two graffiti that are superficially quite similar are **James Bond is a virgin** and **Grumpy is a virgin**. These two graffiti seem to be the same except that different names are used in the subject position. There is a further similarity in that these names are both masculine, even though there is an incompatibility between males and the concept of virginity. But logically, these two statements are very different. The people being referred to are not random males. James Bond was chosen because of all males he is probably the least likely to actually be a virgin. Grumpy was chosen because of all males he is probably the most likely to actually be a virgin, and furthermore, this explains why he is Grumpy.

One of the favorite sex topics of graffiti writers is homosexuality. Sometimes the expression *homosexual* or *homo* is written into the graffito, as in **My mother made me a homosexual, bless her heart**, or as in the dialogue *Enke is a homo.* — He is not. — I am too, or as in the misinterpreted syntactic and semantic graffito, **My mother made me a homosexual. —** *Would she make me one too if I brought her the yarn?* At other times the word *gay* is used, normally as a pun, as in **Ben Gay is hot for your body**, or **The Gay Nineties took place in Greenwich Village**, or **Go gay!** and **Nobody loves you when you're old and gay**. There is even a graffito poem that is based on the ambivalent meaning of *gay* as well as on many other words that have both sexual and nonsexual connotations:

> *I'm so happy, I'm so gay*
> *That's cause I come twice a day.*
> *I'm your mailman.*
> *Knock your knockers,*
> *Ring your bells.*
> *Gee, I bet you think I'm swell.*
> *I can come in any weather*
> *Cause my bags are made of leather.*
> *I don't need no keys or locks,*
> *I just slip it in your box.*
> *I'm your mailman.*

There are other homosexual terms used like the *queer* in **I'm near enuf if you're queer enuf; I'll die laughing while you die trying**, and the *faggot* in **Support Birth Control! Become a faggot**. At other times there is no direct mention, only an implication, as in **My mom dresses me funny**, or **Denny Hoffman loves Tom Chapman; strange but true**. Then there are the homosexual graffiti where there is a certain logical incompatibility, as in **Tiny Tim wears a cross-your-heart bra**, and **My Aunt Harold has a problem**.

Let us now turn to some lesbian graffiti. There is **Have you thanked a lesbian today for not contributing to the world's population explosion?**, **George Wallace is a Jane**, and **All men at Harvard are homosexual except one, and he's a lesbian**. The expression from the lesbian vocabulary that is used most often is *dildo*. There is the **Dildo depth gauge**, the **Dildo floodlight attachment**, and for Christmas we are admonished to give a **Sheaffer pen and dildo set**. But the most mind-boggling reference to this item is the **Goodyear dildo blimp**, and the most homosexual of all is the simple and succinct autosexual statement **I love Me!!!** which brings us to the subject of masturbation.

Graffiti writers may pun in this area: **Do you think masturbation will get out of hand?** They may imply: **If it hangs, fondle it**. They may metaphorize: **An acid trip is mental masturbation followed by spiritual orgasm**. Or they may hypothesize: **I think I've fallen in love with my hand.** — *Thank God you're not ambidextrous*. The reader must supply his own interpretation to this last graffito. If a person were ambidextrous, would this introduce a third party in a love triangle or would it just provide a situation with too much sex (if that's possible) or what?

The most salient quality of incest graffiti is the recurring theme of family togetherness. These graffiti are typically very pleasant and positive in tone: **Incest: A game the whole family can play**. — **Incest and charity are alike; they both start at home**. — **Incest: A family affair**. — **Incest begins at home**. — **Incest is best**. — **Incest is best kept in the family**.— **Incest is like watching TV—the whole family does it**. We found only one exception to this light, airy treatment of incest: **Oedipus was a mother fucker!**

Most of the graffiti relating to prostitution are merely language play with the value system of the writer not reaching the surface. In **Casanova was a pimp**, and **Joe Namath is a pimp for Truman Capote**, there is merely a surprising incompatibility between the subject and the activity being referred to. In **A madam is one who offers vice to the lovelorn** there is a pun on *advice*. Most of the graffiti either take prostitution for granted, as in the above examples, or else are in favor of it, as in **Be ready to serve your country; be a call girl!** and **Support free enterprise; legalize prostitution.** The only statement that put prostitution in a negative light was **Pollution, like prostitution, is any departure from purity.**

There was an occasional reference to swinging, such as **John loves Mary; too bad he's married to Sue, Love thy neighbor, but don't get caught,** and **Jane sits home while Tarzan swings,** but judging from the small number of statements that we found on this subject, swinging is not very important to university students. Rape, on the other hand, is fully represented. In a graffito that has something of the same effect as the end of Shakespeare's *King Lear*, a dirty old man is defined as **a person who rapes a deaf-mute, and then cuts off her fingers so she won't tell.** Then there was the simple incongruity, **Rape — I'll vote for that**, the understatement **Rape is inconsiderate**, and the pun **Rape is an unnegotiated peace.** The definition of Russian Rape as **Ivan Toratitov** has syntactic ramifications since the name "Toratitov" can be viewed as either one word or four. Sometimes there is a comparison of rape with seduction, which after all, have certain aspects in common. For example, there's **Patience is the difference between rape and seduction**, and **Rape: Seduction without salesmanship.** One rape graffito which seems to make sense yet doesn't quite is **Fighting for peace is like raping for war!** Perhaps the writer copied it from **Fighting for peace is like raping for love**, but got confused.

Since graffiti are written anonymously, even a subject as taboo as oral sex can be treated. We are told to **Try to be a** sucksess, and Milking machines suck. We are even told that There is no gravity; the world sucks. And we are furthermore told that Nixon had to see *Deep Throat* three times before he got it down pat, and in pseudo-story-telling form we are told, Meanwhile back at the oasis the Arabs were eating their dates. We can see the effect of advertising on graffiti writers in If he kissed you once will he kiss you again? Be sure! Use Vespray Feminine Hygiene Deodorant.

Commercials have had an important effect on sex-graffiti in general. The *sex* in A day without sex is like a day without sunshine, and SEX: Breakfast of champions was not there in the original versions, nor was *Spanish Fly* in the original version of Spanish Fly makes better loving through chemistry. In some cases the product name remains a part of the graffito, as in Love is like Jello; there's always room for more, and Colonel Sanders' wife is a cock raiser and Colonel Sanders says "The only way to get a better piece of chicken is to be a rooster." What better endorsement could he have for his "fingerlicking" product? Then there are the graffiti which have commercial overtones in a more general way, as in This chair is rated G(IRLS), Sin now—pay later! and You may not approve of free love, but you've gotta admit the price is right.

In comparing graffiti about love and sex, it appears that the love graffiti are typically more tender, as in Lay down, I think I love you. — Love's just not in the making, but in the knowing. — Lovers, like bees, enjoy a life of honey. — Buy land, but invest in love. — Milk-drinkers make better lovers. — I never met a nympho I couldn't love. — Love 'em all; you might miss a good one, or the succinct and somewhat poetic Love is neato peato, and finally the philosophical,

If you love something, set it free.
If it returns, it's yours.
If not, it never was.

Sometimes the love graffito is a bit more flippant, as when we are told that Sweden is a nice place to visit, but I would not want to love there, If loving is an art, we should all aspire to be Picasso, and Remember Girls, the way to a man's heart is through the left ventricle. Or when we are let in on the following dialogue: Love is of God. — *God?* — Yes, God. — Well, I'll be damned! — **Probably.**

There are some negative love graffiti, as in **It's better to have loved and lost**—much better, **Love is a four-letter word,** and **Love isn't the answer; it's the problem.** But the preponderance of love graffiti is positive and the general philosophy of graffiti writers seems to be **Make love, not war,** or better put, **When the Power of Love overcomes the Love of Power, there will be peace.**

The graffiti related to sex in general have a similarly positive tone to them. Some of it is based on puns like **Of all my relations, I like sex best, Sex isn't good for one; but it's great for two,** or **Into the valley of death rode the sex hungry.** Some have a special phonological ring, as **Sex is emotion in motion.** Some relate to university life like **Preserve wildlife**—throw a party, **Conserve water; shower with your steady, Leda's lover is a quack,** or **My place or yours?** Some graffiti are negative (or fake negative) assertions like **Too much sex affects the vision,** or **Sex is like a snowfall**—You're never sure how many inches you'll get. Some are positive assertions, like **Candy is sweet, but sex doesn't rot your teeth,** and **Sex is good exercise.** Some are in the form of questions, like **Is there sex after death?** or **Remember when the air was clean and sex was dirty?** Indeed, just as there seems to be no end to the variety of sex, there seems to be no end to the variety of sex graffiti. And the exciting thing about it is that it's constantly being created all over so that by the time this is published, there will already be new examples just waiting to be collected.

ACKNOWLEDGMENT

My appreciation goes to Frank J. D'Angelo, one of the greatest graffiti collectors of all time, for his help on this article.

[*Editor's Note:* This article was submitted in March, 1977; thus the many dated anti-Nixon graffiti.]

DÉFENSE DE PÉTER
FURZEN VERBOTEN

PROHIBICIÓN DE PEDAR
NO FARTING

ONE TOAST, NO FORK, NO SHEET

AN ITALIAN IMMIGRANT'S STORY

One day I'ma go to Detroit to da bigga hotel. Ina mornin', I go to da stair to eata breakfas'. I tella da waitress I wanna two pisses toast. She bringa me only one piss. I tella her I wanna two piss'. She say "Go to da toilet." I say "You no understan', I wanna two piss' ona my plate." She say "You betta no piss ona you' plate, you sonna-ma-bitch!" I'ma don't even know da lady and she call me sonna-ma-bitch.

Later I'ma go out to eat at da bigga restaurante. Da waitress bringa me spoon anna knife anna butta but no fock. I'ma tell her I wanna fock. She tell me "Everyone wanna fock." I tella her "You no understan', I wanna fock ona table." She say "You betta no fock ona table, you sonna-ma-bitch!"

Den I'ma go back to my room ina hotel, an' there isa no shits ona my bed. I calla da manager an' tella him I wanna shit. He tella me to go to da toilet. I say "You no understan', I wanna shit ona my bed." He say "You betta no shit ona bed, you sonna-ma-bitch!"

I'ma go check outta an' da man at de desk say "Peace to you." I'ma say "Piss on you too, you sonna-ma-bitch. I'ma go back to Italy!"

(Bill C., Miss., 1979)

COMMENTARY

The preceding tale is not a story ridiculing "stupid" Italians, even though popular, trashy books misrepresent such material as "Italian," "Polish" or "Irish" jokes. In fact, the story has nothing whatever to do with Italians.

It is an example of *linguistic humor*, using the convenient and easily-recognized Italian accent as a vehicle to illustrate the tremendous semantic difference vowel length can make. The three minimal pairs, contrasting the long (:) with the short vowels, are the key to this tale:

piece, peace /pi:s/	:	*piss* /pis/
fork /fɔ:k/	:	*fock* /fɔk/
sheet /ši:t/	:	*shit* /šit/

Fork, here the *r*-less variety (New England? South Carolina? Cf. /ka:/ 'car') and pronounced with an open *o*, may be an indication of the geographic background of the originator of this story since *fork* and *fuck* are phonetically not sufficiently close, in most U.S. dialects, to be confused.

As native-born Americans and other cultured speakers of English distinguish very well between long and short vowels, and are aware of the vulgar meanings of the mispronounced words, the story has to feature a character with a poor command of spoken English, such as a recent immigrant or a visitor to this country. Why not a Russian, Portuguese or Albanian? Because their accents are very difficult to represent in writing and are not recognized easily by most readers (or listeners). The Italian accent is widely mocked and is understood by the masses who circulate such tales. The protagonist in this human drama (I used to teach literature, you know) could have been speaking another frequently mocked accent, such as German ("I vant two shitt in mine bett") but the story would have lost much of its warmth and charm since the stereotypical German is not funny.

There is much more to this apparently simple "joke." We can *identify* with the poor fellow. The originator wanted just a simple laugh caused by the mispronounced naughty words, but I'm certain that sociologists, psychologists, folklorists and philosophers (and not to mention Talmudic Scholars and Jesuits) could write long essays on the deeper meaning of this "simple" tale. Without trying to wax philosophical, I do sense an illustration of the Human Condition, a tale of everyday misery, a Kafkaesque nightmare beneath this tale: the outsider, trying to communicate simple requests, is misunderstood again and again, but he is determined to get his wishes across. Yet, because of lacking communication, he is helpless. He becomes frustrated, resigns himself to being misunderstood, and capitulates, finally saying, "To *hell* with it all! Who *needs* this hassle!? I'm going back to my kind, to where I'm understood."

Surely, each of us has been in such frustrating situations where we simply could not get our point across, be it in a foreign country or with co-workers, a spouse, child or parent. Finally, after too much frustration, we become resigned and say, "Oh, *fuck* it! (or civil equivalent) I'm leaving!" We can empathize with the tale's fellow-sufferer and therefore find it so appealing. It strikes a chord.

On a more mundane level, folklorists will recognize the ancient elements of folk tale and fairy tale: *three* events or situations (toast, fork, bedsheet) and *verbatim repetition* ("You no understan', I wanna..." and "You betta no..., you sonna-ma-bitch") which have been used for thousands of years. Unwittingly, the originator of this modern "urban folk tale" utilizes ancient story-telling techniques to which we respond, subconsciously.

The only modern touches are the "Peace" greeting of the desk clerk (?) and especially the blasé, callous, smart-ass or so-what's-new? reply by the waitress, "Everyone wants to fuck." Other than that, and with a change of locale, this tale could have been told in England several hundred years ago.   (R. A.)

MALEDICTA T-SHIRTS

During 1982, we will have a number of iron-on transfers of Maledicta-related matters. You will be notified when these iron-ons are actually available.

colorful speech

★ **Let's have a drink. My mouth tastes like the inside of a Greek wrestler's jockstrap.** (Martha Cornog, Penna. Found in G. Legman's *No Laughing Matter*, p. 477)

★ **You're playing hockey with a warped puck.** ("Crazy." "Carol Burnett Show")

★ **The kid was so obnoxious that his parents had to tie a pork chop to his ear so that the dog would play with him.** (Don Krabbe, Illinois, in letter to Ed.)

★ A Czech insult: **Než ti vodřízli pupeční šňůru tak si s tebou hráli jak s jójem.** "Before cutting your umbilical cord, they played with you yo-yo." (Petr Skrabanek, M.D., Ireland)

★ **May all you ecological bastards freeze to death in the dark.** (Howard Shooshan, Mass., in letter to Ed.)

★ **My dick is so hard a cat couldn't scratch it.** (Common remark while shaving, U.S. Army. Stephen Gregory, Mich.)

★ **May a diarrhetic dromedary defecate in your décolletage.** (To an obnoxious woman. Paul Runey, Va. 1981)

★ **Thanks for.... It was almost as exciting as nestling with a nymph in a nightie.** (Michael Fandal, NY., in letter to Ed.)

★ **Some minimal life form which sucks farts at a diaper service absconded with my *Maledicta*.** (Tom Frillman, Cal., in letter to Ed.)

★ **You're as slick as snot on a marble.** (S. Moe, Cal., an admiring, witty geriatric cat, in letter to Ed.)

★ **Her mother is as busy as the dildo in a fag sultan's harem.** (Merritt Clifton, Québec, in letter to Ed.)

★ **Thanks for sending *Maledicta*. I had so much fun I felt like a whore in a navy yard.** (Bruce Jones, Missouri, to Ed.)

★ **He was happier than a baby in a barrel of tits.** (A comic on the "Tonight Show," 22 Jan. 1981)

★ **He ain't worth shit in a handbag.** *And:* **I don't know whether to shit or wind my watch.** (George Carlin, on a record)

★ **She's a girl who can suck the chrome off a trailer hitch.** (R. Redford's friend about a young woman, in the movie *The Electric Horseman*, 1979)

★ **Colder than the Devil's Prick.** (Feminist reprise to the common "Colder than a Witch's Tit." Jessica Sheridan, Illinois)

★ Heard from a male grade school teacher discussing a sexually active fellow-teacher: **She'll drop her drawers for a mop-handle if you leave it at a forty-five-degree angle.** (Joe Salemi, New York)

★ **It smells like a sack full of sour dick heads.** (Jacquard Guenon, Mich., in letter to Ed.)

★ **Some of my best friends are genitals.** (L. Fischer, Mass.)

★ **May you be like Chicago—chronically plagued by winds.** (Editor, to an annoying "Is it out yet?" inquirer)

★ **Just so that you shouldn't have a loss, may one of your eyes drop in and the other drop out.** (Yiddish curse. Abraham Eiss, NY., in letter to Ed.)

★ **May the smell of their pudenda attract large and horny German shepherds.** (Dave A., Penna., complaining about his slovenly fellow-editors. 1980)

★ **He's so ugly he could open up a branch face.** (Heard from two blacks on the bus. Robert S., Washington, D.C., 1981)

★ **She's so dumb she couldn't add up to 2 without taking off her blouse.** ("Benny Hill Show")

★ **Helloran's bibliographical entry was shorter than the shriveled-up penis of a Hungarian hermaphrodite.** (Editor, referring to some cacademic asshole he once knew)

★ **He's so dumb he thinks manual labor is a Mexican immigrant.** (Editor, read somewhere)

★ **The river is frozen harder than the shady side of a banker's heart.** (Ed McCarthy, Penna., 70, quoted in *Time* magazine, 26 Jan. 1981, p. 37)

★ **You should have been a hemorrhoid because you're such a pain in the ass.** (Novelty card, NY., 1981)

★ Marine to paratrooper: **Only two things fall out of the sky: bird shit and idiots.** (Don Krabbe, Illinois, in letter to Ed.)

★ German insult: **Wenn du so lang wärst wie du dumm bist, dann müßtest du in einer Kegelbahn übernachten.** "If you were as tall as you are stupid, you would have to sleep in a bowling alley." (Editor)

MISCELLANY

♦ Ambrose Bierce's *Enlarged Devil's Dictionary*, ed. by Ernest Hopkins (1967), describes the common housefly as **musca maledicta**, "damned, cursèd fly." (Robert Smith)

♦ **"My sharp Cheddar Balls are back...."** (Advertisement in *The Adventurous Cheeselover: International Cheese Newsletter*, N.Y., March 1981, p. 4. — Thanks for telling us, Gerard)

♦ Found in "Dr. Wing Tip Shoo's X-Rated Fortune Cookies" (N.Y.): **Woman who cooks carrots and peas in same pot, unsanitary. — Stenographer not permanent fixture until screwed on desk. — Girl who sleep with judge get honorable discharge.** (Page Bernstein)

♦ *Q:* What's the difference between a vitamin and a hormone? *A:* You can make a vitamin. ("Benny Hill Show")

♦ John Lahr published the biography of Joe Orton (1978) called **Prick Up Your Ears**. (Rather messy, and painful.)

♦ Does your female sexual partner treat you like your banker? **"Substantial penalties for early withdrawal."**

♦ **Happiness is a Good Screw.** (Advertising on matchbox cover, Tyco Fastening Products, N.Y. — Keith Denning)

♦ *Poetic Justice:* When your brother-in-law who neither smokes, drinks nor swears catches VD. (Roy West)

♦ **Garden Bouquet** Beauty Soap: New brand name for the former **Gay Bouquet** soap. (Henry Madden)

♦ Would you say that a seven-year-old homosexual is a kid who turned prematurely gay?

♦ The headquarters of **Women USA** (Bella Abzug, president) is located in N.Y. City, **76 Beaver St.** (Denison Hatch)

♦ Baltimore Police Commissioner Donald Pomerleau, testifying in a sex discrimination lawsuit: "All women are little balls of fluff in the eyes of the creator." (*Debris* 8, June 1981, p. 2. — John Boston). The Creator must have been blind in the case of Abzug, Friedan & Co.: nothing fluffy about them!

♦ After Tennis Star Billie Jean King's lesbian affair became known, jokes started to fly: *Q:* Who will be B.J.K.'s new sponsor? *A:* Snap-on Tools. — *Q:* How did Billie become champion? *A:* She licked her opponents. — *Q:* Why won't they let Billie play at the World Championship in Holland? *A:* Because she wants to stick her finger in every dike. (Dennis D., Gordon W.)

TOM, DICK AND HAIRY
NOTES ON GENITAL PET NAMES

Martha Cornog

I am sitting in a room with about thirty women. We are all attending a session on "vaginal consciousness raising" at a conference entitled "A View Through the Speculum." [1] The session leader, a beautiful, vibrant woman of a "certain age," asks us each to give the word(s) we use for our own genitals. "Vagina." — "Pussy." — "Pussy. Vagina." — "Cunt." — "Mama's box." — "Henrietta."

Some people, like the last two women, use pet names to refer to their genitals. In *Lady Chatterley's Lover*,[2] the fictional Mellors calls his penis "John Thomas"[3] and Constance Chatterley's vulva "Lady Jane." Names like these (*Mama's Box, Henrietta, John Thomas*) I call genital pet names. They function as proper names[4] and refer to an *individual's* genitals only. In this way, they differ from general slang terms for genitals (e.g., *pussy, bearded clam, box; dick, cock, hog, one-eyed wonder worm*)[5] because they are personal, proper names.

Not only fictional characters like Mellors use pet names: real people name their genitals, too. To date, I have collected over thirty such pet names.[6]

The information given with each pet name follows this pattern (where supplied): significance or meaning of name; circumstances of naming or "christening"; the age of the owner of the genital at the time the name was used; and location.

PET NAMES FOR THE PENIS

Alice: "Put Alice in Wonderland." From Lewis Carroll's book. *See* **Wonderland.** Private language between lovers.

Baby: "Does Baby want to go Home?" *See* **Home.** Private language between lovers. Age 20. Indiana.

Broom: Couple undergoing marriage counseling (*see* text, below). Indiana.

Casey: After Casey Jones, the brave engineer, who took a trip "into the promised land." Private language between lovers. Named by the woman. Age 20. Rhode Island.

Chuck: Middle name of owner. Private language between lovers. Named by the woman during sex play. Age 33. Ohio.

Dipstick: Couple undergoing marriage counseling. Indiana.

Driveshaft: Couple undergoing marriage counseling. Indiana.

Four on the Floor: A car's gearshift. Couple undergoing marriage counseling. Indiana.

Gearstick: Couple undergoing marriage counseling. Indiana.

George: "Let George do it." Age 24. Pennsylvania.

Gnarled Tree Trunk (G.T.T. for short): Shape of penis (heavily veined). Private language between lovers. Named by the woman during sex play. Age 50. Pennsylvania.

Hank: Named by owner at male drinking party (*see* text, below). Age 60. Pennsylvania.

Jason: London, England.7

Jawillbemy: Possibly a shortening of "Jane will be my. . ." Private language of flirtation (couple were not lovers). Age 18. Oklahoma.

Lazarus: "He rises from the dead." Age 33. Washington, D.C.

Little Weese: "Weese" is a Midwestern mispronunciation of owner's surname. Private language within intimate network of three couples. Age 20. Ohio.

Little Willy: Owner named Bill. "Little" is ironic, as "Little Willy" is nine inches long, according to Bill's ex-wife.

Mortimer: Private language between lovers. Named by the woman during sex play. Age 28. Ohio. *See* **Eunice,** below.

Periwinkle: Private language between lovers. May have been used previously by the man.

Peter J. Firestone: "Peter" from common slang for penis,[8] "J. Firestone" from middle initial and last name of owner. Private language between lovers. Age 18. Ohio.

Putz: Yiddish for "penis." Private language within intimate network of three couples. Age 20. Ohio.

Sniffles: Man had slight genital discharge; doctor suggested that maybe he had "caught a cold." Private language between lovers. Age 20. Toronto, Canada. Man (informant) is originally from the U.K.

Winston: "Tastes good, like a cigarette should." Private language between lovers. Age 30. Pennsylvania.

Zeke: Private language within intimate network of three couples. Age 20. Ohio.

▼ ▼ ▼

PET NAMES FOR THE VULVA[9]

Eunice: Old-fashioned name, corresponding to **Mortimer** (*see* above). Private language between lovers. Named by the man during sex play. Ohio.

Henrietta: Pennsylvania.

Home: "Does Baby want to go Home?" *See* **Baby**. Private language between lovers. Age 20. Indiana.

Honeypot: Couple undergoing marriage counseling. Indiana.

Little Monkey: "Can I pet the Little Monkey?" Couple undergoing marriage couseling. Indiana.

Mama's Box: Age 35. Pennsylvania.

Rochester: From the city where she lost her virginity. Private language within intimate network of three couples. Age 20. Ohio.

Virginia Vagina: Alliteration. Private language within intimate network of three couples. Age 20. Ohio.

Wonderland: "Put Alice in Wonderland." *See* **Alice**. Private language between lovers.

Although this list of names is not long, we can discern some patterns of naming, particularly for the penis. Most names of penises fall into one of the following categories:

1. A variation of the owner's name (*Little Willy, Chuck, Peter J. Firestone*).

2. A name suggesting a joke or catchy phrase, usually alluding to erection or sex acts (*Lazarus, Winston*).

3. What Sanders and Robinson call "power slang" [10] (*Driveshaft, Four on the Floor*).

4. Human first names that appealed or occurred to the namer for no reason that could be recalled by the informant. "The Saturday night of Opening Day [of trout season] I can remember vividly. [My father] he was drunker than a warthog.... We get out on the porch [to urinate] and he's...singing 'I took my organ to the party,'...he gets his fly open... and he starts to relieve himself—a fairly steady stream—and he starts talking to his organ and, by God, he calls the thing 'Hank.' He says, 'Aw, look at old Hank here, poor, poor old guy.' And he says, 'You and I, we've been in a couple of tight places together and we've had our ups and downs, but I want you to know, you old sonofabitch'—and this is where he starts shaking it off—'that I outlived you!'.... That was the first time I had heard him allude to 'Hank' [and] I think it was just a spur-of-the-moment thing."

Some of the same patterns occur among the names for vulvas (*Wonderland*, for example). However, I have collected too few names for vulvas to be able to generalize at this point.

Who names genitals? In those cases where I was told the full story by the informant of the "christening" (16 cases out of 33), it was most often a group or couple interaction, or the other partner who produced the name. (For the remaining cases, this information was not available.) Penises seem to be named more often than vulvas.

Why do some people give proper names to genitals? After all, no one names feet, hands or elbows. Genital proper or pet names serve one or more functions.

First, the name(s) can serve as a private language between lovers or other groups of people who know each other well. Such a language permits discussion of sexual matters in front of unknowing friends and parents. The woman who told me about *Peter J. Firestone* said, "We would be sitting at dinner [with his parents] and he would toss off this comment, 'Well, maybe we could double-date with Peter tonight,' and then we'd go, 'Ha, ha, ha,' and hope that his mother didn't see me turn red!" Similarly, the owner of *Winston* and his girlfriend took great pleasure in discussing "Winston's good taste" in front of friends and relatives. One sex manual advises genital naming for this purpose:

> Pat your man's penis during nonsexual moments. Give it a pet name such as "John Thomas," used by Lawrence's Lady Chatterley; or name it after its owner, calling it "Junior" — "David, Junior," "Mark, Junior," etc. A girl I know has long hilarious conversations with someone named Penis Desmond — P.D., for short — who answers her in a high-pitched falsetto voice. This little act is a fun way to humanize a woman's relationship to a man's penis.[11] [Note that here the woman partner is advised to do the naming, and to pick a variation of the owner's name.]

When Sanders and Robinson solicited genital terms from college students, they found that the spouse/lover context elicited the greatest number of idiosyncratic responses, including pet names. To explain this, they quote Mark L. Knapp (*Social Intercourse*, Boston: Allyn and Bacon, 1978, p. 15): "The process of constructing a more intimate relationship eventually reaches the point where we are interacting with the other person as a unique individual rather than as a member of a particular society. Uniqueness in communication simply suggests the adoption of a more idiosyncratic communication system adapted to the peculiar nature of the interacting parties.[12]

In a broader sense, the pet name can also serve as a method of facilitating communication about sex. Many people, particularly women, are uncomfortable with the common generic terms for genitals.[13] One of my informants was a marriage counselor for several years:

> One of the things we frequently encountered were persons who were having a great deal of difficulty verbally communicating

about sex, and the reason was that they were extremely...uncomfortable with what they considered to be profane words, and they were uncomfortable with the official Latin terminology. And what was typically going on, then, was just nothing. With lack of a label, people weren't talking. So...after playing around with it for a while, I thought about the possibility of using made-up words. So we started doing that in therapy [having the couples make up names for body parts and sex acts] and we found it to be very successful. A lot of couples who had had trouble before really got into it, found it very enjoyable and developed a whole new vocabulary for sex organs and sexual acts.... From a therapeutic point of view, it was a very good idea, because, in addition to giving them a label that they could use to communicate and increase the effectiveness of what they were doing,...it [also] created a very nice thing for them to do together. The process of thinking up names and developing this new vocabulary was a very enjoyable process of sharing for most of the couples that tried it.[14]

Finally, the pet name bestows an identity upon the genitals: they have a personality which *is distinct* from the identity of the owner:

The experience of genital excitation parallels the experience of the I in that it has a somewhat detached quality.... In men the penis is often given a name to indicate that it has a degree of independence from the self. It may be called "John," or *le petit homme* [the little man], or "Peter," to denote this independence from the self.[15]

Much current popular literature on sex and psychology describes the alienation and the love/hate relationship men often have with their penises: "...He curses his penis for not performing, as he sweats and strains and informs his partner that *he* really wants to, even though something is wrong with *it*."[16] And Jerry Rubin gives the dialog:

My *penis*: I don't want to get turned on here. This bed is not safe for me.
My *mind*: Shut up! Perform! Don't let me down!...You're humiliating me in front of Rosalie![17]

A man having some of these feelings who gives a pet name to his penis can thereby both wash his hands of what "it" does and also diffuse his anxiety through humor. Lawrence's Mellors illustrates this process:

> The man [Mellors] looked down in silence at the tense phallos, that did not change. —"Ay!" he said at last, in a little voice, "Ay ma lad! tha'art thee right enough. Yi, the mun rear thy head! Theer on thy own, eh? an' ta'es no count o' nob'dy! Tha ma'es nowt o' me, John Thomas. Art boss? of me? Eh well, tha'rt more cocky than me, an' that says less. John Thomas! Dost want *her*? Dost want my lady Jane?... Tell Lady Jane tha wants cunt, John Thomas....[18]

Thus, we have the theme of genitals-as-personality. We can also call this "genitomorphism." It goes much further than the practice of giving proper names to genitals. It reaches into psychology, folklore, literature, art and religion. Included in this theme of genitomorphism are the subthemes of talking genitals (Thompson Motif D1610.6), genitals *talked to* and genitals acting on their own volition. Finally, of course, we have Genital Gods, i.e., phallic worship. Above, I have noted some of the psychological correlates of naming genitals. Gershon Legman discusses the folklore of genitomorphism. In his *Rationale of the Dirty Joke* (First and Second Series), he provides nearly twenty jokes or tales dealing with genitals named, speaking, spoken to, or acting on their own. Several examples, condensed here:

1. Groom on honeymoon to bride: "Honey, would you like to see *Oliver Twist*?"
   Bride: "Why not? I've seen it do everything else!"

2. Prostitute sees reflection of her vulva in a puddle: "There you is, you l'il ol' money-maker!"

3. Man amputates penis accidentally while shaving. Severed penis: "I know we've had lots of fist fights in our time, but I never thought you'd pull a knife on me!"[19]

And a wonderful cartoon was described to me, reportedly published in *The Realist*, of a man holding his penis, *which is saying* (via a cartoon "balloon"), "Not tonight, dear, I have a headache!"[20]

In literature, I have already mentioned *Lady Chatterley's*

Lover. I have found other interesting examples. In *Portnoy's Complaint*, Portnoy has a long dialog with "the maniac who speaks into the microphone of my jockey shorts."[21] Henry Miller, in *Tropic of Capricorn*, gives a long and detailed typology of "cunt personalities."[22] The hero of Petronius's *Satyricon*, Encolpius, has a violent argument with "a part of me which no serious man thinks worthy of his thoughts."[23] Legman cites several additional references from literature.[24]

In the graphic arts, genitals have been depicted as self-contained beings, or as the heads of otherwise human bodies. Fourteen plates in *The Complete Book of Erotic Art* depict this theme,[25] including a delightful series of Japanese prints of a Sumo wrestling match between a penis and a vulva, which ends (not surprisingly) with the penis being engulfed by the vulva/vagina.

Finally, a substantial literature concerns phallic worship. Edwardes gives one example in *The Jewel in the Lotus*, where he describes "the evil *jinee El-A'awer* (one-eyed penis genie), patron spirit of the ravisher."[26]

As Vance Randolph and Gershon Legman point out, "a fascinating monograph could be written on these themes of the speaking privates of both sexes. ..."[27] Genitals *named*, genitals *spoken to*, genitals *acting independently*, and genitals *deified* are related themes. All are subsumed under the broader concept of "genitals-as-personality." But we have yet to understand fully why genitals are personified, the cultural conditions under which personification happens and, finally, what it means to people who say *Henrietta* or *Winston* to genitals.

FOOTNOTES

1. A View Through the Speculum: A Workshop on Vaginal Health and Politics. Sponsored by the Elizabeth Blackwell Health Center for Women. Philadelphia, Pa., May 17, 1980.

2. David Herbert Lawrence. *Lady Chatterley's Lover* (New York: New American Library, 1959), pp. 196-97, 212-14, 283.

3. "John Thomas" is also generalized slang for the penis, as quoted from *The Pearl* by Tim Healey in "A New Erotic

Vocabulary," *Maledicta* 4(2):191, Winter 1980. Mellors, however, uses it as a personal pet name.

4. "Proper names" are explained by David Schwarz as "semantic atoms. They cannot be constructed by a speaker out of pre-existing material; they must be learned individually." (*Naming and Referring: The Semantics and Pragmatics of Singular Terms* [New York: De Gruyter, 1979], p. 51.)

5. For additional terms for genitals, *see* Tim Healey's wonderful compendium [*op. cit.*, pp. 181-201] and "Naming the Vulvar Part" by Clyde Hankey [*Maledicta* 4 (2): 220-22, Winter 1980].

6. All owners and informants, with the exception of *Jason*'s and *Sniffles*'s owners, were U.S. citizens. None was self-identified as homosexual. I do not know if the patterns of genital naming by homosexuals are different in any way from heterosexual patterns.

7. *Jason* was the name a male stripper gave his penis, reported in "A Big Gland for the Little Ladies." [*Oui* 4(3):13, March 1975.] Was *Jason* looking for the Golden Fleece?

8. *Firestone* is a pseudonym for the surname of the owner.

9. I was going to call this section "Pet Names for the Vagina" until I read Mildred Ash's "The Vulva: A Psycholinguistic Problem" [*Maledicta* 4(2): 213-19, Winter, 1980, with accompanying mnemonic].

10. Janet Sanders and William Robinson. "Talking and Not Talking About Sex." *Journal of Communication* 29(2):22-30, Spring, 1979, p. 28.

11. Xaviera Hollander. *Xaviera's Supersex: Her Personal Techniques for Total Lovemaking* (New York: New American Library, 1976), p. 134.

12. Sanders and Robinson. *Op. cit.*, p. 29.

13. Sanders and Robinson's data suggest that women have fewer terms for sexual parts and acts than men, and verbalize less about sex, particularly about their own genitals. (*Op. cit.*, pp. 27-28.)

14. David Weis. Personal communication. Dec. 12, 1980.

15. Alexander Lowen. *Fear of Life* (New York: Macmillan, 1980), p. 87.

16. Herb Goldberg. *The New Male: From Self-Destruction to Self-Care* (New York: William Morrow, 1979), p. 120.

17. Jerry Rubin and Mimi Leonard. *The War Between the Sheets* (New York: Richard Marek Publishers, 1980), p. 68.

18. Lawrence. *Op. cit.*, pp. 196-97.

19. Gershon Legman. *Rationale of the Dirty Joke: An Analysis of Sexual Humor.* First Series (New York: Grove Press, 1968), pp. 285-86, 301, 371, 490, 750-51. Second Series *No Laughing Matter* (New York: Breaking Point, 1975), pp. 169, 229, 236-37, 589, 597, 604-05, 629, 874-76, 878-89. One of these tales is treated at greater length in Vance Randolph and Gershon Legman, "The Magic Walking Stick," *Maledicta* 3(2): 175-76, Winter, 1979. The three jokes given come from First Series, p. 490 and Second Series, pp. 229, 605.

20. Arno Karlen. Personal communication. April 10, 1981.

21. Philip Roth. *Portnoy's Complaint* (New York: Random House, 1969), pp. 126-28. (Cited by Legman, *op. cit.*, Second Series, pp. 586-87.)

22. Henry Miller. *Tropic of Capricorn* (New York: Grove Press, 1961), pp. 194-95. (Cited by Legman, *op. cit.*, First Series, p. 371.)

23. Quoted by Robert S. De Ropp in *Sex Energy* (New York: Delacorte Press, 1969), p. 125.

24. Legman. *Op. cit.*, First Series, pp. 750-51; Second Series, p. 237.

25. Phyllis and Eberhard Kronhausen. *The Complete Book of Erotic Art*, Volumes 1 and 2 (New York: Bell Publishing, 1978); plates 146, 326 in Vol. 1; plates 23, 123, 130, 335, 337-46 in Vol. 2.

26. Allen Edwardes. *The Jewel in the Lotus* (New York: Julian Press, 1959), p. 109.

27. Randolph and Legman. *Op. cit.*, p. 175.

CANADIAN SEXUAL TERMS

Reinhold Aman *and* Grace Sardo

In 1978, Grace Sardo, an undergraduate student at McMaster University in Hamilton, Ontario, wrote a socio-linguistic paper, "Our Sexist Language: An Investigation of Male/Female Taboo Words." Students and a few others from southern Ontario were given a questionnaire with 16 key words and were asked to list all synonyms they knew for these 16 terms. Ms. Sardo divided her informants into a Control Group and a Random Group, collected the data, and established detailed statistics showing words per informant provided, standard deviation, etc., and used the material for her feminist paper.

Reinhold Aman edited and annotated the material for this presentation, extracted and arranged the vocabulary items into the 32 lists published below, divided the terms collected into responses from males and from females, alphabetized the lists, and corrected various misspellings.

Certain shortcomings of the questionnaire supplied to the informants are evident, such as mixing verbs, nouns and adjectives, as well as not distinguishing between terms for *male prostitute* and *female prostitute*, *male masturbation* and *female masturbation*, *vulva* and *vagina*, and the absence of related terms such as *scrotum, ejaculation, climax*, and others. However, on the whole, the terms gathered provide an interesting insight into present-day sexual vocabulary used in southern Ontario.

The 16 key words are grouped by terms applying to males only (*Man, Male Homosexual, Penis, Testicles, Erection*), to females only (*Woman, Female Homosexual, Prostitute, Vagina, Breasts, Menstruation, Pregnant*), and a third group of terms applying to both sexes (*Buttocks, Kissing, Masturbate, Sexual Intercourse*).

LISTS

MAN (*synonyms elicited from males*): achiever, adolescent, boss, boy, breadearner, breadwinner, brother, buck, buddy, bus driver, chap, dominant protector, dude, esquire, father, fellow, friend, gent, gentleman, God, grandfather, guy, homemaker, homo sapiens, human, husband, jerk, leader, male, manager, man of the house, masculine sex, nephew, person, prick, serviceman, son, stud, uncle.

MAN (*synonyms elicited from females*): aggressor, ape, babe, bastard, better half, bloke, boss, boy, boyfriend, breadwinner, brother, butch, chap, chauvinist, dog, donor of sperm, dude, egoist, exploiter, father, fellow, friend, gentleman, grandfather, guy, homo sapiens, hunk, husband, initiator, jock, lad, lover, macho image, male, masculine sex, mister, No. 1, old man, partner, person, pimp, powerful, screw, sir, son, strong, stud, turkey, uncle, victim, worker.

MALE HOMOSEXUAL (*males*): AC/DC, bent, butch, clockwork orange, cocksucker, deviant, drag queen, fag, faggot, fairy, fink, fruit, gay, gayboy, homo, homo sapiens, homophile, homosexual, ignorant woman, individual, invert, kook, male, man, pansy, person, pouf, queen, queer, sissy, strange, suckhole, switch-hitter, weirdo, woman.

MALE HOMOSEXUAL (*females*): AC/DC, Alice, ass bandit, bugger, butch, closet queen, cream puff, deviant, different, effeminate male, fag, faggot, fairy, feminine, fruit, fruit puff, fruitcake, gay, gayboy, he/she, homo, human, individual, john, lesi, leslie, man, nice guy, pansy, prick, queen, queen in drag, queer, raving queen, stud, swell, weirdo.

PENIS (*males*): big stick, bird, bone, boner, cock, dick, dink, dong, dork, feat, genital, glory, gun, hanger, hardon, John Thomas, joint, joystick, knob, machine, meat, meat hook, member, mickey, muscle, one-eyed worm, organ, pecker, peter, pickle, pisser, pistol, poker, pole, priapus, prick, rat, rod, shaft, staff, staff of life, stick, thing, tool, wand of life, wang, weapon, wiener, wire.

PENIS (*females*): big boa, big stick, birdie, bone, candlestick, centerpiece, cock, crotch, dick, dicky, dildo, dink, dipstick, dong, flashlight, gun, hammer, hotdog, joint, joystick, knob, kolbassa [Polish: *kiełbasa* "sausage"], love gun, love muscle, manhood, male ego, meat, noodle, organ, pecker, peepee, pee shooter [*wordplay*], personal, peter, phallus, pickle, pistol, pole, prick, privates, rat, rod, sausage, sex organ, sexual organ, six-incher, shaft, shmuck, stick, thing, tool, turkey neck, wang, weapon, wee man [*wordplay*], wiener, wienie.

TESTICLES (*males*): bags, balls, cherries, *cojones* [Spanish], cubes, eggs, family jewels, golf balls, grapes, hairy bag, jewels, leather, lover nuts, meat balls, nuts, pool balls, rocks, sack, scrotum, stones, testes.

TESTICLES (*females*): bag, bags, balls, berries, brass monkey [from "cold enough to freeze the balls off a brass monkey"?], chestnuts, crotch, family jewels, gonads, jewels, knockers, love nuts, male sex organ, marbles, nuts, organ, plums, prairie oysters, rocks, sac, sack, scrotum, spermmakers, stones, testes.

ERECTION (*males*): big, bone-on, boner, construction building, engorged, excited, firm push, flagpole, get-it-up, hard, hard stiff, hard-on, horn, horny, hot, proud, ready, rod, stand-up, stiff, stiffer, stiff prick, tall building, teninch, throbber, thrust, tumescence, up.

ERECTION (*females*): arousant, boner, constructing, excitement, frozen, get-it-up, hard, hardness, hard-on, heavy, high, horny, lover's nuts, rod, stiff, stiff cock, stiff prick, stiffness, stimulation, up.

WOMAN (*males*): aunt, babe, baby-sitter, beauty, beaver, better half, bimbo, *bint* [Arabic, "girl, daughter"], bird, bitch, broad, chattel, chick, companion, creator, crumpet, cunt, dame, darling, daughter, dog, dolly, female, female counterpart, feminine, fox, friend, gal, gash, girl, girlfriend, grandmother, hen, homo sapiens, honey, housewife, human, lady, lovely, lover, mistress, momma, mother, niece, nurse, old lady, person, piece of ass, prostitute, secretary, sex symbol, sexy, Sheila, sister, spouse, sweetheart, temptress, waitress, wench, whack, whore, wife, woman of the house, wren.

WOMAN (*females*): angel, adult counterpart, babe, baby, bearer of children, *bint* [Arabic: "girl, daughter"], bird, bitch, broad, chick, child, companion, cunt, dame, daughter, doll, female, feminine sex, fairer sex, fox, friend, gal, girl, grandmother, hag, homemaker, homo sapiens, honey, housewife, lady, lover, madame, mate, Miss, mother, Mrs., Ms., No. 2, old girl, old lady, old maid, piece, piece of ass, second sex, sister, slut, slave, spinster, strength, sweetie, toots, victim, virgin, weaker sex, wench, wife, whore.

FEMALE HOMOSEXUAL (*males*): AC/DC, beaver-eater, bitch, butch, dyke, fag, fay, fem, gay, homo, homosexual, les, lesbian, lezzy, non-Anita-Bryant, odd, queen, queer, sapphist, sickie, sister, tribadist, weirdo.

FEMALE HOMOSEXUAL (*females*): butch, butch broad, deviant, dyke, female, gay, homo, les, lesbi, lesbian, lesbo, lessie, lesy, queer, sappho, sister, virago, weirdo.

PROSTITUTE (*males*): bitch, call girl, chippie, courtesan, deviant, dog, douche bag, easy lay, expensive, floozy, harlot, hooker, lady of pleasure, lady of the night, mother, nymph, nympho, pleaser, pervert, pro, pushy, red light girl, sexy, sleeze, slut, street girl, streetwalker, strumpet, tart, teaser, trick, wench, whore, woman, woman of the night.

PROSTITUTE (*females*): bitch, boy, business woman, call girl, cock sucker, cock teaser, courtesan, douche bag, evil woman, floozy, hooker, hosie, hose bag, lady in red, lady of the evening, lady of the night, lay, loose woman, madame, piece, pig, pro, prostie, saloon girl, screw, scuz bag, self-sell, sleeze, sleeze bag, slut, streetwalker, stripper, tart, tramp, travelling secretary, vamp, whore, wild woman, woman, womankind, work, working girl.

VAGINA (*males*): beaver, beaver pelt, box, bush, cavern, crack, crevice, crotch, cunt, dirt chute, douche, front bum, furburger, genitalia, glory, guiff [?], hole, home-sweet-home, honey pot, love hole, love mound, mound, muff, nether lips, organ, patch, pie, piece, private parts, pudenda, pussy, screwhole, sex, slit, slot, snatch, triangle, twat, valley, vulva.

VAGINA (*females*): beaver, big V, birth canal, box, bun, bush, candle holder, canal, cave, cherry, clit [!], cookie, crack, crotch, cunt, donut, furburger, ginny, hairy pie, hole, juice box [*wordplay on* "jukebox"?], labia, lips, lower lips, man hole, muff, opening, orifice, passage, peepee, pelt, pie, pit, playpen, pussy, sex organ, snapper, snatch box, tube, tunnel of love, twat, twit, Y.

BREASTS (*males*): balloons, big ones, boobs, bosom, bottles, bouncers, bulbs, bumps, bumpers, bristols, bust, butes, cans, chest, glands, globes, hangers, headlights, jelly rolls, jugs, knockers, lungs, mams, mammaries, mammary glands, melons, milkers, mounds, nipples, norts, orbs, pectorals, playthings, potatoes, promontories, puppies, set, teats, tits, tomatoes, udders.

BREASTS (*females*): balloons, bank accounts, bazooms, boobies, boobs, bosom, bust, cans, chest, coconuts, drobes, female anatomy, fried eggs, grapefruits, handful, headlights, jugs, juts, knockers, mammaries, mammary glands, melons, milk dairies, milk jugs, molehills, mounds, nipples, norts, nuts, pillows, set, tits, stacked, watermelons.

MENSTRUATION (*males*): bleeding, curse, drip, flags, flying, friend, getting wet, menses, monthlies, monthly, natural process, on the bun, on the rag, period, problem, rag, ragging, red wings, ragtime, stop sign, that time, three-day wait, time of the month, visitor, yuk.

MENSTRUATION (*females*): bleed, bleeding, blood, blood flow, blood week, buddy, Charlie, cramps, curse, cycle, excoriation, flow, flushing, friend, foe, glad rags, George, jinx, monthly, on the rag, ovulation, pain, period, plague, rag, rag time, red flag, sick, that time of the month, thing, time of the month, unpregnant, visitor, woman's cycle, womanliness.

PREGNANT (*males*): bearing child, belly, big, bread in the oven, breaded, bun in the oven, caught out, expectant, expecting, fat, filled with child, fucked, full, great with child, having a baby, heavy, huge, in the family way, in the pudding club, knocked up, mother-to-be, nine months, not a book reader, popped up, problem, round, up the shoot [chute], up the stump, with child.

PREGNANT (*females*): banged up, big trouble, bun in the oven, conceived, conception, expectant, expecting, full of something, having a baby, having a kid, in a condition, in a motherly way, in the family way, in the hangar, in the oven, knocked up, mother-to-be, motherhood, motherly way, one in the oven, swelled belly, under construction, up the stump, with child.

BUTTOCKS (*males*): anus, arse, ass, asshole, backside, bat, behind, bottoms, bum, buns, butt, caboose, can, cheeks, derrière, dirt shute [chute], fanny, hearts, lower limits, moon, orbs, parts, posterière [*wordplay*: posterior + derrière], rear, rear end, rester, rump, tail, trailer.

BUTTOCKS (*females*): arse, ass, back end, backside, behind, bottom, B.T.M. [= bottom], bum, bums [= bum + buns?], buns, butt, can, cheeks, derrière, fanny, fat, ham, hips, keister, loaves, low bottom, moon, pork chops, posterior, rear, rear end, rectum, rump, seat, slats, tail, thighs, tush [from Yiddish *tokhes*].

KISSING (*males*): blue bird, crooning, embracing, french kissing, frenching, gum, in rapture, loving, making out, necking, osculating, pecking, petting, pressing lips, smackeroos, smacking, smooching, snugging, spooning, sucking, touching.

KISSING (*females*): buss, embracing, enjoying, french kissing, frenching, hugging, making out, muck-muck [?], necking, pecking, petting, puckering up, sharing, smacking, smooching, snuggling, sucking.

MASTURBATE (*males*): auto-eroticism, auto-stimulation, beat it, beat off, beating off, beat the meat, blow your load, choking my chicken, ejaculate, feel oneself, fighting, fingering, fucking off, getting off, getting your rocks off, hand job, hand work, have it off, jack off, jerk off, making do, manual override, milk the snake, ooze, playing with self, play with yourself, pounding, pull my wire, pull my prick, pulling wire, putt peter, relieving yourself, self-abuse, self-excitation, self-manipulation, self-pleasuring, self-relief, tossing off, touching up, whack off.

MASTURBATE (*females*): auto-eroticism, beat the meat, enjoying oneself, excite, finger job, fingering, fucking, hand job, hand trip, having fun, jacking off, jerk off, jerking off, making do, making the soup, one-man show, playing with yourself, physical pleasure, release, self-abuse, self-fulfillment, self-stimulation, sex stimulation, tension release, whack off, whacking off.

SEXUAL INTERCOURSE (*males*): balling, banging, beast with two backs, braise, coitus, connect, copulate, couple, doing it, deflower, end away [?], frying bacon, fucking, get it, get it on, getting dicked, getting it off, getting laid, getting one's oats, getting together, getting your rocks off, going at it, going all the way, going to bed, get breaded, hammering away, have carnal knowledge, having it off, heavy petting, humping, in rapture, jumping, lay, lovemaking, lucky, making it, making love, making out, mating, piece, poke, pork, pumping, rattling, relief, riding, riding high, rock & rolling, score, screwing, securing, sex, shafting, shagging, shoving it in, sleeping, slipping a length, stuffing, take advantage.

SEXUAL INTERCOURSE (*females*): adultery, balling, bang, banging, blow job, coitus, copulation, diddle down, doing it, eating out, fifty different ways, fool around, fornicate, fucking, gang bang, get it on, get lucky, getting laid, getting your rocks off, go to bed, going all the way, having sex, horseback riding, humping, lay, lovemaking, loving, lard, making babies, making it, making love, making out, orgy, pleasure, pork, score, screwing, sex, shack up, shag, snag, sleep with, sucking, tail, tail ass, togetherness, whoopee.

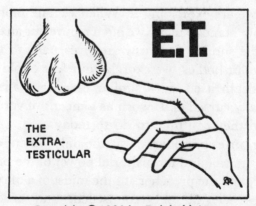

E.T.

THE
EXTRA-
TESTICULAR

Copyright © 1983 by Reinhold Aman

ITALIAN BLASPHEMIES

Giuliano Averna
Co-translated and Annotated by
Joseph Salemi

I

Swearing and cursing are very common in Italy. Although the practice is impolite, and a sin in the eyes of religion, most Italians — regardless of their social level — frequently use blasphemy. Perhaps centuries of religious domination, both temporal and spiritual, in extremely close proximity to the central power of the Catholic Church, have driven them to it.

We are all well aware that there are many ways to exorcize something hostile or inimical to us. When we speak of death we are exorcizing it. When we talk more or less freely about homosexuality we often relieve our anxiety concerning the subject. When we refer casually to the signs of age on our bodies, we exorcize our fear of old age and perhaps death itself. In a similar manner, Italians have traditionally cursed and sworn as a means of verbal exorcism, and they continue to do so today.

For centuries blasphemy was the only way of escaping the legal, moral, and inquisitorial power of the priest, the confessor, and the preacher. In the midst of a life of privations these clerics told, counselled, and ordered the wretched majority of the populace to continue suffering and obeying in the hope of a heavenly reward. Meanwhile, the dream of a land flowing with milk and honey was realized daily in the castles and palaces of the rich.

God is clearly the catalyst for the majority of these blasphemies, but we also find expressions that mention Christ, the Madonna, the sacraments, and so on. I have listed here about one hundred expressions in which God's divinity is blasphemed or insulted, along with some euphemisms. They have all been collected from the Italian language and its various dialects.

II

Abbreviations:

cal. dialect of Calabria	*rom.* dialect of Rome
emil. dialect of Emilia	*sic.* dialect of Sicily
ferr. dialect of Ferrara	*tosc.* dialect of Tuscany
lig. dialect of Liguria	*ven.* dialect of Veneto
mil. dialect of Milan	*venez.* dialect of Venice
par. dialect of Parma	*veron.* dialect of Verona

Dio assassino! *That assassin of a God!*

Dio 'ssasino! (ven.) *That assassin of a God!*

Dio beco! (ven.) *Horned God! God with a beak!* This imprecation refers to the horns of cuckoldry. The blasphemy would then have the same force as **Dio cornuto!** *Beco* (Venice, Veneto) and *becco* (standard Italian): "he-goat"; "beak"; "cuckold."

Dio bestia! (ven.) *That beast of a God!*

Dio bestialone! *That big beast of a God!* In Italian the suffix *-one* is a pejorative addition that connotes both largeness and derogation.

Dio birbo! (ven.) *That rascal of a God!*

Dio bonino! (tosc.) *Good God!*

Dio brigante! (ven.) *That bandit of a God!* Brigands and bandits have always been a part of Italian life.

Brigante de Dio! (ven.) *That bandit of a God!*

Dio brutt! (emil.) *Ugly God!*

Dio brutto! (ven.) *Ugly God!*

Dio buono! *Good God!*

Dio campanile! (venez.) *That bell tower of a God!* In Venice and Veneto, *campanile* is also pronounced *canpanile.*

Dio cane! *That dog of a God!*

Dio can! (ven.) *That dog of a God!*

Can de Dio! (mil.) *That dog of a God!*

Dio 'hane! (tosc.) *That dog of a God!*

Dio can-arino! (ven.) *That canary of a God!* This and the following two items are examples of verbal stops, designed to suggest *cane* "dog."

Dio can-oro! (ven.) *That singer of a God!*

Dio can-tante! (ven.) *That singer of a God!*

Dio cara! (ven.) *Dear God!*

Dio caro! (ven.) *Dear God!*

Dio cangi! (lig.) *Dear God!*

Dio cornuto! *Cuckolded God!* See **Dio beco!**

Dio culattiere! (venez.) *That sodomite of a God!* From *culatta*, the rump, the seat of the pants.

Dio fiol! (ven.) *That son of a God!*

Dio ladro! (ven.) *That thief of a God!*

Dio mamma! (ferr.) *That mother of a God!* "Mother" in this imprecation should be understood in the literal sense, not as the shortened form of *motherfucker*, a meaning which the term almost always carries in American malediction.

Dio madonna! *That Madonna of a God!*

Dio mas-cio! (ven.) *That boy of a God!* Another verbal stop, perhaps to suggest the term *mascalzone* "rogue, blackguard." *Mas-cio* also means "pork."

Dio mat! (ven.) *That madman, lunatic of a God!*

Dio nimale! (par.) *That animal of a God!*

Dio nimel! (par.) *That animal of a God!*

Dio porco! *That pig of a God!*

Dio porc! *That pig of a God!*

Dio prete! *That priest of a God!* In a country with a strong anticlerical tradition the term *prete* is often used pejoratively. *Strozzapreti* ("It strangles priests") is the name of several Italian dishes. According to Robert Di Pietro, this term is derived from the priests' reputation of being big, greedy eaters. Naming a dish *strozzapreti* thus indicates that it is so generous that it would even choke a priest.

Dio sagrasco! (rom.) *That sacrament of a God!* (**Dio sacramento!**) The sacrament referred to is the Eucharist or Christ's body. **Corpo di Cristo!** ("Body of Christ") is a very old Italian blasphemy, and there was no end of trouble in Italy when the Church switched from Latin to the vernacular in its services. Instead of saying *Corpus Christi* in Latin during Mass, priests had to say *Corpo di Cristo*, thus introducing blasphemy into the heart of the liturgy.

Dio sagraschio! (rom.) *That sacrament of a God!*

Dio sagrataccio! (rom.) *That sacrament of a God!*

Dio sagrato! (rom.) *That sacrament of a God!*

Dio sborà! (ven.) *God jacked-off! That jacked-off God!* From *sborar(e)* "to ejaculate."

Dio serpente! (ven.) *That snake of a God!*

Dio sarpente! (ven.) *That snake of a God!*

Dio scanpà! (ven.) *God ran off!*

Dio scapà da lett! (par.) *God escaped from bed!*

Dio scapà da lett senza scarpi! (par.) *God escaped from bed without shoes!* This and the following forms help reduce the blasphemy by their expansion.

Dio scapà da lett senza gambe! (par.) *God escaped from bed without legs!*

Dio scapà da lett in bicicletta! (par.) *God escaped from bed by bicycle!*

Dio sallarga! (rom.) *Expanding God!* Euphemism for **Dio sacramento!**

Dio s'allarga! (rom.) *Expanding God!*

Dio serenella! (rom.) *Cloudless God!* 19th century, military use.

Dio travo! (ven.) *That beam of a God!*

Dio impalato! (tosc.) *That shafted God!*

Dio rospo! (tosc.) *That toad of a God!*

Orco Dio! (ven.) *That pig of a God!* Euphemism for **Porco Dio!**

Orco zio! (ven.) *That pig of a God!* Double euphemism.

Per Dio! *By God!*

Per brio (par.) *By God!* Euphemism.

Par bio! (par.) *By God!* Euphemism.

Pebbio! (rom.) *By God!* Euphemism.

Peddio! (rom.) *By God!* Euphemism.

Peddio sagranne! (rom.) *By holy God!* Euphemism.

Peddio sagraschio! (rom.) *By holy God!* Euphemism.

Peddio de legno! (rom.) *By wooden God!* Euphemism.

Perdio sagrato! (rom.) *By holy God!*

Perdio santo a le bocie! (veron.) *By holy God playing* bocce! *By holy bowling God!* Blasphemy reduced by expansion.

Pardia! (veron.) *By God!* Euphemism.

Par die! (veron.) *By God!* Euphemism.

Par didedi! (veron.) *By God!* Euphemism.

Pardiu! (cal.) *By God!* Euphemism.

Pardeu! (cal.) *By God!* Euphemism.

Parbeu! (cal.) *By God!* Euphemism.

Pardena! (cal.) *By God!* Euphemism.

Perdena! (cal.) *By God!* Euphemism.

Perdeu! (cal.) *By God!* Euphemism.

Porco Dio! *That pig of a God!*

Porco zio! *That pig of a God!* Euphemism; *zio* means "uncle."

Porki dia! *That pig of a God!* Euphemism. Sometimes *porco* is written with a *k*, just as *cazzo* "prick" is seen written as *kazzo*.

Porco diose! (ven.) *That pig of a God!* Euphemism.

Porco madono! (ven.) *That pig of a Madonna!*

Sacher Dieu! (mil.) *Holy God!* Cf. the French *sacrebleu!* where *bleu* "blue" is a phonetic euphemism for *Dieu* "God." In French, however, *sacre* has retained the original double meaning of the Latin *sacer*: "holy" and "accursed." Thus *sacrebleu!* means "damned God!"

Sangue di Dio! *Blood of God!*

Sangue de Dio! (ven.) *Blood of God!*

Sangue de bio! (rom.) *Blood of God!* Euphemism.

Sango de bio! (par.) *Blood of God!* Euphemism.

Sanguanon de bia! (mil.) *Blood of God!* Euphemism.

Sandiocan! (ven.) *That dog of a holy God!*

Santo Dio! *Holy God!*

Santi dia! (sic.) *Holy God!*

Santu dia! (sic.) *Holy God!*

Vaca dio! (ven.) *That cow of a God! That whore of a God!* — *Vaca* "cow" is one of the most common insults meaning "whore."

Zio porco! (ven.) *That pig of a God!* Euphemism; *zio* "uncle."

Zio cane! (ven.) *That dog of a God!* Euphemism.

Zio can! (ven.) *That dog of a God!* Euphemism.

Zio schitaron! *That chickenshitting God!* — *Schito* is "chicken shit," and *schitarar* means "to defecate," especially in reference to chickens.

III

We have seen, although our sampling is limited, how practically any attribute or adjective can be effectively conjoined to the name of the divinity in order to create a blasphemy or an imprecation. Some blasphemies are restricted to specific regions and dialects, while others are common to vulgar and popular Italian.

A widely used one is *Dio cane!* ("That dog of a God!" or "You dog of a God!"), euphemized in various ways by using words that begin with *ca-*, i.e., the first syllable of the word *cane* "dog." A euphemism is thus created inasmuch as the word is different, but since the stress falls exactly on the first syllable, it creates the same emotive situation of the original *Dio cane!* In some expressions of the Venetian dialect we have instead a kind of verbal stop. Consider those words that begin with the syllable *can-*, the form for *cane* in the Venetian dialect. When these words are spoken in blasphemies, their pronunciation is held in suspension before completing the word, as if to recall the word *can* prior to varying it at the last moment to *can-ario*, *can-tante*, and so on.

The form *Dio sagrasco!* and its variants originated in the dialect of Rome, and in the early part of the nineteenth century the great Roman poet G. G. Belli recorded them in his sonnets. These sonnets, by the way, are a mine of many other words and expressions from Belli's Roman dialect.

In any case, the simplest of all euphemisms for Italian blasphemies and imprecations are the terms *orco* (for *porco* "pig"), and *zio* "uncle" (for *Dio* "God"). In the first, the dropping of the initial letter avoids the actual insult, while in the second the word changes its meaning completely. But since the sounds represented by *d* and *z* are both dentals, their pronunciation turns out to be quite similar.

Many Italians are convinced that by saying *Orco Dio!* and *Zio cane!* they are not blaspheming. The point to be made is this: whenever an individual utters imprecations involving the divinity it is blasphemy. Many persons have actually been persuaded by clerics that by using this sort of euphemism one does not blaspheme. Nevertheless, from a psychological and linguistic perspective, we have no choice but to disabuse them of this comforting notion. One always blasphemes when one uses an expression that links the word *God* with a more or less derogatory or offensive attribute, even when the words are altered orthographically or phonetically.

It is useless to seek to evade this reality. Blasphemy is a deeply rooted impulse in every individual, fixed in the human mind by millenia of religious training and inculcated piety. After all, everything comes from God, even the hammer that hits our finger and makes us cry out *Porco Dio!* He is the source of the missed bus that makes us yell *Zio cane!* and of the small daily misfortunes that prompt us to mutter *Orco zio!* Both the atheist and the believer blaspheme, using the pure blasphemy or the euphemism indiscriminately. It makes no difference. One man simply denies God while the other affirms him.

Perhaps these locutions are without significance in the long run. But some of them have been repeated for many centuries, with only slight variations. Our task is to catalog and report them; others will have to explain them.

"Kojak! Banacek! Toma! Kung-Fu!"

Note the abundance of voiceless stops and fricatives in his ejaculations. 5-10-74.

A GLOSSARY OF COMMON TERMS USEFUL FOR BEGINNING TEACHERS IN THE PUBLIC SCHOOL SYSTEM OF NEW YORK

Joseph Salemi

I. INTRODUCTION

The following glossary was composed in 1969, when I had the gross misfortune to be a teacher in the public school system of New York City. Those were troubled times — a protracted strike in the previous year had embittered parents and teachers, the Board of Education was a bloated, bureaucratic nightmare, and "community control" had not yet been exposed for the corrupt farce that it is. Schools were arenas where teachers, parents, administrators, and local political hacks battled over promotions, prerogatives, and purse-strings, while students remained untamed and untaught.

In this Hobbesian war of all against all, I was stationed at John Ericsson Junior High School in Brooklyn. A more pungent sinkhole of educational squalor could not be imagined. Discipline in the school was erratic at best — one strove mightily to keep a little order in one's classroom, but the halls and cafeteria were pure anarchy. Worse than disruptive students, however, was a faculty composed largely of backstabbing political climbers and timeserving unionized incompetents. I spent two years there, before fleeing back to graduate school.

What was I to do in such a purgatory, during the long

stretches between paychecks and holidays? Well, as Juvenal said, *difficile est saturam non scribere*. I wrote this glossary because, faced with the absurdity of the situation, it was impossible to do anything else. The following definitions are meant to reflect not just one school in one time period, but the entire mindset fostered by professional educationism and its concomitant imbecilities. I wish I could say the glossary was outdated. It isn't.

II. GLOSSARY

Administration: Those persons whose function it is to maladminister the school.

Assembly: A weekly gathering of the student body, for the purpose of impressing upon them the utter vacuity and boredom of school.

Board of Education: A group of superfluous appointees, dedicated to the proposition that it is better to make things artificially difficult rather than naturally easy.

Books: Originally the main tools of learning, books contain information in convenient form. It is traditional for every school to have a huge number of books, and to order countless more every semester. However, since most of the students and a sizeable number of the teachers are illiterate, the presence of this vast quantity of books is largely ceremonial.

Building Assignment: Every teacher is obliged to serve as a hostage five times per week, covering what is known as a *building assignment*. The teacher either walks the gantlet in the student cafeteria, or is placed as a sacrificial lamb at exits or in corridors. Building assignments are the principal occasions for the death or mutilation of teachers.

162 • Reinhold Aman

Bus: To transport a group of inferior students to a distant school, for the purpose of degrading the quality of *education* (q.v.)

Chancellor of the Board of Education: A person of limited intelligence whose function is to think up hypothetical problems and impose them on the school system as a whole.

Community: Those persons in a given locality who generate enough noise and disorder to attract the attention of the press. A true community is always composed of minorities; white communities are considered part of the *establishment* (q.v.)

Custodian: The person in charge of maintaining the school premises. Some people have wondered whether the custodian is a real person or a legend, since he is very rarely seen. However, inasmuch as broken windows are occasionally repaired and jimmied locks now and then replaced, it is probably safe to assume that he actually does exist.

Diploma: A document of no intrinsic importance, routinely given to all students who meet certain minimum attendance requirements.

Education: An obsolete concept involving the transmission of knowledge and wisdom, long rejected by the Board of Education for more electrifying concepts such as integration and larger budgets; the name, however, is retained for sentimental reasons.

Establishment: An imaginative concept, existing in the minds of those who make up the community. The establishment is the source of all corruption, oppression, and evil. However, when the community gains control and sets up its own establishment, this is known as *participatory democracy* (q.v.)

Faculty Conference: A monthly penitential exercise, directed by the administration.

Forms and Papers (*includes memos, circulars, notices, records, lists, plans, and documents of all kinds*): A minor divinity, devoutly worshipped by the Board of Education and administrators. No school can be operated without the sanctified presence of the requisite *Forms and Papers*, and daily rituals of obeisance and adoration must be performed in their honor. At certain times of the year, entire days are set aside exclusively for the worship of *Forms and Papers*. During these holy days the religious celebrations reach a fevered pitch.

Guidance Counsellor: An amateur psychologist with an abnormal devotion to teenagers. The guidance counsellor's function is to contradict everything a teacher says, and accept without question whatever a student says. The guidance counsellor — who is usually a pathetic, middle-aged female — hopes in this way to recapture her lost youth.

Intelligence: A character trait in certain children which the Board of Education discourages; its presence in a teacher is grounds for dismissal.

Lesson: A diversionary tactic by which a teacher keeps a given group of students relatively quiet and seated for forty minutes. A teacher must think up and perform five lessons before he is allowed to leave the school for the day.

   1. Lesson Aim: The purpose of the lesson. This is invariably to keep the students quiet and seated.

   2. Lesson Plan: A paper that the teacher keeps on his desk, to convince passing administrators that he is prepared to *teach* (q.v.)

Letter Box: One of the chief ways of distinguishing a teacher from an administrator. A teacher's greatest wish is to see that his letter box is empty; an administrator cannot pass an empty letter box without putting something into it.

Literacy: The ability to read and write clear, intelligible English sentences. Persons suffering from this disorder are automatically disqualified from joining a school's administration.

Participatory Democracy: A form of mob rule in which only members of the community may participate.

Paycheck: A bribe that one accepts to put up with the idiocies of the school system.

Principal: A person in a figurehead capacity, of dubious usefulness, whose function is to harass teachers from time to time.

> *Assistant Principal:* A subordinate of the principal who carries out harassment in greater detail. One of the chief functions of the assistant principal is to convince himself and the teachers of his own indispensability.

Racism: The belief that quality alone, and not race, should determine grades, appointments, and promotions in the school system.

> *Anti-racism:* The belief that race, and not quality, should determine grades, appointments, and promotions in the school system.

School Secretary: A hellish virago who mans the front desk at every school. Her personality is a combination of consuming envy of teachers, dripping contempt for students, and bootlicking adulation of administrators. Unfortunately, teachers are obliged to approach the school secretary for a variety of things, including *paychecks* (q.v.)

Security Guard: A musclebound cretin who roams the halls under the influence of alcohol or hashish. His task is to maintain order and discipline, and he is perfect for the job, having spent several years studying these subjects in Dannemora and Sing Sing.

Student: A person incarcerated in school, having been sentenced from birth to a period of not less than twelve years imprisonment in public institutions.

Supplies: Materials useful in teaching. Since supplies are items of incalculable preciousness (chalk, pencils, and yellow paper), they are kept under lock and key. No teacher can receive them without a written request, composed in the proper tone of obsequiousness.

Teach: To generate a series of coherent sounds, for the purpose of convincing administrators of one's usefulness, and keeping students quiet.

Time Clock: The central fetish in every school. Once in the morning and once in the afternoon, the faithful queue up to pay homage to this idol. If said homage is not paid at precisely the right time and in precisely the right manner, one may be excommunicated by the *school secretary* (q.v.)

Union Representative: A snivelling coward who is adept at extorting contributions from teachers for the political action fund, but who always finds an excuse for not helping a teacher in disputes with the administration.

"They called me a *what*?"

"YOUR MOTHER'S LIKE..."

FORMULA IN CONTEMPORARY AMERICAN RITUAL INSULTS

Simon J. Bronner

The hallways and playgrounds of schools are great places to hear insults hurled back and forth in a game-like atmosphere. Just recently I walked down the corridor of Penn State's Capitol Campus and noticed a group of burly young men engaged in a battle of words. "Why don't you get a *real* job?" Tony said to his pal, snickering. "Your mother," John retorted. "That's a low blow; speaking of low blows, how's your mother?" The group of five guys could be heard laughing and muttering to each other. In defense John exclaimed, "Well, your mother's like a railroad track—laid all over!" but Tony got the better of John, according to the audience, with "At least my mother doesn't use telephone poles for tampons!" With chortling and an air of play the group entered the classroom and prepared for work. This scene is repeated quite often across the country in schools and even in factories as friends "kid around" by verbally playing with insults. As the settings and players and formulas for insults are repeated, so the event takes on the character of ritual.

Part of the appeal of insulting is that once the basic structures for them are mastered, one can freely substitute in, and improvise upon, insult forms. A person can show his skill and creativity, become a recognized member of a group, and entertain himself and others by learning the appropriate settings and subjects for ritual insults. In fact, the persistence of ritual insults in oral tradition can be partially explained by their ease of recall. Why are they easily remembered? They are usually brief, have a clear structure, and like a script depend on cues which signal appropriate responses. In addition, the forms of insults are similar to other traditional genres, such as proverbial comparisons and riddles, which reinforce already familiar insult forms. Such easily remembered insult forms can be employed in a variety of situations and relationships, both joking and hostile, although the distinctions between joking and hostility are admittedly vague. An individual can usually rattle off many insults based on knowledge of their basic forms. Thus a person has the potential for an instant verbal defense, the possession of a valued ability to respond quickly, or in other words to have a biting "comeback." Yet another skill is to judge the proper times and people to act out these insult games.[1] You don't want to be like the college football player prone to cursing at formal dinners to whom the coach told to say nothing at the next one he attends. "My, you're being quiet tonight," one of the guests said to the star player. "Is anything wrong?" — "No," the player growled, "Coach doesn't want me to fuck-up!"[2]

The forms of American ritual insults are varied, but certain types appear distinctive. One category consists of the form, **Your mother is like...**, as in "Your mother's like a fan — turn her on and she blows," "Your mother's like a police station — dicks going in and out," "Your mother's like the freeway — everyone getting on and off," or "Your mother's like a door knob — everyone gets a turn." This form exhibits similarities with the structure of the proverb and riddle. Alan Dundes and Robert Georges have suggested that a riddle is a "traditional verbal expression which contains one or more descriptive elements, a pair of which may be in opposition; the referent of the element is to be given."[3] The descriptive element consists of the topic, defined as an apparent referent, and the comment, defined as an assertion about the topic. This really isn't as difficult as it may appear at first glance. In the case of "Your mother's like a fan—turn her on and she blows," *mother* is the topic and *fan* is the comment. The difference between the form of the insult and that of a riddle is that the referent in the insult is expressed as an action and is not guessed but is declared. An important characteristic of the referent action is a degree of surprise or incongruence which injects a humorous element into the insults. The unexpectedly large, small, grotesque, or exaggerated action and the clever analogy suggest incongruence, absurdity perhaps, and humor. The technique of incongruence is intrinsic to other humorous genres as well, such as jokes and riddle-jokes.[4]

As in other formulaic statements, substitutions in the statement are made which retain the basic form and concept of the insult. Thus "Your mother's like a birthday cake—everyone gets a piece," "Your mother's like the telephone company—her rates go down at night," or "Your mother's like a bowling ball—always getting laid in alleys" repeats the topic-comment descriptive element, pause, and referent action structure. Substitutions within the bimembral construction of the insult often repeat traditional insults or proverbial comparisons, but once the form is familiar, the teller can improvise easily. The process trains the teller to use simile and analogy and to substitute words using the same formulaic concept and sense of drama. Take, for example, "Your mother's like a cup of coffee—hot, black, and ready to be creamed," "Your mother's like an old Ford—used, rusty, and easy to get," "Your mother's like a bus—guys getting on and off all night," and "Your mother's like a lollipop—she gives everybody a lick."

Another formulaic device used in "Your mother is like…" insults is threefold repetition. The completeness expressed by enumeration of three elements in American culture also injects a finality to insults.[5] We have three basic classes, three strikes (and you're out), three branches of government, and three basic parts to a sentence (subject, object, verb). Dick Cavett recently indicated the entrenchment of threes when he unwittingly asked his guest on his television show, "What are *some of the three things* that make a good doctor?"[6] In insults, including three elements gives the statement an aesthetic balance. "Your mother's like a dollar — wrinkled, green, and spent" and "Your mother's like a bowling ball — black, gets fingered, and gets laid down alleys" are examples of this device.

Americans also like oppositions. We talk of "on the one hand, yet on the other" and we match one player versus another. We are asked whether we are *pro or con*. In insulting, this pattern is also found. One player usually squares off against another, and the structure of "Your mother's like…" is usually divided into two opposing parts. "Your mother's like the temperature" is opposed by "she goes down at night," and "Your mother's like the sun" is similarly matched by "she goes down at night." This structure seems as natural as having opposing ends of a balancing scale. One element must be as strong as the other and the proper structure depends on their balance.

A second insult form, **Your mother got…** expresses a simple declarative statement. Many of these insults express traditional motifs concerning remarkable organs.[7] By tracing these motifs found in Stith Thompson's *Motif-Index of Folk Literature* we have an inkling of the longevity and wide circulation of some ideas expressed in insults. "Your mother got three tits," for example, has an analog in Motif F546.2, "Women with three breasts," found in Irish and Indian traditions. Still another common insult, "Your mother got a dick," which I often collected from adolescent boys, reflects Motif F547.2, "Hermaphrodite. Person with both male and female sexual organs," found in Greek, Icelandic, and American Indian traditions. Motif F547.6.1, "Remarkably long pubic hair," found in Irish tradition, is indicated by the oft-repeated insult appearing in both black and white American traditions, "Your mother got hair on her pussy that sweep the floor." I do not wish to overstate the significance of motifs, but present them to suggest a traditional corpus of images permeating the American ritual insult tradition. The body of traditional motifs represents one basis for substitutions in the structure of insults. So we can note the traditional fear of insects and "cooties" in "Your mother got lice," "Your mother got crabs," or even "Your father got fruit flies—his banana died!"

Another distinctive insult form which also uses traditional motifs is **Your mother so... she...** The basic structuring principles involve the use of hyperbole, especially about remarkable organs. "Your mother's tits are so big, she needs roller skates to move them," "Your mother smells so bad, she uses Raid for crotch spray," and "Your mother's so low, she could walk under a pregnant ant" are examples of this form. The "so... she..." form contains a bimembral structure that includes a topic-comment descriptive element and referent action. Thus, the common insult "Your mother's so low, she has to look up to see the curb," contains *mother* as the topic, *low* as the comment, and *look up at the curb* as the referent action. And like much of folklore these insults have variants, such as "Your mother's so low, she can play handball against the curb," or even "Your mother's so low, she plays 'Sea Hunt' in whale spit!"

Insults do not always contain both the topic and comment in the descriptive element, but usually retain the bimembral construction. One form which often eliminates the comment is found in the **I went to your house...** form.

The predominant image compares the home to garbage cans or sewers. "I went to your house, but they said you moved two sewers up," "I went to your house, but the garbage men already emptied it," and "I walked in your house, I stepped on a cigar butt, and your mother said, 'Who turned off the heat?'" are typical insults collected in different cities in the East and South. The latter insult includes the comment, "I stepped on a cigar butt," although the action of "I went to" may be considered an implicit comment. Such insults strike at the fragile components of the teller's existence: family and home. Home life often incited insults because group members' domestic situations were frequently unknown to others in the group. Mothers and homes were easy prey for abuse since no firm base of truth existed; thus exaggerations rested comfortably on a base of belief rather than concrete information. Indeed, insults often were a means to evoke information from a group member by an indirect method. The insults against home attacked the Victorian image of cleanliness and order; the taboo against ritual dirt is embedded in many of the insults in circulation: "I went to your house but I couldn't get in — I didn't have a dime," "I went to your house — you need two sticks to get in there, one to hold up the roof and one to frighten off the alligators," "I went to your house for dinner — the flies led the way," and "In your house the rats are so big, the mice have to carry switchblades."

Personal insults such as "He said you were a frigid homosexual, but I defended you — I said you weren't," and response forms such as "Go fuck yourself" or "Eat my crusty shorts" commonly found in oral tradition underscore the combination of defense and offense in the content of insulting. Both categories of insults do not rely on a single structural form, but rather vary from simple epithets or curses to proverbial comparisons or rhymes. They may steer the game toward a different type of insult; for example, from "Your mother's like…" to "I went to your house…" In many instances, personal insults and response forms are a formulaic device to introduce the actual verbal duel or signal its end, thus providing a framing effect for ritual insult events. If this frame can be expressive, all the better: "I used to wear clothes like you, then my father got a job," "If I had a face like yours, I'd sue my parents for damages," "If shit was electricity, you'd be a powerhouse," and the proverbial "Your ass is grass and my fist is a lawnmower!"

Since ritual insults depend on responses to certain verbal cues, the insulting takes on an event character. Certain cues such as curses frame a duel for the players and for the watchful audience. In fact, routines based on the bantering of cues and responses emerge. The routines may be used for amusement outside a formal verbal duel, or they may advance a formal contest-in-insults, a ploy which allows the players to mentally prepare elaborate insults. A typical routine concerns scatological themes.

X: Eat shit!
Y: What will I do with the bones?
X: Build a cage for your mother.
Y: Your mother…

Several routines also mention intercourse.

X: Go fuck yourself!
Y: At least I can.
X: Sure, that wooden dick helps out a lot.
Y: Yeah, but the fairies complain about the splinters you leave.
X: At least I don't leave skidmarks like you.

These cues and responses in ritual insulting provide an escalating technique that furthers the game until its conclusion. Provocations by third parties can reinforce the escalation, and they often provide secondary cues.

Other insult types exist in oral tradition such as **I'd… you, but…, If I want any… I'll…, If you had… you**

would be..., and **If you won't... I won't...** Many of these personal insults consist of conditional statements again structured by a bimembral construction that delineates a descriptive element and referent action. "I'd hit you, but shit splatters," "If I want any lip out of you, I'll pull down my pants," "If you had brains you'd be dangerous," and "If you won't tell anybody I got a wooden dick, I won't tell anybody you've got splinters in your mouth," are, respectively, examples of such forms. The fundamental brevity and incongruence intrinsic to insults remain.

The selection of particular images used in insults, whether it be sex, bodily appearance, poverty, or manliness, depend on local preferences and references. For example, Oneonta, New York, informants usually stated, "I could have been your father, but a dog beat me over the fence," while New York City informants typically used "up the stairs" instead of "over the fence." The rationale for this substitution lies in Oneonta's housing spaces, which are denoted by fences, in contradistinction to New York City, which contains many apartment dwellings. Another local reference such as "You must get your clothes at John Bargain Stores" probably means little to players outside of New York City, but Woolworth's or some other reference may be substituted in other locales. Knowledge of sensitive topics for the receiver of insults also affects the selection of insults by the attacking player.

Particular groups or individuals often select particular insults unique to them. One informant repeated the phrase "Eat my crusty shorts" so often that when I mentioned the insult to others in the group, they would associate it immediately with him. Apparently inspired by the previously mentioned comeback for "Eat shit!", a response that was often stated for "Eat my crusty shorts!" was "Can I make soup out of it?" Similarly, certain subjects, such as oral sex or homosexuality, appeared more frequently among some groups than others. One Brooklyn group developed a routine from constant repetition of such images.

X: You want to scratch your chin? My balls itch.
Y: Keep talking; it tickles my balls.
X: You didn't get no round mouth from sucking on doorknobs.
Y: If you won't tell I got a wooden dick, I won't tell you got splinters in your mouth!

Related to this routine is the angry response, "Blow me!" which is perhaps as bad as "Get fucked!" In America it is truly better to give than to receive.

In addition to subjects, certain words or word compounds are individualized. If "motherfucker" is common to many blacks, "fuckwad," "shithead," and "dickface" are equally pervasive among particular white groups. These compounds are also formulaic to the degree that their structure overshadows the logical content of the insults. In San Diego, California, I heard a woman call her roommate a "dickbrain." "Isn't that usually 'dickface'?" I asked. "It's the way it sounds that makes it; I always liked dickbrain better," she answered. I then asked, "But what *is* a dickbrain?" She looked rather surprised at me and said, "Why it's a jerk." *Dickbrain*, then, is not a description of external appearance but rather a use of formula for expressive effect.

Participants in ritual insults could rarely make clear their personal aesthetics of ritual insults. Yet such aesthetics are clearly implied. It appears obvious that heavy usage of rhymes in insults by blacks is not paralleled by whites. Rather, metaphor, simile, and analogy are preferred techniques to white males. The movements and gestures of players also play an important aesthetic function by enhancing the expressive effect of the insult. Deliveries of insults commonly assume a "tough" stance with deliberate intrusion into the other player's personal space. We can see the impact of this strategy when we note those familiar photos of managers nose-to-nose with umpires. Even without dialogue we know that verbal abuse is occurring. Such delivery strategies, coupled with the value of fluidity of speech, embellish already-known insults or highlight new ones. Even if the audience knows the "old" insult, the audience waits to see *how* you tell it. A good reaction to an insult and delivery during a duel encourages the repetition of that insult in another setting.

The use of formula for enacting insults became especially apparent to me when some of my colleagues at Indiana University began to try out ritual insults on me after they saw my publications on the subject. Most of these people were not even personally familiar with "dozens" or "ranking" traditions, but they unconsciously used formulas to create insults, especially when they could not remember a specific insult's content. In the Folklore Institute one day I made a disparaging remark to which a folklorist friend replied, "That's a dirty crack; speaking of dirty cracks, how's your mother?" I asked him then if he had been reading my articles and was waiting to spring that on me. "Yes," he said, "They're very useful. Your mother's like a telephone pole — always standing on a corner." When I told him that insult was not in my collection, he claimed "Well, it sounds like it could be." What he had unwittingly done was substitute an appropriate metaphor in a formulaic construction, a typical technique of oral tradition. When I mockingly complained that as a scholar he, and others, were destroying the sanctity of my study as well as taking the insults out of their natural contexts, the answer from another folklorist was, "I defended you, though; someone said you weren't fit to live with pigs, I said you were." This incident reminds me that scholars, like most human beings, take a certain joy in being offensive, and given the proper inspiration will display verbal abuse by using formulaic techniques. After all, even greater joy for my colleagues seems to come from being insulting to researchers of insults (but at least my mother still loves me!).

To sum up, the structure of ritual insults performs functions that cannot be separated from social and psychological factors. The structure allows for the ease of recall and the ruling of perfomance intrinsic to the ritual insult tradition. While formula supplies the organizing principles for the ritual insult tradition, it also plays an aesthetic function: the strengthening of the expressive effect of insults. No wonder then that I felt compelled when coming upon Tony and John's contest-in-insults to glare and say, "Hey, you kiss your mother with that mouth?" to which Tony replied, "Why don't you get a real job?" And so the ritual repeats and varies. "That's a dirty crack; speaking of dirty cracks..."

NOTES

1. This essay is an expansion of a section of my "'Who Says?': A Further Investigation of Ritual Insults Among White American Adolescents," *Midwestern Journal of Language and Folklore* 4 (1978), 53-69. Unless otherwise indicated, the examples of ritual insults cited here derive from collections I made in New York City; Clifton, New Jersey; Otsego County, New York; and Greenville, Mississippi, between 1971 and 1977; and Harrisburg, Pennsylvania, between 1981 and 1982. A classified listing of collected insults is found in my "A Re-examination of White Dozens Among White American Adolescents," *Western Folklore* 37 (1978), 118-28. — The use of the term "formula" in the present essay refers to a "group of words which is regularly employed under the same metrical conditions to express a given essential idea." (From Albert Lord, *The Singer of Tales* [Cambridge, Mass.: Harvard University Press, 1960], p. 30.)

2. A variant of this tale collected at the University of Illinois is reported in Ronald L. Baker, "The Folklore of Students," in *The Handbook of American Folklore*, ed. Richard M. Dorson (Bloomington: Indiana University Press, 1983).

3. Alan Dundes and Robert Georges, "Toward a Structural Definition of the Riddle," *Journal of American Folklore* 76 (1963), 111-18. The quote is on p. 113.

4. See Elliott Oring, "Everything is a Shade of Elephant: An Alternative to a Psychoanalysis of Humor," *New York Folklore* 1 (1975), 149-60; Simon J. Bronner, "Structural and Stylistic Relations of Oral and Literary Humor," *Journal of the Folklore Institute* 19 (1982), 31-45.

5. See Alan Dundes, "The Number Three in American Culture," in *Every Man His Way: Readings in Cultural Anthropology*, ed. Alan Dundes (Englewood Cliffs: Prentice-Hall, 1968), 401-24.

6. "The Dick Cavett Show," aired on PBS, 10 July 1979.

7. Motifs mentioned here are from Stith Thompson, *Motif-Index of Folk Literature*, 6 vols. (Bloomington: Indiana University Press, 1966). International tale-types also indicate contests-in-insults: Type 1093, "Contest in Words"; Type 1094, "Contest in Cursing." From Anntti Aarne and Stith Thompson, *The Types of the Folktale* (Helsinki: Folklore Fellows Communication, 1961).

When I went with the pickers,
One cherry-harvest time,
I left at home my knickers,
The easier for to climb.

My ladder-boy, young Tommy —
A lad just turned fourteen —
Seemed driven well-nigh balmy
By scenes he'd seldom seen.

Our jests grew broad and merry
As we worked the day-long line.
I plucked full many a cherry,
And then he pluckèd mine.

Or so he thought. I knew it
Was needless he should know
That he'd been beaten to it
By others, long ago.

From *A Shropshire Lass* by
*Tryphemia Tregaskis (1882-1980)

inflicting Jewish Mother and the prudish Jewish Wife. The result is an indiscriminate use of JAP, Jewish Wife, Jewish Mother, and Jewish Woman as the main character in such jokes, totally botching up the joke. *Oy*, those *goyishe kep!*

Please keep me abreast of the newest jokes. In our next volume, I will thank all benefactors who have sent me kakological and other items. The material that you send me is very slowly being put into a data base, for quick retrieval, later on. The computerization of my research is a slow process, but once finished, it will be far more efficient than the present method of putting your information on 3 by 5" cards, and searching manually. When the material is on computer disks, all I have to do is ask the machine to pull out all jokes or terms of abuse attacking certain targets (such as lesbians) and in a few seconds all lesbian jokes pop up on the screen or can be printed out. Similarly, all material dealing with certain shortcomings (such as kinky hair or being dirty) can be searched and compiled quickly.

So, keep your photocopies and clippings coming. I have already more clippings than a workaholic *mohel*, but new jokes and variations appear almost daily.

II. KAKOLOGIA

When does a "black gentleman" become a "nigger"?
— *As soon as he leaves the room.*

What do you get when you cross a Negro with an Oriental?
— *A car thief that can't drive.*

What's the difference between poverty and a Jewish wife?
— *Poverty sucks.*

Have you heard of the Jerry Falwell designer jeans?
— *They have one right leg and a welded zipper.*

What do you get when you cross an orangutan with Jerry Falwell?
— *An ignorant, uneducated asshole that likes bananas.*

Why didn't Jesus like to eat M&M's?
— *Because they kept falling through his hands.*

Why did the West Germans elect a new chancellor?
— *Because they were tired of the same old Schmidt.*

What's the difference between a vulture and a Jewish mother?
— *The vulture waits until you're dead before it eats your heart out.*

How can you tell when a Jewish American Princess has an orgasm?
— *She drops her nail file.*

What's black and white and has a dirty name?
— *Sister Mary Elizabeth Fuck.*

Did you hear about the gay rabbi?
— *He kept blowing his shofar.*

What's long, black, and has an asshole at each end?
— *The line at the welfare office.*

What does a French-Chinese prostitute do?
— *She sucks your laundry.*

What do you call an overweight Chinese?
— *Chunk.*

Why don't Frenchmen eat flies?
— *Because they can't get their little legs apart.*

What do Jackie Onassis and Bambi's mother have in common?
— *They both fuck for bucks.*

Why can't Santa Claus have any children?
— *Because he comes only once a year, and that's down the chimney.*

Why don't Polish cheerleaders do the splits?
— *Because they stick to the floor.*

How do you get four gays on a bar stool?
— *Turn it upside down.*

Have you heard about the queer burglar?
— *He couldn't blow the safe, so he went down on the elevator.*

Why can't you circumcise Iranians?
— *Because there is no end to those pricks.*

Why is Ray Charles smiling all the time?
— *Because he doesn't know he's black.*

How do you get 17 Yankees into a car?
— *Tell them it's heading for Houston.*

What do you get when you cross an Indian with a black?
— *A Sioux named "Boy."*

What do you get when you cross Bo Derek with Sammy Davis, Jr.?
— *A ten of spades.*

Why are there no black mountain climbers?
— *Because their lips explode at 5,000 feet.*

How do you say "Fuck you" in Jewish?
— *"Trust me."*

What's the perfect woman like?
— *She's three feet tall, doesn't have any teeth, and the top of her head is flat so you can put your beer down on it.*

What's twelve inches and white?
— *Nothing!*

What's the longest six years in a Negro's life?
— *Third grade.*

What do you call a faggot with a broken tooth?
— *An organ grinder.*

What's the difference between Nancy Reagan and a tampon?
— *No difference. They're both stuck up cunts.*

What evidence do we have that Adam and Eve were not black?
— *No one, including God, has ever been able to take a rib away from a nigger.*

Why are a woman's asshole and pussy so close together?
— *So when she gets drunk you can carry her home like a six-pack.*

What's a hillbilly virgin?
— *An eight-year-old who can run faster than her brothers.*

Why did so many black soldiers die in Vietnam?
— *Because when someone yelled "Get down!" they got up and danced.*

Why is San Francisco like granola?
— *Because once you get past the fruits and nuts, all you have left is flakes.*

What do you get when you cross a gorilla and a computer?
— *A Harry Reasoner.*

What goes into thirteen twice?
— *Roman Polanski.*

What's brown and full of holes?
— *Swiss shit.*

Why don't Polish women use vibrators?
— *Because they chip their teeth.*

What is a blood vessel?
— *Four Negroes in a '57 Chevy.*

Why were Helen Keller's legs yellow?
— *Because her dog was blind, too.*

Why do Italians wear pointed shoes?
— *So they can get the cockroaches in the corners.*

What's the cheapest way to grease your car?
— *Run over a Puerto Rican.*

Why did God make come white and urine yellow?
— *So that Italians could tell if they were coming or going.*

Why are Polish men such lousy lovers?
— *Because they always wait until the swelling goes down.*

Why don't Polish mothers breast-feed their babies?
— *Because it hurts when they boil their nipples.*

What do these numbers have in common: 214, 781, 6, 355?
— *They are adjoining rooms in the Warsaw Hilton.*

What's Monaco's new national anthem?
— *"She'll be coming around the mountain."*

What is long and black and stinks?
— *The unemployment line in Detroit.*

Did you hear about the two Indians who were on "That's Incredible"?
— *One held a job, and the other quit drinking.*

How does a Mexican know when it's time to eat?
— *When his asshole stops burning.*

How many blacks does it take to shingle a roof?
— *Six, if you slice them thin enough.*

How do you keep black kids from jumping up and down?
— *Put Velcro on the ceiling.*

And how do you get them down?
— *Get a Mexican and tell him they're piñatas.*

What is nine miles long and has an asshole every thirty inches?
— *The St. Patrick's Day Parade.*

Did you hear about the rich Texas WASP who after 20 years finally satisfied his wife?
— *He bought her a lesbian.*

What's the difference between love and herpes?
— *Herpes is forever.*

How do we know that God wants us to eat pussy?
— *Because He made it look like a taco.*

What's the last thing that goes through a bug's mind as it hits the windshield?
— *Its asshole.*

Why do tampons have strings?
— *So you can floss after eating.*

What goes "Mark, mark!"?
— *A dog with a harelip.*

What's green and hops from bed to bed?
— *A prostitoad.*

What did Adam say to Eve?
— *"Stand back! I don't know how big this thing gets."*

Where do you get virgin wool?
— *From ugly sheep.*

What happened to the girl who went fishing with six fellows?
— *She came back with a red snapper.*

What's a coolie?
— *A quickie in the snow.*

What's a black test-tube baby called?
— *Janitor in a drum.*

What's the difference between a nurse and a BMW car?
— *Some people have never been in a BMW.*

Why do flies have wings?
— *To beat the Pakistanis to the garbage cans.*

What is Puerto Rican cole slaw?
— *Just like American cole slaw, except it has hair in it.*

What do you call a Pole who marries a Negro?
— *A social climber.*

What is a Jewish Princess's favorite wine?
— *"I wanna go to Miami!"*

How do you tickle a Jewish Princess?
— *"Gucci, Gucci, goo!"*

Why don't Newfies golf?
— *Because they can't tell their ass from a hole in the ground.*

What did Abraham Lincoln say when he woke up from
a five-day drinking spree?
— *"I freed the who???"*

How can you tell when a Polish woman is menstruating?
— *When she is wearing only one sock.*

What disease is common among Polish women?
— *Toxic Sock Syndrome.*

Why did Begin invade Lebanon?
— *To impress Jodie Foster.*

How can you tell cowboy boots from engineer boots?
— *Cowboy boots have the shit on the outside.*

What's the difference between JELL-O and a Jewish woman?
— *JELL-O jiggles when you eat it.*

Why don't congressmen like bookmarks?
— *Because they prefer bending over pages.*

What's the Congressional Record?
— *Four pages a night.*

Did you hear about the senator who fell asleep with a book in his lap?
— *He woke up with a page between his knees.*

Where do senate pages come from?
— *Some from the senators' home state. Others were reared in Washington.*

Did you hear about the new entomological drink in California?
— *It's called malathion cocktail. One sip and your fly falls down.*

How do they announce the station break on Radio Israel?
—*"This is Radio Israel, twelve hundred on your dial. But for you, ten ninety-five."*

Did you hear about the Pole who studied five days for his urine test?

What are the first three words a Mexican child ever hears?
— *"Attention, K-Mart shoppers..."*

What are the first three words a black child learns?
— *Coup De Ville.*

What does a Jewish American Princess make for dinner?
— *Reservations.*

What did Natalie Wood and William Holden want for Christmas?
— *Henry Fonda and John Belushi.*

What's long and black and hard and smells like pussy?
— *Billie Jean King's tennis racket handle.*

What's an African Moanback?
— *The guy who stands behind the garbage truck and yells "Mo'an back!"*

How did Stevie Wonder know he was black?
— *He felt his lips.*

Why don't Mexicans like blowjobs?
— *Because they screw up their unemployment checks.*

What's the difference between a circumcision and a crucifixion?
— *In a crucifixion, you throw away the whole Jew.*

What happens when you shoot a black in the head?
— *You put a bullet hole through his radio.*

What happens when a Jew with a hard-on runs into a wall?
— *He skins his nose.*

What's the square root of 69?
— *8 something.*

What do the Starship Enterprise and toilet paper have in common?
— *They both circle Uranus for Klingons.*

What's a definition of gross?
— *When your girlfriend throws her panties against the wall and they stick.*

What do you call a truckload of vibrators?
— *Toys for twats.*

What do designer jeans and a cheap motel have in common?
— *No ballroom.*

What's the difference between dark and hard?
— *It stays dark all night.*

What do you call a female clone?
— *Clunt.*

What's the difference between a rooster and a hooker?
— *A rooster goes "Cock-a-doodle-do!" and a hooker says "Any cock'll do."*

What did Little Red Riding Hood say when the wolf threatened to eat her?
— *"Eat, eat, eat! Doesn't anyone just* fuck *any more?"*

What's the difference between "Oooh!" and "Ahhh!"?
— *About three inches.*

Why did God give Mexicans noses?
— *So they have something to pick in the off-season.*

What's the word for today?
— *Legs. Now go home and spread the word.*

What is gray and comes in quarts?
— *An elephant.*

Did you hear about the epileptic who had a fit at the amusement park?
— *Four people jumped on him. They thought he was a new ride.*

Why do bees buzz?
— *You'd buzz, too, if you had your honey between your legs.*

What do you call a happy Roman?
— *Gladiator.*

What do you do when your Kotex catches fire?
— *Throw it on the floor and tampon it!*

What do soy beans and dildos have in common?
— *Both are meat substitutes.*

What is red and has seven dents?
— *Snow White's cherry.*

What do African elephants use as vibrators?
— *Epileptic pygmies.*

What's the difference between a young hooker and an old hooker?
— *Vaseline and Poly-Grip.*

How do you make a dead baby float?
— *Two scoops of ice cream and one scoop of dead baby.*

What's the ultimate rejection?
— *When your hand falls asleep while you're masturbating.*

What do you call a guy from Gary, Indiana, with a 12-inch cock?
— *A Hungarian.*

Where is an elephant's sex organ?
— *On his feet. If he steps on you, you're fucked.*

What do you call a man who puts his tool into another man's mouth?
— *A dentist.*

What do lesbians get before they get married?
— *A liquor license.*

How did Brigham Young get his name?
— *When he asked for more women, he had a head cold and said, "Bri'g 'em, but bri'g 'em young!"*

Why was the tailor fired?
— *Because he couldn't mend straight.*

What's a mixed blessing?
— *When your 16-year-old daughter comes home at 3 a.m. with a Gideon Bible under her arm.*

What's alimony?
— *The screwing you get for the screwing you got.*

Did you hear about the flasher who wanted to retire?
— *He changed his mind and decided to stick it out another year.*

What's a concubone?
— *A male concubine.*

Who was the first soft-drink manufacturer?
— *Adam. In the Garden of Eden, he made Eve's cherry pop.*

Who was the first carpenter?
— *Eve. She made Adam's banana stand.*

What did the one gay sperm say to another gay sperm?
— *"How do you find an egg in all this shit?"*

What's the difference between a dyke and a lesbian?
— *The dyke kick-starts her dildo.*

What's the definition of a *rugged* woman?
— *One who kick-starts her own vibrator and rolls her own tampons.*

What does a gay whale do when he meets up with a submarine?
— *He bites off its tail and sucks out the seamen.*

Why did God create gentiles?
— *Well, somebody has to pay retail!*

Why did Jesus cross the road?
— *Because He was nailed to a chicken.*

What do you call a nun with one leg?
— *Hopalong Chastity.*

Why did the Baptists outlaw fucking?
— *Because it may lead to dancing.*

What did the Valley Girl say to the black before giving him a blowjob?
— *"Ooooh, gag me with a coon!"*

How do you pick out the Polish dykes at a lesbian convention?
— *They are the ones picking up men.*

What's the difference between Jewish women and the Bermuda Triangle?
— *The Bermuda Triangle swallows seamen.*

Why do blacks think about sex all the time?
— *You would, too, if you had a head full of pubic hair.*

Why do they call the camels the Ships of the Desert?
— *Because they are full of Arab seamen.*

Why do car salesmen call blacks "Doo-duhs"?
— *Because many black car buyers ask, "Do duh cah come wif a radio? Do duh cah come wif air conditionin'?"*

How do you bathe Haitians?
— *You don't. You just let them wash up on shore.*

What do you call a black hitchhiker?
— *Stranded.*

Why did the Wave want to get out of the Navy?
— *Because she found out that a 21-inch Admiral was a TV set.*

What is the Hungarian recipe for making an omelet?
— *First you steal two eggs....*

How do you know that Earl Mountbatten had dandruff?
— *They found his Head & Shoulders on the beach.*

Why did Argentine Head of State Galtieri buy a glass-bottom boat?
— *So he could look at his air force.*

What's the difference between Minnesota and yoghurt?
— *Yoghurt has culture.*

Why do all the football fields in Iowa have artificial turf?
— *So the cheerleaders won't graze after the game.*

What did the leper say to the prostitute?
— *Keep the tip.*

Did you hear about the gigolo in the leper colony?
— *He was doing fine until his business started falling off.*

What do you call a leper in a hot-tub?
— *Stew.*

What do you get when you cross a penis with a potato?
— *A dick-tator.*

What do you get when you cross a prostitute with an elephant?
— *A 4,000-pound whore who does it for peanuts.*

What's the Great American Dream?
— *Two million niggers swimming to Africa, with a Jew under each arm.*

What's the new version of "Mother Hubbard"?
— *Old Mother Hubbard lived in a shoe / She had so many children she didn't know what to do. So she moved to Atlanta.*

Why does Dolly Parton buy her clothes at Datsun?
— *Because that's the only place where she can get a 280-Z.*

What would you call one thousand feminists at the bottom of the ocean?
— *A start.*

Why can't the United Nations (UN) be in Connecticut (CT)?
—*Because it would result in CUNT.*

Why does the Pope always kiss the ground when he gets off the airplane?
— *Because the pilot is Polish, too.*

Why do newborn babies have a soft spot in their head?
— *So the nurses in the neonatal ward can carry five of them at one time.*

What is this? [Stick out tongue]
— *A lesbian with a hard-on.*

What did Jim Brady say when he was shot?
— *"I need this job like I need a hole in the head!"*

And what did Brady say a few days later?
— *"I've got half a mind to quit this job."*

Why won't Ronald Reagan let Jim Brady ride in an open limousine?
— *Because Jim's head whistles.*

How do you babysit a black kid?
— *Wet his lips and stick him on the wall.*

Where did Prince Charles spend his wedding night?
— *In Diana.*

Why didn't the little Greek boy run away from home?
— *Because he couldn't leave his brothers behind.*

What's a Jewish porno film?
— *Ten minutes of sex and 50 minutes of guilt.*

Why do Jewish women use golden diaphragms?
— *Because they want their men to come into money.*

Name a biceptual athlete.
— *Arnold Schwarzenegger.*

Did you hear about the new German microwave oven?
— *It seats twelve.*

What's the difference between a Jew and a pizza?
— *A pizza doesn't scream when you stick it in the oven.*

How can you spot an Italian airplane?
— *Look for hair under its wings.*

How can you tell that a woman is wearing pantyhose?
— *When she farts, her ankles swell up.*

What do you call a gay Jew?
— *A Heblew.*

What do you call a black skindiver?
— *Jacques Custodian.*

What do you call a beautiful girl in Poland?
— *Tourist.*

What's black and white and has three eyes?
— *Sammy Davis, Jr. and his wife.*

What kind of meat do priests eat?
— *None.*

What's yellow and ugly and sleeps alone?
— *Yoko Ono.*

Why did God give blacks rhythm?
— *Because He fucked up their hair.*

How do you keep five blacks from raping a white girl?
— *Throw them a basketball.*

What do you get when you cross a Mexican with a faggot?
— *A señor-eater.*

How did Helen Keller's parents punish her?
— *They rearranged the furniture.*

What is Jewish foreplay?
— *Two hours of begging.*

How does a French girl hold her liquor?
— *By the ears.*

How do you fuck Elizabeth Taylor?
— *Roll her in flour and look for the wet spot.*

What's black and shines in the dark?
— *Oakland, California.*

Why does Lady Diana want a divorce?
— *Because she expected that all rulers have 12 inches.*

Have you heard about the new Jewish tire?
— *It's called* Firestein. *It stops on a dime and then picks it up.*

What do you get when you cross a black, an Eskimo, and a prostitute?
— *A snowblower that doesn't work.*

How can you tell when an Iranian reaches puberty?
— *He takes his diaper off his ass and puts it around his head.*

Why can't an employer let a Puerto Rican take a coffee break?
— *Because it takes too long to retrain them each time.*

How does a German tie his shoes?
— *With little knotsies.*

Why do blacks smell?
— *So blind people can hate them, too.*

Why does Nancy Reagan always climb on top?
— *Because Ronnie can only fuck up.*

Why is New York City so quiet on Sunday mornings?
— *Because all the Italians have gone to the cemetery. The Jews have gone to Long Island. The Irish were out drinking on Saturday and are hung over. The blacks were out mugging and are in jail. The Puerto Ricans can't get their cars started. And the Poles think it's Tuesday.*

CATALAN BLASPHEMIES

Joan J. Vinyoles

Catalan, a Romance language related to Spanish and Provençal, is the official language of Andorra and the native tongue of about six million speakers in Catalonia and parts of Aragon, Roussillon, Valencia, and the Balearic Islands.

The utterances below — blasphemies, euphemisms and exclamations — are arranged by blasphemies involving the name of God, Christ, Virgin Mary, the Saints, Biblical Persons, and others that desecrate Catholic liturgical objects. Most utterances that do not expressedly name God or other sacred persons are considered euphemisms, not blasphemies. Utterances beginning with **mecàgum...** (a contraction of *me cago en*) "I shit on..." are the most blasphemous ones, followed by those beginning with **vatua...** (a contraction of *voto a*) "I curse..." The remaining ones are exclamations not necessarily considered blasphemous. Those beginning with **Mecàgum...** "I shit on..." and ending in **de Déu** "of God" are not thought to be blasphemous; the "of God" element merely intensifies or potentiates one's angry outburst. For example, if one cannot get a door open, one exclaims *Mecàgum la porta de Déu!* "I shit on the door of God!" — comparable to U.S. English "This goddamn (fuckin') door!"

Mecàgum often is euphemized to *mec, meca, mecascum, mecatxum, mecatxus* or the Spanish *mecachis.* The intensifying prefix *re-* is here translated as "double-." Also, several euphemistic utterances were not translated, as they are meaningless.

I. GOD
1. God

Mecàgum Déu! *I shit on God!*

Mecàgum Ceuta! *I shit on Ceuta!* The name of this African city is derived from *Déu > seu > Ceuta.* This and the following utterances are constructed with euphemisms of *Déu* "God."

Mecàgum dé! Apocope of *Déu.*

Mecàgum dena! From *Déu nat* "born God" *> deuna > dena.*

Mecàgum Dénia! *I shit on Denia!* The name of this city in Valencia is derived from *Déu > dena > Dénia.*

Mecàgum des! Apocope.

Mecàgum deu! *I shit on ten!* From *Déu > deu.*

Mecàgum deula! From *Déu nat* "born God" *> deuna > deula.*

Mecàgum deuna! From *Déu nat.*

Mecàgum deure! *I shit on duty!* From *Déu > deuna > deure.*

Mecàgum el de dalt! *I shit on Him above!*

Mecàgum ell! *I shit on Him!*

Mecàgum neu! *I shit on snow!* From *Déu > neu.*

Mecàgum redera! *I shit on behind!* From *redéu > redena > redera,* an incorrect but common metathesis of *darrera* "behind."

Mecàgum setze i mig! *I shit on sixteen and a half!* From *Déu > deu > setze i mig.*

Mecàgum seu! *I shit on His!* From *Déu > seu.*

Mecàgum Sivilla! *I shit on Seville!* The name of this Spanish city is derived from *Déu > Ceuta > Sevilla,* Cat. *Sivilla.*

Vatua dell! *I curse Him!* From *Déu* and *ell* (*el* "he").

Vatua deuxes! From *Déu* > *deuxes.*
Vatua nell! From *dell* > *nell.*
Vatua redell! From *redéu* and *ell.*
Vatua renell! From *redell* > *renell.*
Redena! From *re-* (intensifier) and *dena.*
Redéu! *Double-God!* or *God Again!* From *re-* (intensifier) and *Déu.*
Déu, redéu i mecàgum Déu! *God, Double-God, and I shit on God!*
Mecàgum Déu de Déu! *I shit on God's God!*
Mecàgum Déu de Déu, Déu de redéu! *I shit on God's God, on Double-God's God!*
Mecàgum Déu i la verge Maria! *I shit on God and the Virgin Mary!*
Mecàgum Déu i l'hòstia divina! *I shit on God and the divine host!*
Mecàgum Déu i sa Mare! *I shit on God and his Mother!*
Mecàgum Déu i tots els sants! *I shit on God and all the saints!*
Mecàgum Déu, mecàgum Déu i mecàgum Déu! *I shit on God, I shit on God, and I shit on God!*
Mecàgum Déu sagrat! *I shit on the sacred God!*
Mecàgum Déus de Déus! *I shit on the Gods of Gods!*
Mecàgum el Déu de Bagà! *I shit on the God of Bagà!* (A Catalonian village.)
Mecàgum el Fill de Déu! *I shit on the Son of God!*
Mecàgum el nom de Déu! *I shit on the name of God!*
Vatua el món! *I curse the world!* This and the next five are euphemisms.
Vatua el món dolent! *I curse the evil world!*
Vatua nada! Probably from *nom de* "name of."
Vatua nada deuxes! Probably from *nom de Déu* "name of God."
Vatua nada l'ou xarbot! *I curse the unfertilized egg!*
Vatua non! Probably from *nom de.*

2. Christ

Mecàgum Cristo! *I shit on Christ!*

Mecàgum Maria Cristina! *I shit on Mary Christina!* This and the following ones are euphemisms.

Vatua crispu sangrinyat! *I curse bleeding Christ!* Humorous euphemism of *Crist sangrant*.

Vatua listo! From *Cristo* > *listo*, Spanish "ready, clever."

Cristina! *Christina!*

Recristina! *Double-Christina!* From the intensifying prefix *re-*.

Recristina marinera! *Double-Christina the sailor!* (Feminine form.)

Recristina puta! *Double-Christina the whore!*

Recristo! *Double-Christ!*

Mecàgum el Crist crucificat! *I shit on the crucified Christ!*

Mecàgum les cinc llagues de Crist! *I shit on the five wounds of Christ!*

Mecàgum la sang de Cristo! *I shit on the blood of Christ!*

3. Body Parts of God

Mecàgum el cap de Déu! *I shit on the head of God!*

Capde! *Head of…!* This and the next two are euphemistic exclamations.

Captecreus! *Head of the Cross!*

Captemins!

Mecàgum el cap de Déu ver! *I shit on the head of the true God!*

Mecàgum el cony de Déu! *I shit on the cunt of God!*

Mecàgum el cor de Déu! *I shit on the heart of God!*

Mecàgum el cor d'aital senyor! *I shit on the heart of the so-called Lord!* Euphemism.

Mecàgum el cul de Déu! *I shit on the arse of God!*

Mecàgum el cul d'aital! *I shit on the arse of the so-and-so!* Euphemism, as are the next three.

Mecàgum el cul de tal! *I shit on the arse of the so-and-so!*

Mecàgum el cul sagrat! *I shit on the sacred arse!*
Vatua cul! *I curse the arse!*
Mecàgum el fetge de Déu! *I shit on the liver of God!*
Mecàgum el nap de Déu! *I shit on the cock of God!*
Mecàgum els collons de Déu! *I shit on the balls of God!*
Mecàgum la fel de Déu! *I shit on the gall of God!*
Mecàgum la figa de Déu! *I shit on the cunt of God!*
Mecàgum la pixa de Déu! *I shit on the prick of God!*
Mecàgum la sang de Déu! *I shit on the blood of God!*
Mecàgum la sang d'un banc, el fetge d'una cadira i les arrels del campanar! *I shit on the blood of a bench, the liver of a chair and the foundations of the belfry!* Euphemism.
Mecàgum la sang d'un toro quan està vermella! *I shit on the red blood of a bull!* Euphemism.
Mecàgum les freixures de Déu! *I shit on the entrails of God!*
Mecàgum res de Déu! *I shit on nothing of God!*

4. God—Man Relationship

Mecàgum el Déu que et va fer! *I shit on the God who made you!*
Mecàgum el Déu que et va fotre! *I shit on the God who fucked you!*
Mecàgum el Déu que et va inventar! *I shit on the God who invented you!*
Mecàgum el Déu que et va matricular! *I shit on the God who matriculated you!*
Mecàgum el Déu que et va parir! *I shit on the God who bore you!*
Mecàgum el Déu que t'aguanta! *I shit on the God who sustains/tolerates you!*

II. VIRGIN MARY AND THE SAINTS
1. Virgin Mary

Mecàgum la Mare de Déu! *I shit on the Mother of God!*

Mecàgum la mar! *I shit on the sea!* Euphemism, as the following ones.

Mecàgum la mar salada! *I shit on the salty sea!*

Mecàgum la mar serena! *I shit on the calm sea!*

Mecàgum la mare del Tano! *I shit on Tano's mother!* (Personal name.)

Mecàgum la puta Mare de Déu! *I shit on the whore Mother of God!*

Mecàgum la puta de Déu! *I shit on the whore of God!*

Mecàgum la puta divina! *I shit on the divine whore!*

Mecàgum la puta d'oros! *I shit on the whore of diamonds!* Euphemism.

Mecàgum Maria Santíssima! *I shit on the Very Holy Mary!*

Mecàgum Maria Santíssima de Déu! *I shit on the Very Holy Mary of God!*

2. Body Parts of Mary

Mecàgum el cony beneit! *I shit on the blessed cunt!*

Mecàgum el cony sagrat! *I shit on the sacred cunt!*

Mecàgum els collons de Maria Santíssima! *I shit on the balls of the Very Holy Mary!*

Mecàgum la figa de Maria Santíssima! *I shit on the cunt of the Very Holy Mary!*

3. Saints

Mecàgum sant(a)...! *I shit on Saint...[name]!*

Mecàgum la cabellera de sant(a)...! *I shit on the hair of Saint...!*

Mecàgum la cort celestial! *I shit on the celestial court!*

Mecàgum els dotze apòstols! *I shit on the twelve apostles!*

Mecàgum les barbes de sant Pere! *I shit on the beard of Saint Peter!*

Mecàgum la fava apostòlica! *I shit on the bean (= glans) of the apostles!*

Mecàgum tots els sants fotuts en una bóta i Déu per tap!
I shit on all the fucking saints inside a bottle and God for a cork!
A *bóta* actually is a leather wine bag.

Mecàgum una bóta plena de sants i Déu per tap! *I shit on a bottle full of saints and God for a cork!*

III. BIBLICAL AND ECCLESIASTIC PERSONS

Mecàgum el bisbe de Segòvia! *I shit on the bishop of Segovia!*

Mecàgum Judes! *I shit on Judas!*

Mecàgum els collons del capellà! *I shit on the balls of the priest!*

Mecàgum els collons del Pare Sant / del Sant Pare! *I shit on the balls of the Pope!*

Mecàgum el Pare Sant! *I shit on the Pope!*

Mecàgum la pell de Barrabàs! *I shit on the skin of Barabbas!*

Mecàgum la raspa de Caifàs! *I shit on the kitchen-maid of Caiaphas!*

Mecàgum la Santíssima Trinitat! *I shit on the Holiest Trinity!*

IV. LITURGICAL OBJECTS

Mecàgum el copó! *I shit on the ciborium!*

Mecàgum la forma! *I shit on the unleavened bread!*

Mecàgum l'hòstia! *I shit on the host (eucharistic bread)!*

Mecàgum l'olla! *I shit on the stew pot!* From *hòstia* > *olla*. This and the next seven are euphemisms.

Mecàgum l'os! *I shit on the bone!* Apocope.

Mecàgum l'os pedrer! *I shit on the stomach's bone!* (i.e., something nonexistent).

Mecàgum l'os pedreta! Variant of preceding.

Mecàgum l'ospedrera! Variant of preceding.

Mecàgum l'osti! Apocope.

Mecàgum l'òstima! From *hòstia* > *osti* > *òstima*.

Mecàgum l'ou! *I shit on the egg!* From *os* > *ou*.

Rehòstia! *Double-host!* From prefix *re-* and *hòstia*.

Òndia! From *àndia* and *hòstia*.

Òsmia! From *hòstia* > *òsmia*.

Òsmit! From *osti* > *òsmit*.

Ospa! From *hòstia* > *ospa*.

Òstic! From *osti* > *òstic*.

Osticana! From *òstic* > *osticana*.

Ostimeta! From the diminutive of *òstima*.

Ostres! *Oysters!* From *hòstia* > *ostres*.

Mecàgum l'hòstia beneita! *I shit on the blessed host!*

Mecàgum l'hòstia consagrada! *I shit on the consecrated host!*

Mecàgum l'hòstia de Déu! *I shit on the host of God!*

Mecàgum l'hòstia divina! *I shit on the divine host!*

Mecàgum l'hòstia puta! *I shit on the whore of a host!*

Mecàgum l'hòstia puta consagrada! *I shit on the consecrated whore of a host!*

Mecàgum l'hòstia sagrada! *I shit on the sacred host!*

Mecàgum la santa forma! *I shit on the sacred unleavened bread!*

Mecàgum l'hòstia, mecàgum Déu! *I shit on the host, I shit on God!*

Mecàgum Déu, en la creu i en el fuster que la feu (i en el fill de puta que va plantar el pi)! *I shit on God, on the cross, and on the carpenter who made it (and on the son-of-a-whore who planted the pine)!*

V. VARIOUS

Mecàgum el gall de la passió! *I shit on the cock of the Passion!*

Mecàgum el rentamans de Pilat! *I shit on the lavatory of Pilate!*

Mecàgum els claus de Crist! *I shit on the nails/spikes of Christ!*

Mecàgum les claus de Sant Pere! *I shit on the keys of Saint Peter!*

Mecàgum les arrels del campanar! *I shit on the foundations of the belfry!*

Mecàgum la tomba de Crist! *I shit on the tomb of Christ!*

Mecàgum els quatre pilars que aguanten la cagadora de Crist! *I shit on the four posts that hold up the shithouse of Christ!*

VI. COMMON VARIOUS INTERJECTIONS
1. Lightning

Llamp de Déu! *God's lightning!*
Llamp del cel! *Heaven's lightning!*
Llamp de Déu, llamp de redéu! *God's and double-God's lightning!*
Mal llamp de Déu! *God's bad lightning!*

2. Wrath

Ira de Déu! *God's wrath!*
Reïra de Déu! *God's double-wrath!*
Ira de bet! Euphemism.
Iba de bet! Euphemism.
Ingra de bet! Euphemism. According to Joan Corominas, *ingra* is derived from *d'engre* = *ingle.*
Mala reïra de Déu! *God's bad double-wrath!*
Reïra de nell! *His double-wrath!* Euphemism, from *ell* = *el* "he"
Fure de Déu! *God's fury!*

SOURCES CONSULTED

Beaumatin, E. *Recherches sur la censure verbale: L'euphemisme dans le catalan parlé de Barcelone.* 1980.
Bernadó, J. and F. Prat. *Sobre els signes fònics usats en les relacions home-bèstia.* 1980.
Plaza, C. *El renec i la paraulota dels pagesos a Barberà de la Conca.* 1980.
Oral sources and the collection of the *Gerinel Archive.*

The Editor wishes to thank Prof. Frank Nuessel for his help with Catalan difficulties.

WINDY WORDS
A GLOSSARY OF EUPHEMISMS FOR THE EXPULSION OF INTESTINAL GAS

Bob Burton Brown

Said a printer pretending to wit:
"There are certain bad words we omit.
It would sully our art
To print the word F...,
And we never, oh, never, say Sh.."

Some people, especially women over forty, simply cannot bring themselves to use the word *fart*. Although this word may be an appropriate Anglo-Saxon expression commonly used in many classics of English literature and today on every school yard in America by even the most innocent of children, it is still considered vulgar and offensive to some folks (especially the editors of big publishing houses and major book distributors). So, it has become a tradition to invent all sorts of euphemisms — most of them silly or childish — to cover the subject; anything to keep from coming right out and saying it.

We often simply let our farts go unnamed, using instead some indirect pronoun reference, such as "it" or "one" or "them" or "those": "Did you do *it*?" – "I let *one* go" – "He has been letting *them* all night" and "He lets *those* all the time."

When we feel we must call them something more specific, our cultural habit has been to give them disgustingly "cute" little names, something palatable to squeamish mothers and amusing to small children. What did you call "them" at your house? Barks? Poots? Smells? Snappers? Sniffles? Stinkies? Toots? Whiffles?

These are, of course, all euphemisms. A euphemism is a figure of speech by which a delicate word or expression is substituted for one which is considered harsh or indelicate. "Breaking wind" and "passing gas" have been the most acceptable euphemisms in literary circles for many years, but these sound so stilted, so old-fashioned, that one almost never hears them in ordinary conversation.

See if you can find your family's favorite euphemism in the following glossary. If not, will you please send it to me, as I would like to add it to this ever-expanding list of "windy words."

bark a sharp report, as in a "barking" gun, makes this a natural for a noisy passage of gas: "Are you barking for your supper or because of it?"

barking spider a gentle, family-type expression to cover the subject in reasonably good humor: "Did I hear a barking spider just now?" or "It's about time to call the exterminators; those barking spiders are back again."

beanie a childish choice, relying on supposition of cause for its identification rather than the end result, as in "Was that your beanie I heard?" or "Do your beanies always smell that bad?"

borborygmus internal farting, the rumbling sounds made by the movement of gas in the intestine, as in a "growling stomach," "belly noise," "gut mumblings," when your stomach "talks to you." Not very useful, since most people will not understand what you are talking about.

bowel howls not really delicate enough to qualify, but nicely descriptive for locker-room talk. Some euphemisms increase rather than ameliorate the impact.

breaking wind very descriptive, and perhaps the most acceptable euphemism in literary circles, but terribly stilted, and dated, too.

Bronx cheer an oral imitation of a sputtering fart, employed to take advantage of a psychological moment which will not wait for the passage of the real thing. Used as a euphemism in "Are you giving me the raspberry?" or "Here's what I think of that...."

bucksnorter a farting hunter who, when tromping through the woods with a buddy, stops, lifts his leg, lets one rip, and then says: "Did you hear that buck snort?"

cushion creeper a muffled fart that seems never to end, and lingers — both the sound and the smell — in, around, and on the soft cushion of an over-stuffed chair or sofa. "I've had about all of your cushion creepers I can take."

cutting the cheese how folks in Indiana describe it when someone lets an especially stinky fart, as in "Cutting the cheese is not allowed in the living room."

elephant on my back an announcement that you are about to let one rip, intended to dupe some gullible fool (or child) into making an innocent inquiry or investigation — then "getting it" with a well-timed blast. Also, one may inquire of a suspected culprit, "Is there an elephant on your back?"

exterminal gas a quasi-technical term coined by my youngest son to describe particularly smelly expulsions of intestinal gas — the kind that could exterminate you, or provide overwhelming evidence that the expulsor is afflicted by something terminal.

flatulence gas with class; whatever fancy folks blow out their ass.

flatus farts with status; a puff of wind; gas generated in the stomach or bowels.

gas or **gassy** mothers who have traditionally had real difficulty bringing themselves to use four-letter Anglo-

Saxonisms often prefer to describe flatulence as "gas," as in "You seem to be awfully gassy today" or "Was that your gas?" or "I just passed some gas."

house frog another family-type term often used to explain the situation nicely, as in "What was that?" – "Just a house frog." – "Okay." An outside equivalent may be found in the question "Who stepped on that frog?" or "Is that damned frog loose again?"

it an all-purpose term for whatever four-letter word we feel we must avoid, as: "Okay, you guys, which one of you did it?" or "It just slipped out."

one what prudes call an expulsion of intestinal gas, as in "Did you just let one?" – "Yes, and that *one* is enough."

one-cheek sneak when little boys in short pants fart while seated on a flat wooden bench or chair.

pain an indirect reference to discomforting flatulence, sometimes used as a euphemism, as in "Did you just have a pain?" Or as a confession in "That was a terrible pain I got rid of."

painting the elevator in a Jewish neighborhood, after you have just let a real stinker on an elevator (thinking you are all alone) and somebody gets on at the next floor, you wrinkle up your nose and say, "They must have just painted this elevator." In our family we all know what it means when one of us asks, "Who painted the elevator?"

passing gas pretty straight-forward, but it always reminds me of a cartoon I saw once of several bicyclists pedaling by a gasoline pump held by a disappointed service station attendant on a lonely highway in the desert, with the caption "Passing Gas."

pets what French-Canadians call farts; and farting is called "petting"—not because they are fond of it, and not to be confused with the pawing of eager lovers; short for the French word *pétard*, meaning "to crack, to explode, to break wind"—in other words, a French fart.

poop a noun, used as a euphemism for anything that comes out of the anus; often a term of pseudo-endearment, as in "You old poop!"

poot an interjection used to express disgust. In the South it is a popular euphemism for fart, especially among the women-folk.

puff as in "a puff of wind," exappropriated as a verb all too often, as in "I hope all those beans we ate for supper don't make us puff all night."

pumping gas a childish euphemism for farting—a confusion of the kind of gas Daddy puts in his car with the kind he puts out of his rear-end.

raspberry the equivalent of "Bronx cheer," a mouth-fart, used as an expression of derision to let others know that you are displeased with them. A spluttering noise made while sticking the tongue out, which translates: "I fart on thee!"

rattler a reverberating blast powerful enough to rattle cups and saucers, or, perhaps, even the windows and doors of rickety buildings—like army barracks.

S.B.D. the abbreviation for the worst kind of fart—the silent-but-deadly; in medical circles, this is called a "tacit" fart.

shooting rabbits what one says Down East when one hears a fart of unknown origin: "Somebody is shooting rabbits!" or "Are you the one that's been shooting rabbits all night?"

silent horror a very smelly fart inflicted upon another without fair warning; illegal chemical warfare, something akin to mustard gas.

smell or **smelly** too obvious to merit comment: "Mommy, I let a smelly."

snappers beans, for obvious reasons; served every Saturday night throughout New England, "to put life into the old boy!" Also used to describe what happens after the beans have had a chance to work.

sniffle the women and children in my ex-wife's family used this word, both as a noun and as a verb, to cover their flatulence as sweetly as possible. Personally, I never liked the term. On my side of the family a "sniffle" was something we blew out of our nose.

sputter sound imitations are sometimes useful: "I've been sputtering (*or* spluttering) all day." However, one can go too far with this if the imitation is too close to the real thing, as in "Who just 'sphtttttt'?"

squeaking chair a clever way to bring the passage of gas to public attention, asking: "Are you sitting in a squeaking chair?" or "I think my chair squeaks." A variation on this theme can be: "Is there a mouse in here?"

stepping on a frog if you have ever stepped on a frog, or can imagine the complaints the frog would give you if you did; no further explanation is necessary.

stink or **stinky** boys let "stinks" but nice little girls call theirs "stinkies."

storm implies a strong and dangerous wind, invariably noisy, as in "Is that your storm I hear?" – "Yes, my stomach is really storming (*or* howling) today."

toot a mild euphemism for a particularly melodious fart. The Yankee equivalent of the South's "poot." Some families use the variation **tootles**.

whiff a windy-sounding term that makes your meaning clear. "Somebody just whiffed; I can smell it!" Variations: **whiffles** and **whiffling**.

wind as in "Was that your wind?" or "I sure feel windy today" or "Standing downwind of you can be dangerous." Sometimes referred to as a **howling wind.**

THANK YOU
FOR NOT
FARTING

A Maledicta Card

RITUAL AND PERSONAL INSULTS IN STIGMATIZED SUBCULTURES
GAY - BLACK - JEW

Stephen O. Murray

Although which attributes are considered pejorative may vary from culture to culture, speech acts recognized as insults probably exist in all cultures. Speech *events* involving sequences of insults are characteristically (though not exclusively) used by those whose silence is not cutting. For instance (1) is a speech event involving two children,

(1) A: **You're fat.**
B: **Well, you're stupid, so there!**

comprised of two speech acts, both of which are insults. *A* labels *B* with a disvalued characteristic and *B* retaliates.

Ritual insults can be distinguished from such literal *personal* insults by the greater outlandishness of characterization, and by the chaining of successive insults. The negative characterization in a ritual insult is patently not true. This literal implausibility must be obvious to the participants. Particularly to the insulted person the "not serious" frame (Bateson 1972) must be made clear. Metaphorical exaggeration and rhyme are two means to signal the "playing insult" frame (Labov 1973:123). The second distinction between ritual and personal insults is that each retort is linked to the preceding insult, prototypically by rhyme, but also by building on the semantic foundation of the first insult or making a "play" on its words.

The goal of the retorter[1] is to silence his[2] opponent—to "strike him dead" with "lightning" repartee. What constitutes an appropriate response to a personal insult differs from what constitutes an appropriate response to a ritual insult. The appropriate response to a personal insult is fight or flight if the insult is made by someone of relatively equivalent status, to passively "take" it from someone of superior status, or to ignore it (at least at the times of the interaction) from someone of inferior status (and to have the upstart punished later by someone else). A personal insult (to an adult) is overt aggression. In subcultures with exaggerated sense of personal honor, such as the white planter caste of the antebellum American South, or 19th-century European officer corps, an insult was a prelude to a duel.[3] A ritual insult, however, is an invitation to "play" in a contest of wits.[4] The appropriate response is verbal rather than physical violence. *Within* a group, violence in any form other than verbal is regarded as a failure to match wits. Playing with strangers risks misinterpretation of the frame and may lead to fights (Labov 1972; Kochman 1970). To deny a patently exaggerated statement with rational argumentation is just as silly (and hence damaging) as resorting to physical force.

According to Radcliffe-Brown (1940), in a joking relationship "one is by custom permitted and in some instances required to take no offense" (195), but "taking abuse," i.e., accepting the insult with aplomb, is not positively valued in ritual insult exchanges. There, aplomb is at most only of instrumental value: one must not become so upset as to be unable to think of a good retort. Good performance requires taking the offensive, and taking offense is an obstacle to that. In addition to this distinction between ritual insults and joking relationships in terms of response, the two differ in participants. Joking relationships exist between persons in some set structural relationship (e.g., if one must accept denigrating jokes from mother's brother), whereas ritual insults are exchanges by peers. The locus of joking relationships is the family, whereas ritual insults occur in peer group idle hours (Abrahams 1962:219; Howell 1973). Ritual insults occur in several North American subcultures. The one in which they are most prominent is that of urban black adolescents (Dollard 1939, Golightly and Scheffler 1948; Abrahams 1962; Kochman 1970; Mitchell-Kernan 1971; Labov 1972). A folk art form consisting of rhymed retorts has been found in black ghettoes across North America. Black youths who do badly in schools and are classified as "verbally deficient" show a highly developed linguistic competence along with verbal artistry and keen sociological and psychological perception in speech events of their vernacular culture, including ritual insults (Labov 1972, 1973). In the simplest and most ubiquitous example,

(2) A: **Motherfucker!**
    B: *Your* mother.

B turns A's jibes back on A's family. Verbal deftness in twisting the original insult is highly prized. Escalating coarseness is common, but neither necessary nor sufficient. To somewhat simplify the rules for reply, given (a), (b) is a failure and (c) a success:

(3) A: T(B) is x
    B: T(A) is x
    C: T(A) is y, and y is worse than x (Cf. Labov 1972)

in which T is the targeted person, A and B are speakers, x and y are insulting attributes. The insulted person (B) cannot simply repeat the same form, saying the insulter is also x, but must produce some other insulting characterization of A: y might be an escalation of x, a twist on it, or some other attribution from within the same semantic domain. Memory is more important than invention in "the heat of battle," at least for rhymed retorts; *ad hoc* responses likely sacrifice rhyme (reported already waning by Dollard 1939). However, ritual insults that are not rhymed are more difficult to recognize—for participants as for analysts. Unrhymed insults with the same content as rhymed insults are more likely to be taken seriously. So, although in one sense it is easier to play when the retorts do not need to rhyme, other distancing devices are needed to distinguish the game of ritual insults from the serious and sometimes lethal business of personal insults. More bizarre and outrageous forms of accusations are often relied upon to signal this distance.

TOPICS OF BLACK YOUTHS' RITUAL INSULTS

Reanalyzing the contents of the corpora of ritual insults reported in studies of the speech of black youths, one can see that the most frequently mentioned theme is sexual receptivity. That of one's mother is most frequent (as in 4), but the wantonness—or at least accessibility—of other relatives (5) or oneself (6) also occasion comment.

(4) **Your mother's like a police station: dicks going in and out all the time.** (Labov 1972:140)

(5) **It takes twelve barrels of water to make a steamboat run. It takes an elephant's dick to make your grandmammy come.** (Kochman 1970:158)

(6) **Roses are red. Violets are blue. I fucked your mama, and now it's for you.** (Abrahams 1962:212)

Blackness is a second theme of black ritual insults. Early work emphasized self-hatred and rejection of blackness both in the sense of skin color and in the sense of "country" or "low-down nigger" behavior. Insults such as "You so black you sweat Super Permalube oil" seem to denigrate blackness, but Kochman (1970:158) argued that whiteness—again, either shade or culture—may also be a target.

Abrahams (1962) similarly suggested that "aping" or "selling out to" white culture are weighty charges. Deviance from culturally appropriate behavior is not monotonic and varies from group to group. Labov (1972:133) reported the following whiteness insult:

(7) **Your mother so white she have to use Mighty White.**

A third major theme is poverty. Recurrent forms include **Yo' so poor...**, **Yo' family so poor...**, **Yo' mother eat...**, **Yo' mother raised you on...**, and **I went to your house and...** [some grotesque event occurred], e.g.,

(8) **I went to Money house and I walked in Money house. I say — I wanted to sit down, and then, you know, a roach jumped up and said, "Sorry, this seat is taken."** (Labov 1972:136-7)

(9) **Yo' moma eat Dog Yummies.**

Remarks like the last may be taken personally and lead to fights, denial, or flight — even within a peer group. Eating dogfood (9) is not outlandish in urban American ghettoes. Neither is the presence of cockroaches (8), so simply calling attention to such phenomena is not innovative. Greater than normal abundance or boldness must be asserted, as in (8).

Labov (1972:134-5) proposed the following as the basic black ritual insult form:

Your mother so ... she ....

Surprisingly, Labov's collection of ritual insults had a much narrower topic range than earlier, more impressionistic collections. In the insults Labov reported, only characteristics of mothers were mentioned (fathers in some retorts). Another common topic, according to Abrahams (1962:211) is homosexuality of fathers or brothers, e.g.,

Your brother like a grocery store: he take meat in the back.

Dollard (1939:5) also noted incest and passive homosexuality as "frequent themes." In passing, Labov (1972:166) mentioned a "large class of ritual insults which impute homosexuality to the antagonist," but he apparently ignored those data. Thus, mothers are not the only topic of black youths' insults, although they may be mentioned in all three of the classes here suggested: sexual receptivity, blackness, and poverty.

DEVELOPMENTAL INTERPRETATIONS

Adolescents, especially urban black male adolescents, must learn to defend themselves in the hostile world outside the home. Dollard (1939), Abrahams (1962), and Kochman (1970) regarded ritual insults as conditioning the victim to rough treatment. While taunting may train one to maintain composure (Goffman 1957), this is only a negative precondition for success in insult interchanges. The retort is the positive accomplishment. Insult interchanges provide training for the fast-thinking, fast-talking skills used to outwit and out-talk representatives of the dominant social order, such as welfare workers, police, schoolteachers, and hostile majority group members encountered in unofficial interaction.

Cutting loose from the mother (the dominating socializing force in early years) is a part of growing up emphasized in accounts of black insults. Ridiculing femininity and weakness may be means to independence, to masculinity (Abrahams 1962:213-4; cf. Devereux 1937; Levy 1973), and to making the transition from mother-centered childhood to masculine peer-group-centered adolescence (Labov 1972). Mothers' expressed approval of masculinity and the general denigration of women in American culture facilitate this.

As Dollard (1939) recognized, projection also plays a large part: projection of homosexual feelings and of aggressive feelings about one's mother. She cannot be attacked, but peers' mothers can (Abrahams 1962:214).

Finally, the importance of play in the acquisition of communicative competence has been emphasized by Hymes's followers (see Bauman 1974, 1976; Kirshenblatt-Gimblett 1976).

To generalize statements about ritual insults as characteristic of stigmatized groups, the remainder of this essay reports exchanges of insults from the two other subcultures analyzed in *The Survival of Domination* (Adam 1978). The miniscule Jewish data were witnessed in Detroit. The more abundant gay data are drawn from naturally-occurring interactions in Toronto, Edmonton, Tucson, Detroit, and San Francisco.

TOPICS OF GAY RITUAL INSULTS

The three basic themes found in the content analysis of reported black ritual insults recur in gay insults, if a more general gloss is substituted for "blackness." Sexual receptivity, degree of conformity to the stigmatized culture, and relative income are more general categories capturing corpora from the two subcultures.

Unlike black ghetto boys, gay men do not usually make remarks about the mothers of those they wish to insult. As adults, usually not living with parents, their parents are not visible to prospective insulters. And having made the adolescent adjustment to leaving the childhood world of the mother, gay men are less obsessed with these problems — folk prejudice to the contrary notwithstanding.[5] Even among hustlers the same age as the black youths studied, mothers are not a topic.

The most common theme of black ritual insults is sexual receptivity. The sexual behavior of one's whole family can be of central concern to an adolescent, and is particularly likely to be in a culture where kinship is central and one is held responsible for the sexual behavior of other family members (see Carrier 1975; Glazer 1976), but for most American adults, only statements about the individual threaten one's reputation.

Contempt for sexual receptivity from the dominant culture is shared by some within the gay community,[6] as, indeed, are negative judgments about homosexuality itself (Ashley 1979, 1980). Stigmatized subcultures are by no means immune to the values and prejudices of the majority culture (Humphreys and Miller 1980; Mitchell-Kernan 1971; Ashley 1979:218).

Hayes (1977) and Ashley (1979, 1980) suggest that "camp" is dead, overestimating the homogeneity of the contemporary gay world. As Murray (1982) showed modeling disparate conceptualizations of "gay community,"[7] the advent of a "Stonewall generation" (i.e., those whose gay identity crystallized after the 1969 Greenwich Village riots) did not result in an overnight change of self-conception everywhere. Not only are there still "pre-Stonewall" queens, even in New York and San Francisco, but new ones are being socialized (what Robert Patrick termed "the queen machine"). Members of the "post-Stonewall" or "clone" generation are too committed to hyper-masculinity with its strong, silent presentation of self to engage in repartee on any topic. Indeed, conversation of any sort is markedly deviant in many encounters in the institutions of contemporary gay ghettoes. It must be kept in mind, therefore, that in what follows, a minority of a minority are being described. "Clones" may "camp" in some social gatherings, while "queens" are neither an extinct nor a vanishing species.

The classic queens accepted feminine labels, seizing thereby the advantage of being able to denigrate others' masculinity without defending their own. Being penetrable is one thing, but being too-penetrable is and was an attribute that can be targeted, as in the following:

(10) A: **We can't afford to lose another sofa** [disappearing up your distended anus].

B: **Your ass is so stretched you should put in a drawstring.**

A: **Word is you've had your dirt-shute mack-tacked.**

B: **And you wall-papered your womb.**

A: **Where do you find tricks who'll rim your colostomy?**

B: **You douche with Janitor in a Drum.**

A: **Slam your clam.**

B: **Slam it, cram it, ram it, oooh, but don't jam it.** [demonstrating]

A: **Cross your legs, your hemorrhoids are showing.**

B: **You need to strap yours forward so you'll have a basket.** [male genitalia implied otherwise lacking]

A: **Better than back-combing my pubies, like you do. Preparation H is a great lubricant.**

B: [pointing at *A*] **This girl's hung like an animal — a tsetse fly.**

A: **Four bulldogs couldn't chew off this monster.** [fondling himself]

B: **I don't think even a bulldog would want *that* in its mouth. Besides, I've seen chubbier clits.**

A: **Peeking under the door in the washroom again?**[8]

Most of the insults derogate the other's masculinity, although the "oooh" acknowledged that *B* was not adverse to getting fucked. From enlarged anuses the exchange moved to diminutive penises. In the following exchange *A* had just been fucked while *B*, his roommate, had been in the next room. *A* begins by implying that *B* had gone into the bathroom to masturbate:

(11) A: **Sitting on the toilet with your toy up you again?**

B: **Darling, you already have the only *man* in the house in you. He can't very well be two places at the same time —**

A: **And you *do* need to fill yourself with something.**

B: **What's it to you?** [a stop signal]

A: **But if you can't get anything that's alive, can't you at least get something that was alive once?**

B: Like what? Rob the morgue like you usually do?

A: Nah, they'd turn away. You wouldn't feel a carrot, what about a pumpkin?

B: What about *your* handle? [a come-on]

A: Not available.

B: Oh, no! [mock horror] You mean that hunk you're with is a woman like us?

A: Wouldn't you like to know?

B: How could I not know? I hear every thrust he makes and every gasp from you.

A: So you know, why ask?

B: Yeah, I know; your hands are in love with your cock.

A: Takes two hands to handle a Whopper.

B: That's why you'd be perfect for me.

A: Shit! They should shoot rockets up your ass. Then maybe you could feel it.

B: You mean if you fucked me I wouldn't feel anything?

A: You could try a shotgun. Bullet'd probably get lost, though.

B: You should get lost — or stick to taking it up the ass. You should put in a toll gate. Then we could pay the phone bill.[9]

In this exchange (not all of the speech acts being insults), *B* acknowledges not only sexual receptivity, but desire for *A*. The latter makes him vulnerable to rejection and *A* doesn't charge *B* with being receptive, but with being too fucked out to feel being fucked. Nor does *B* attack *A* for being fuckable (the masculine self-image of *C*, the guest, is, however, potentially open to comment).

Too much sexual activity of any sort may be a source of envy, and hence of comment, e.g.,

(12) A: It's time to pull in your horns. [inhuman phallic apparatus]

B: At least I can get it up. [in implied contrast to *A*'s impotence]

Not being able to attract men may be noted (as in 11), but attracting too many can also draw derogatory comment, as in the last thrust in (11) and

(13)A: **Ships passing in the night have nothing on you.**
   B: **Me? Your bedroom looks like the Hong Kong harbor —**
   A: **Sailors smell sea food.** [said in a bragging tone]
   B: **You forget: Hong Kong harbor is full of junks.**

Looking worn-out is often attributed to sexual hyperactivity as in

(14) **Where were you last night? Your eyes look like roadmaps.**

Just as it is possible to be too black or not black enough, it is possible to be too overtly gay on the one hand, or to pretend not to be gay on the other. While there is clearly an overtness/covertness continuum, the appropriate place on it to be varies considerably in the opinion of cliques and individuals. In any milieu in which various gay networks are mixed (especially queens and clones), comment can be aroused by what is deemed inappropriate ("trashy") behavior. There is *no* level of overtness which cannot be faulted be someone as either "flaunting it" or as "trying to hide it." Still, it is the latter that occasions the "bitchiest" comment. "Closet queens" are said to wear "crystal veils," i.e., disguises transparent to other gay men. Closetry is an acceptable topic for insult among queens, clones, and even the most politically-correct politicos. The following examples all were produced by self-identified clones (in social gatherings):

(15) **You're 'bout as straight as a fever chart in a malaria ward.**
(16) **You're about as straight as a rattlesnake ready to strike.**
(17) **You straight? Yeah, like Highway One curving up the California coast.**

And then there is the retort to ostensibly straight researchers:

(18) **Writing a book, eh? What better way to get material than on your knees.** [i.e., in position to fellate]

In (19) the possibility of bisexuality is challenged:

(19)A: Nobody can dance at two weddings? Which is it?
   B: How would you know? You can't dance at all?

The extended examples above include recurrent charges of being too overtly homosexual (a "flaming queen").

Pretensions other than to masculinity form the next most frequent class of insults, although they may revert to comments on pretensions to masculinity, as when one person in a gay bar was rhapsodizing about his new car, and the person beside him stage-whispered,

(20) Too bad he had to hock his cock. [get fucked rather than fuck to get it]

"Tackiness" rather than poverty is the charge applied to substandard expenditure as in

(21) Nice car, but where do you put it when they lock the park? [i.e., the target does not own a house with a garage; he spends his life engaged in sex in the bushes of public parks]
(22) Don't most parties include booze?

If value and taste must be granted, "piss elegance" can be invoked:

(23) Christ! You can't turn around in here without breaking something. [fragile antiques]

The rule seems to be, "If you can't deny it, devalue it." This rule applies to more than purchased objects. For instance, one well-hung man on the gay beach seemed overly proud of the size of his penis, so another commented (in another stage-whisper):

(24) That's no cock; it's just the handle to turn him over with. [cf. (11) on "handle"]

Also on the beach, the following exchange culminates in a devaluation:

(25)A: I have him wrapped around my little finger.

B: The only thing you ever had wrapped around your finger was a piece of elastic to remind you who you are, and you lost that.

A: I get more men than you can count. [possibly this could be interpreted as an insult to B's mental ability, but it was probably intended as a personal insult]

B: Tricks are for kids.

In (26) another desirable condition (having a lover) is devalued:

(26)A: You're like a railroad track: laid all over the country. [apt because B had not been around of late]

B: I got married.

A: Some old troll.

B: You ain't ever seen him.

A: Anyone who'd go with you I'd never look at; I know what he must look like to wanna fuck you. Who wants something looks like he already groun' up in the meat grinder?

B: Honey, I the meat grinder. You stick it up, I does the turning.

A: I'd be too 'fraid.

B: So lil' you'd get lost?

A: Ain't nobody ever called it little before. [though swaggering, this breaks frame as argumentation rather than retort]

B: Don't matter how big it is if you don't know how to use it.[10]

B devalues penis size and A devalues having a lover.

Pretentiousness is a more global category than relative affluence, but charges of pretentiousness overlap charges about sexual identity and sexual behavior. Sexual identity, cultural identity, and relative affluence gloss non-overlapping categories; pretentiousness cross-cuts them just as attributes of mothers cross-cut black ritual insults.

CONTENT OF JEWISH RITUAL INSULTS

There are parallels to black and gay uses of ritual insults in North American Jewish communities, in which wit and quick repartee are also valued, and the same themes reappear. Sexually nonconforming behavior seems to be universal (although the norms for appropriate behavior vary). Second, just as it is possible to be too black or not black enough in appearance and behavior, or too overtly gay or too "closeted," it is possible to be judged too assimilated — "denying your heritage" — or too stereotypically Jewish. Lacking money or throwing it around are also occasions for insults. While informants make these generalizations, I have not collected examples, except the following about "denying one's heritage" and (horrors!) emulating blacks:

(27) A: **Where dja get those shvartse clothes?**
 B: **At least I don't look like I just got off the boat!**
 A: **No? You look like you're getting *on* the boat — to Africa!**
 B: **Not everyone wants to look like a rabbi, you know.**
 A: **Something's wrong with rabbis? You're not Jewish anymore?...**

This exchange took place in northwest Detroit (1977) between old friends who hadn't seen each other recently. Whereas *B* considered the opening sally as ritualized, *A* may not have been playing even with his first question. Clothes are, or course, an important symbol of cultural identity, and the entire conversation (including the discussion following the exchange quoted) dealt with what is the appropriate amount of Jewish visibility. Intra-familial discussions of this topic are a widely-noted feature of Jewish life in North America.

CONDITIONS FOR PLAYING

Black: The entire black population cannot be characterized by participation in ritual insulting. Labov (1972:255-

92) split the population of black urban youths into two groups: those who participate in gang street culture and those who do not. For the latter he borrowed the folk label "lame." "Lames" do not know the slang, nor how to verbally duel, and so on. This gross dichotomy is important, because it is a rare indication that many black youths do not command the vernacular, nor engage in the verbal games of that culture. Unfortunately, neither Labov nor other observers have estimated what proportion of the population is "lame."

Just as knights made careers of jousting, Southern gentlemen, *samurai*, and Prussian officers careers of dueling (Flynn 1977), some regular participants in subcultural settings build up a reputation for verbal dueling and become specialists within a network. In Labov's study, "Boot" stands out as the master craftsman of insults. His superiority at playing the game is recognized by other gang members, who often refuse to engage him in verbal duels. Since "communicative competence" is stratified, the recognized masters frequently must hold back, waiting for worthy opponents on whom to test their wits (teachers are reported to be too pathetic to bother with "showing them up").

Gay: Just as being a young urban black does not automatically imply participation in street culture or even passive knowledge of vernacular games, being gay does not automatically give one comprehension of gay argot or competence in verbal game-playing. Most self-styled "queens" have probably played insults, but not all are very good at being witty rather than gross. And most gay men would be insulted to be labeled "queens" and have never been involved in extended exchanges like those reported here. One part of the stereotype of gay people held by others is that they spend much of their time "bitching," "backbiting," "cutting each other down" (Adam 1978). Very few gay men and seemingly still fewer lesbians spend an appreciable amount of time verbally dueling. The rarity of ritual insults in the many hours of participant observation in gay political groups, in other "post-Stonewall" institutions and various gay circles suggests that only a minority of those who frequent gay settings engage in the sort of stylized repartee discussed here.[11]

There are a few specialists, like "Boot." On special occasions, one group's champion dirt-talker may do battle with another's specialist for entertainment of all, as in (10). Since not everyone is an active participant (and still fewer accomplished in the art), the question becomes, "Who will insult whom when and where?"

The first condition is that the insulter cannot be trying to pass as anything he is not—a social success, rich, or, especially, straight. Those passing do not want attention focused on them: they are too vulnerable to devastating rejoinders to wield weapons of insult in public (private expressions of contempt are another matter altogether).

Second, insulting seems to be a skill more developed among what might be called "the doubly damned"—black gays and gay transvestites. Both are likely to encounter denigrating remarks from other gay men as well as from straight people. A sharp tongue is a weapon honed through frequent exercise, and is a survival skill particularly of "drag queens." Generally, aggressive self-denigration is an art of oppressed people. It is not the black youths who lead sheltered lives ("lames") who "play the dozens," but, rather, those most exposed to racist aggression.

Third, insults seem more the provenance of older, more closeted gay men than of younger, publicly self-accepting gay men (although as noted above, there are young queens and young closet queens and the "arts of oppression" are not about to be lost). The variables of age and openness are confounded: young, closeted males may lack a peer group of likewise closeted friends, while older closeted men frequently have networks of closeted friends (Warren 1974; Covelli 1978), and some openly gay men have predominantly straight networks.

Generational differences can be attributed to a number of factors: greater self-acceptance, stronger group norms of self-acceptance, lower status ("less to lose"), less experience of "pre-Stonewall" self-loathing and repression, and the formative influence of gay liberation. The last dampened insults interpretable as self-loathing, but recourse to insults focused on "tackiness," "piss elegance" and closetry continued. The "post-Stonewall" or "clone" generation is distinctly less verbal, but people whose experience and outlook are "pre-Stonewall" continue to pour out of the provinces, the suburbs, and sometimes even cities with gay ghettos, so generation cannot easily be linked to age or birth order. Date of birth is less important to "generation" than when one came out: gay people of divergent ages who came out into a particular gay world belong to one generation, while two gay people of the same age who came out at different ages (may) belong to different generations. Access to information about the existence of other gay people, the presence of gay role models, and the particular experience of oppression and challenge to it affect *how* one is gay (not *whether* one is homosexual).

Standard sociological independent variables other than "generation" and "passing" do not seem to affect the distribution of insulters: not class, not education, though possibly race.

Having made these assertions about who plays, let us turn briefly to the questions of "when" and "to whom." The latter defied specification, because almost anyone can become the target for outlandish insults — friends, enemies, strangers. Anyone perceived as an affront to one's sensibility, a poacher on one's territory, or a potential rival may be targeted. Nevertheless, some individuals seem to be the butt of an inordinate share of insults.

Most gay ritual insults occur within exclusively gay settings. The presence of rivals of long standing or of regular
targets accounts for many exchanges. New persons may
become targets by breaching the expected order of the
situation — especially if they are unaware of what that expected order is. "Tourists" or persons wandering into gay
settings by accident are especially likely to be the victim
of displays of wit and/or outrageous behavior (Cavan 1963;
Lee 1978), displays for which they are rarely prepared with
adequate retorts. If the insulter is mistaken in identifying
a "tourist," more spirited retorts will be made.

Of the gay insults outside gay settings, many occur near
gay territories. Against bypassers, "tourists," and "fag-
bashers," tongues sharpened on peers cut loose on
"straights." As Mezzrow and Wolfe (1969:198) noted of
black adolescents

> What they were sharpening in all this verbal horseplay was their
> wits, the only weapon they had. Their sophistication didn't come
> out of moldy books and dicty colleges. It came from opening their
> eyes wide and gunning the world hard. [*Dicty* = black dialect for
> "pretentious vocabulary." –*Ed.*]

Various "queens" — especially those identifiable targets for
straight aggression or with black skins — have been performing their own guerilla theater in the streets for a long time,
using keen perception and sharp words to demand acceptance, or to annihilate any who would deny it. Such "play"
is, quite literally, "self-defense." Although many denigra-
tions stem from, and perpetuate, collective self-hatred, at
least some undermine the oppressive cognitive structure,
attacking those who deny the group. However much they
may be practiced on stigmatized fellows, the skills of quick,
acute perception of others and lighting repartee are used
against the group's oppressors.

NOTES

A preliminary report of some of these data was presented at the 1977 annual meeting of the American Sociological Association in Chicago. The author wishes to acknowledge the encouragement and the comments of Niyi Akinnaso, Keith Basso, Philip Blumstein, Meredith Gould, Joseph Hayes, John Lee, Dennis Magill, Brian Miller, Terry Moss, Kenneth Payne, William Simon, and one of the anonymous referees for the *American Sociological Review*. The ignorance about ethnography and about the world revealed by other referees should be documented, but as is argued in this essay, it's no fun insulting the verbally incompetent. Nevertheless the idiocy of the demand for a "control group" from one referee for *Qualitative Sociology* must be mentioned.

1. Dittmar (1976:227) is simply wrong by claiming that "the whole point is to outdo the other in the coarseness of the insult."

2. The masculine pronoun is used throughout because both the existing literature and the observations reported here deal with male peer groups. Carolyn Dirksen, Meredith Gould and Deborah Spehn have assured me that black girls do not lack in ritualized repartee but have not provided examples.

3. "What was ritualized in dueling days was the glove-slap, whereupon the offended party gave to the offender the right to choose weapons. What the writer misses is that even when things went that far, an actual duel was not common — most got bogged down in preparations" (anonymous referee comment).

4. Joking was conceived by Radcliffe-Brown (1940) as a means to avoid conflict, but humorous sallies are examples of aggression and conflict, not conflict avoidance (Lyman 1971; Howell 1973).

5. As Adam (1978) showed, the dominant group projects a mother obsession on groups it inferiorizes: the omnivorous Jewish mother, the black matriarch, and the castrating homosexual-genic mother are all creations of the dominant group's imagination (see also Murray 1984).

6. Participants in stigmatized subcultures do not possess a wholly distinct culture (Mitchell-Kernan 1971; Humphreys and Miller 1980): one of the reasons for the prefix.

7. Consideration of "gay community" as a technical term is provided by Murray (1979).

8. This exchange followed a Canadian Thanksgiving dinner and involved two masters of the art both in their early 30s. They were performing for the other guests.

9. Both participants were in their late teens. The exchange was reconstructed, so this is not a direct transcription. However, A accepted it as capturing what had been said accurately (B shortly after the exchange evicted A).

10. Both participants were gay black males in their late teens. The exchange took place in the heart of the "valley of the clones," i.e., at Castro and 18th Streets in San Francisco.

11. In Guatemala City, Murray (1980) showed that the same terms for "homosexual" are not shared by those involved in homosexual cruising. Most of the terms in Rodgers (1972) and Ashley (1979, 1980) were unknown to San Francisco gay men I queried, although known generative principles allowed some to be decoded correctly.

REFERENCES

Abrahams, Roger D.
1962 "Playing the Dozens," *Journal of American Folklore* 75:209-20.
1974 "Black Talking in the Street," pp. 240-62 in R. Bauman and J. Sherzer, *Explorations in the Ethnography of Speaking.* Cambridge: University Press.

Adam, Barry D.
1978   *The Survival of Domination.* New York: Elsevier.
Ashley, Leonard R. N.
1979   *"Kinks and Queens*: Linguistic and Cultural Aspects of the Terminology for *Gays," Maledicta* 3:215-55.
1980   "'Lovely, Blooming, Fresh and Gay': The Onomastics of Camp," *Maledicta* 4:223-48.
Bateson, Gregory
1972   *Steps to an Ecology of Mind.* San Francisco: Chandler.
Bauman, Richard
1974   "Verbal Art as Performance," *American Anthropologist* 77:290-311.
1976   "The Development of Competence in the Use of Solicitational Routines," *Working Papers in Sociolinguistics* 34:1-16.
Carrier, Joseph M.
1975   "Urban Mexican Male Homosexual Encounters." Thesis, University of California, Irvine.
Cavan, Sherri
1963   "Interaction in Home Territories," *Berkeley Journal of Sociology* 7:17-32.
Covelli, Lucille H.
1976   "A Gay Friendship Network." Thesis, University of Toronto.
Devereux, George
1937   "Institutionalized Homosexuality among the Mohave," *Human Biology* 7:498-527.
Dittmar, Norbert
1976   *Sociolinguistics.* London: Arnold.
Dollard, John
1939   "'The Dozens': Dialectic of Insults," *American Imago* 1:3-25.
Flynn, Charles P.
1976   *Insult and Society.* Port Washington, NY: Kennikat.
Glazer, Mark
1976   "On Verbal Dueling among Turkish Boys," *Journal of American Folklore* 89:88-91.
Goffman, Erving
1957   "Embarrassment and Social Organization," *American Journal of Sociology* 62:264-71.
1963   *Stigma.* Toronto: Prentice-Hall.

Golightly, Cornelius and Israel Scheffler
1948 "Playing the Dozens," *Journal of Abnormal and Social Psychology* 34:104-5.

Howell, Richard W.
1973 *Teasing Relationships.* Addison-Wesley Module 46.

Hayes, Joseph J.
1977 "Language and Language Behavior of Lesbian Women and Gay Men." *Ms.*

Humphreys, Laud and Brian Miller
1980 "Stigma and the Emergence of Culture," in J. Marmor, *Homosexual Behavior.* New York: Basic Books.

Kirshenblatt-Gimblett, Barbara
1976 *Speech Play.* Philadelphia: University of Pennsylvania Press.

Kochman, Thomas
1970 "Toward an Ethnography of Black-American Speech Behavior," pp. 145-62, in R. Whitten and J. Szwed, *Afro-American Anthropology.* New York: Free Press.

Labov, William
1972 *Language in the Inner City.* Philadelphia: University of Pennsylvania Press.
1973 "Linguistic Research in American Society," pp. 97-129, in E. Hamp, *Themes in Linguistics.* The Hague: Mouton.

Lee, John Alan
1978 *Getting Sex.* Toronto: General.

Levy, Robert I.
1973. *The Tahitians.* Chicago: University Press.

Lyman, G. Peter
1971 "On Male Chauvinist Humor," *Phalanstery Review* 3,10:9-11

Memmi, Alberto
1968 *Dominated Man.* Boston: Beacon.

Mitchell-Kernan, Claudia
1971 *Language Behavior in a Black Urban Community.* Berkeley: Language Behavior Research Laboratory.

Murray, Stephen O.
1979 "Institutional Elaboration of a Quasi-Ethnic Community," *International Review of Modern Sociology* 9:165-77.
1980 "Lexical and Institutional Elaboration: The 'Species Homosexual' in Guatemala," *Anthropological Linguistics* 22:177-85.
1982 "Labels and Labeling: Prototype Semantics of 'Gay Community'." *Working Papers of the Language Behavior Research Laboratory* 51.

1984   "Psychoanalytic Fantasies in Black and Gay," in S. Murray (ed.), *Cultural Diversity and Homosexualities.* New York: Irvington.

Radcliffe-Brown, A.

1940   "On Joking Relationships," *Africa* 13:185-210.

Rodgers, Bruce

1972   *The Queens' Vernacular.* San Francisco: Straight Arrow.

Stanley, Julia P.

1970   "Homosexual Slang," *American Speech* 45:45-50.

1974   "Gay Slang, Gay Culture," American Anthropological Association meeting, Mexico, D.F.

Warren, Carol A. B.

1974   *Identity and Community in the Gay World.* New York: Wiley.

"How dare you question our journalistic integrity and professional objectivity, you disgusting little perverted commie pinko fag?"

HOWARD UNIVERSITY LAW SCHOOL
FINAL EXAMINATION

I. CONSTITUTIONAL LAW

A dude commit armed robbery. After he be arrested, the dude be hungry and ax the police to get him some chicken wings and a RC Cola. The police refuse and give him a bologna sandwich and water instead. Has the dude's constitutional rights been violated?

II. BANKRUPTCY

Lionel wish to open a bean pie factory. He borrow $100,000 from the SBA. One week later, Lionel file a bankruptcy petition due to economic fluctuations. Can Lionel keep his Cadillac?

III. DOMESTIC RELATIONS

Sylvester have not paid his non-support money to Yolanda for his and Yolanda's 14 children. This weekend, Sylvester want to take the children to the Coliseum to see the Jackson Five. Can Yolanda refuse to let Sylvester take the children?

IV. BANKING AND FINANCE

Clifton rob the Consolidated Bank and be running down Clay Street with the Man in hot pursuit. When Clifton hear the dogs and siren less than 50 feet away, he observe Tyrone walking out Slaughter's Lobby. He saunter up to Tyrone with sweat pouring down his face and looking over his shoulder and say "Say, Brother, would you like to purchase $50,000 worth of readily negotiable securities for $25.00?" Whereupon Ty, an economic adviser for HUD, say, "I'll give you $20.00 now and $5.00 next week." Clifton then consummate the transaction with the "right-on" handshake and black power salute.

(1) If Ty be caught, can he give Bondsman Elkins the securities to hold as collateral for his bond?

(2) Can Clifton consider the $5.00 that Ty owe him as accounts receivable for the current tax year?

V. INSURANCE

Willard pass on to his final reward in a razor fight after procuring a debit insurance policy for $2,000.00. After a two-week period of bereavement, Lawyer Mimms meet with the family and friends to discuss the estate.

(1) Do Haverty's Furniture Company have a shot at the insurance proceeds?

(2) Willard have not cashed his last welfare check. Can his devoted friend Corroledda sign his name to the check and keep the money?

VI. REAL PROPERTY

Alphonso "Nite-Batch" Jones have not paid the property taxes on the house he inherit from his Uncle Billy Jones for the past 12 years. Before the Sheriff can sell the property, the stove in the living room ignite and reduce Nite-Batch's house to ashes.

(1) Under these unfortunate circumstances, do Nite-Batch still have to pay the taxes?

(2) How much time do Model Cities have to replace the house?

(3) If Nite-Batch park his Grand Prix with gangster whitewalls where the house used to be and live in it, do he have to pay real property tax on the Grand Prix?

VII. PATENTS AND COPYRIGHTS

Isador obtain a grant from the Federal Afro Studies Administration to study the impact of the automobile on the black
man. He invent a swivel stand for his auto TV and apply
for and receive a U.S. patent. While on a lecture tour, Ford
Motor Credit Company successfully repossess his Mark IV.

(1) Would the Neighborhood Legal Aid Society be successful in their suit in U.S. District Court against Ford
Motor Credit Company for patent infringement?

(2) Assuming Isador prevail in his suit, can he be reim-
bursed for Greyhound passage back to Richmond?

VIII. TORTS

Deaconess Alvina Jackson, unmarried, give birth in the
Fellowship Hall of Zion Church to a boy, Hiawatha, who
depart this life shortly after being born. Since Deaconess
Jackson have been deprived of extra welfare money, can
she sue the midwife, Sister Olivetta Simpson, for medical
malpractice?

IX. MATHEMATICS

(1) The judge give a dude 20 years for selling smack,
with 10 suspended. How much time do the dude have
to serve?

(2) Alreatha have 100 food stamps. She steal 15 more
from Violina and send 10 to Florida. How many food
stamps do Alreatha have?

(3) Braxton have been in an automobile accident. He
get Lawyer Smith to settle the case for $9,000.00.
Lawyer Smith's fee be one-third. How much have
Lawyer Smith rip Braxton off for?

X. BIOLOGY

Circle the animal which is not seafood: (a) Catfish (b) Heel
(c) Crabs

Sickle Cell Anemia is caused by licking food stamps.
( ) True ( ) False

XI. SOCIAL STUDIES

Who founded the free clinic at the Medical College of
Virginia?

What were the dudes' names who led the Attica revolt?

Name at least three of the Soledad Brothers.

In the space provided below, give a detailed account of
black history in the United States before 1951.

(Submitted by P. Bernstein)

**"I want you bunch of thieving shysters
to defend me on a slander charge."**

AGEIST LANGUAGE

Frank Nuessel

Elders in our society are a heterogeneous group.[1] Membership in this sector of our society is unrestricted as to gender, race, religion, national origin, and handicap. In fact, Matthews (1979:68) has observed that "old age is not a social category with a simple definition or an obvious membership. It is a social category with negative connotations, but, because of the ambiguity surrounding membership, to whom negative attributes may be imputed, is unclear." In practice, assignment to this category of society is usually defined by an arbitrary chronology, physical appearance, and patterns of behavior. Participation in this open-ended group is normally viewed as highly undesirable and unpleasant. This explains why some people tend to lie about their age or conceal it. Moreover, the social stigma attached to aging accounts for the ever-increasing number of cosmetic products (hair dye, skin discoloration ointments, etc.) designed to mask the superficial signs associated with the aging process. The related upsurge in surgical procedures (facelifts, hair implantation, etc.) is a more radical example of such gerontophobia.

The expression "ageism" was first coined by Robert N. Butler, former Director of the National Institute on Aging, in 1967 (Butler, 1969, 1975). Verification of the lexicalization of this notion is confirmed because this neologism now has a separate entry in *The American Heritage Dictionary of the English Language* where the term is defined as "discrimination based on age; especially discrimination against middle-aged and elderly people" (Morris, 1979:24).

The lexicon of ageist language is substantial (Nuessel, 1982). Such maledictology provides an excellent domain for the empirical verification and confirmation of Aman's (1973, 1977) prototypical onomastic questionnaire for eliciting data on deviations from the norm, shortcomings, and flaws. The present study constitutes a preliminary inventory of ageist terminology in the English language.

The difficulty associated with defining who is an elder is also manifested in the complexity of selecting a suitable term for describing this group. Ward (1979:165) reports ten terms (**senior citizen, retired person, mature American, elderly person, middle-aged person, older American, golden ager, old timer, aged person**, and **old man/old woman**) for this sector of the community. Many of these are euphemisms, i.e., they involve the substitution of a supposedly innocuous phrase for one which is considered patently offensive.[2] The sheer number of such expressions constitutes a linguistic record and indictment of society's phobic reaction to inclusion in this classification.

Humorous labels for elders are numerous: **geriatric generation, Geritol generation**, and **Lawrence Welk generation**. The activist political organization (Consultation of Older and Younger Adults) founded by Maggie Kuhn and popularly known as the **Gray Panthers** is yet another appellation with half-menacing, half-comic overtones. Even the adjectivally-derived noun **elderly** is stigmatic because this word has been employed by media reporters who have traditionally portrayed this social subdivision in a negative and derisive fashion. Another euphemistic term is **agèd** (also used adjectivally). At present, the emerging, acceptable lexical item for this diverse group is **elder**.

242 • Reinhold Aman

Ageist language comprises two separate categories. One domain includes words whose specific denotation refers to elders. The other component includes lexical items whose connotation or intensional meaning is normally associated with elders.

Many ageist words are particularly pernicious in their deprecatory impact because they denigrate people on the basis of both age and gender (Matthews, 1979; Sontag, 1972). **Beldam(e), biddy, crone, granny, gremalkin, hag, trot** (archaic), and **witch** relate to women who possess unpleasant physical attributes or who comport themselves in a socially unacceptable manner. **Bag, bat**, and **battle-ax(e)** allude to women with major personality defects. Although the latter terms are not age-specific, these words are frequently prefixed by the adjective **old**. These hybrid syntagms, consequently, reinforce the disparagement of female elders. The semantically neutral **maid** in conjunction with **old** and the term **spinster** combine unflattering ageist and sexist references. Likewise, **little old lady** suggests impotency based on age and sex. In this same vein, an old wives' tale, is idol gossip engaged in by elder idle females.

Disparaging terminology marked for age and sex exists for males also. **Codger, coot, gaffer, geezer**, and **greybeard** all portray this group wrongfully by attributing unacceptable behavior to its membership. **Old goat** and **dirty old man** invoke perceptions of lecherous men with misguided sexual inclinations. The acronym **D.O.M.** (*Dirty Old Man*) is frequently employed. To this repertoire of ageist words may be added the following distasteful colloquialisms:[3] **baldy, back number, bottle-nose**, and **mummy**. In addition to this list, labels preceded by the descriptor **old** are also negative: **cornstalk, crank, fart, fool, fossil, fuck, fuddy-duddy, fussbudget, grouch, grump, guard** (a collective term), **miser**, and **reprobate**.

All of these phrases allude to repugnant and antagonistic idiosyncracies. **Oldster** and **old-timer** are currently considered unacceptable designations. The term **dotard** (see *dotage, dote*) is unspecified for gender yet marked for age. **Decrepit, doddering, frail, infirm, rickety**, and **superannuated** are all specific ageist designations for physical decline. **Antediluvian, obsolete, old-fashioned**, and **outmoded** are qualities that normally refer to objects or ideas. Their more recent application to elders reflects society's disdain for this group of people. Many other qualifying adjectives are not age-related but are commonly linked to elders: **cantankerous, constipated, cranky, crotchety, eccentric, feebleminded, flabby, frumpy, fussy, garrulous, grouchy, grumpy, over-age** (a relative term), **peevish, rambling, silly, toothless, withered, wizen, wizened**, and **wrinkled**. Each one of these epithets is an objectionable or unattractive physical, mental or behavioral trait.

In fact, few favorable expressions exist to allude to elders. Positive, age-specific attributions are indeed exiguous (e.g., **august, experienced, mature, mellow, sage, seasoned, veteran, well-versed, wise**). In fact, many of the adjectives that refer to age in an auspicious sense carry favorable connotations only when applied to objects (alcoholic beverages, certain foods, and various handicrafts). Thus when *old* refers to wine or lace, this is a good property. Likewise, *aged* ascribed to brandy, cheese and wood is an excellent characteristic. Yet when assigned to people, these two terms (**aged, old**) are normally pejorative.

In addition to the denominations for the collective membership of elders, the terminology for the state of being aged is numerous. Many of these phrases—**anecdotage** (a blend of *anecdote* plus *dotage*), **declining years, second childhood, over the hill, twilight years**—imply decadence, decline or foolish activity. Words of Latin derivation such as

longevity and **senectitude** seem to be neutral. Other Latin derivatives for this status are **anility, caducity, debility, decrepitude, dotage, infirmity,** and **senility**. Again, most of these de-adjectival nouns which contain the same negative allusions as their derivational sources. The fact that they are erudite terms fails to conceal their euphemistic intent.

A few other ageist phrases are noteworthy. **Generation gap**, a neologism of the 1960s, focuses on the polarization of young and old people in our youth-oriented society (see note 3). **Convalescent center** is a frightening euphemism for a segregated concentration camp for elders. The pleasant and euphonic descriptive names (**Friendship Manor, Pine Tree Villa, Tendercare**) for these urban ghettoes conceals the fact that such sites are the penultimate repositories of their charges. Even the term **geriatric ghetto** has been employed to describe this form of virtual incarceration.

Even a few verbs may be considered ageist in their intent. The admonition **to act one's age** is a warning to elders to behave in a customary manner expected (even demanded) by society. The verbal expression **to show one's age** is sexist because it normally requires a [+ female] subject. This expression refers to the overt manifestations of the normal aging process (wrinkles, so-called age spots, etc.).

In summary, ageist language is insidious and nefarious because such parlance distorts or degrades its victims. The lexicalization (i.e., standardization of clichés about this group) facilitates verbal abuse of elders. Eventually, such maledictions can lead to far more serious mistreatment as evidenced by the current media accounts concerning the mistreatment of elders by their own children and by nursing home personnel.

NOTES

1. Holmes (1983:116-17) cites Rose (1965) who suggests that the aged may be considered a clearly identifiable subculture because of patterns of interaction, and common interests and problems. Levin and Levin (1980:95) also take the position that elders are a minority group because they are victims of ageism. Many sociologists dispute such a categorization. In this regard, Matthews (1979:60) states that "except for a few obvious correlates of old age, such as collecting pensions and social security, there are few behavorial prescriptions that apply specifically to the aged and not to adults generally. At the same time, however, age is an attribute that has social meanings and is taken into account in social interaction." Streib (1965) also concurs that the aged do not comprise a minority group.

2. Fischer (1978:94) states "...praise words invented for old people... such as *senior citizen* are often laden with a heavy freight of sarcasm."

3. Fischer (1978:91-92) observes that many of the terms of elder abuse (*gaffer, fogy, greybeard, old guard, superannuated*) were simply redefinitions of earlier non-offensive lexical items. Moreover, the increasing number of such opprobrious phrases in the late 19th and early 20th centuries reflect urban and industrial society's tendency to favor the young (Holmes, 1983:171; Sokolovsky, 1983:117).

REFERENCES

Aman, Reinhold. 1973. *Bayrisch-österreichisches Schimpfwörterbuch.* Munich: Süddeutscher Verlag.

———. 1977. "An Onomastic Questionnaire," *Maledicta* 1:83-101.

Butler, Robert N. 1969. "Age-ism: Another Form of Bigotry," *The Gerontologist* 9, 243-46.

———. 1975. *Why Survive Being Old in America.* New York: Harper and Row.

Fischer, David. 1978. *Growing Old in America.* Expanded Ed. Oxford: Oxford University Press.

Holmes, Lowell D. 1983. *Other Cultures, Elder Years: An Introduction to Cultural Gerontology.* Minneapolis: Burgess Publishing Co.

Levin, Jack and William C. Levin. 1980. *Ageism: Prejudice and Discrimination Against the Elderly.* Belmont, CA: Wadsworth Publishing Company.

Matthews, Sarah. 1979. *The Social World of Old Women: Management of Self-Identity.* Sage Library of Social Research, vol. 78. Beverly Hills, CA: Sage Publications.

Morris, William (ed.), 1979. *The American Heritage Dictionary of the English Language*. Boston: Houghton-Mifflin Co.

Nuessel, Frank. 1982. "The Language of Ageism," *The Gerontologist* 22:3, 273-76.

Rose, Arnold M. 1965. "The Subculture of Aging: A Framework in Social Gerontology." In: Arnold M. Rose and Warren A. Peterson (eds.), *Older People and Their Social World*. Philadelphia: F.A. Davis Co.

Sokolovsky, Jay. 1983. *Growing Old in Different Societies: Cross-cultural Perspectives*. Belmont, CA: Wadsworth Publishing Co.

Sontag, Susan. 1972. "The Double Standard Again," *The Saturday Review* (September 23), 29-38.

Streib, Gordon. 1965. "Are the Aged a Minority Group?" In: Bernice Neugarten (ed.), *Middle Age and Aging*, 35-46. Chicago: University of Chicago Press.

Ward, Russell. 1979. *The Aging Experience: An Introduction to Social Gerontology*. New York: J.P. Lippincott Company.

AN AGEIST LEXICON

Definitions in this glossary are from three sources: (1) numbers only in parentheses refer to Morris (1979); (2) parenthetical references with Fischer and number refer to Fischer (1978); and (3) those glosses with no parenthetical references are the author's creation.

act one's age *v.* to behave as suitable for (13)

agèd *n., adj.* contemporary euphemism for *old* or *elders*

anachronism *n.* anything out of its proper time (46). Meaning extended to elders to indicate that this group of people is out of step with current society.

anecdotage *n.* garrulous old age or senility (used humorously) (49)

anile *adj.* of or like an old woman (52)

anility *n.* the state of being anile

antediluvian *adj.* very old; antiquated; primitive (55)

back number *n.* an anachronistic old man (Fischer, 92)

bag *n.* an unattractive woman (slang) (99)

baldy *n.* a person whose age is evidence by loss of hair

bat *n.* an ugly or nagging woman; shrew (112)

battle ax(e) *n.* an overbearing woman; virago (slang) (113)

beldam(e) *n.* an old woman, especially one who is loathsome or ugly (120)

biddy *n.* a garrulous old woman (slang) (130)

bottle-nose *n.* an alcoholic old man (Fischer, 92)

caducity *n.* the frailty of old age (186)

cantakerous *adj.* ill-tempered and quarrelsome; disagreeable; contrary (198)

codger *n.* an old man (informal) (258)

constipated *adj.* reference to a supposed chronic condition of elders

convalescent center *n.* a warehouse for elders (euphemism)

coot *n.* a foolish old man (292)

crank *n.* a grouchy person; an eccentric (304)

cranky *adj.* ill-tempered, peevish; odd, eccentric (309)

crone *n.* a withered, witchlike old woman (315)

crotchety *adj.* capriciously stubborn or eccentric; perverse (316)

debility *n.* the state of abnormal bodily weakness; feebleness (340)

declining years *n.* old age (euphemism)

decrepit *adj.* weakened by old age, illness, or hard use; broken down (344)

decrepitude *n.* the state of being decrepit; weakness, infirmity (344)

dirty old man *n.* lecherous aged male

doddering *adj.* feeble-minded from age; senile (387)

D.O.M. *n.* acronym for DIRTY OLD MAN

dotage *n.* second childhood; senility (392)

dotard *n.* a senile person (392)

dote *v.* to be foolish or feeble-minded, especially as a result of senility (392)

eccentric *adj.* departing from or deviating from the conventional or established norm, model, or rule (411-12)

fart *n.* a mean, contemptible person (vulgar slang) (476)

feeble *adj.* lacking strength; weak; especially frail or infirm (481)

feebleminded *adj.* mentally deficient; subnormal in intelligence; dull-witted; stupid; foolish (481)

flabby *adj.* lacking firmness; loose and yielding to the touch; lacking force or vitality; feeble; ineffectual (497)

fogy *n.* a person of old-fashioned habits and outmoded attitudes (508)

fogyish *adj.* having the attributes of a FOGY

fogyism *n.* having the traits of a FOGY

fool *n.* one who shows himself, by words or actions, to be deficient in judgment, sense, or understanding; a stupid or thoughtless person (511)

foolish *adj.* lacking good sense or judgment; silly (511)

fossil *n.* one that is outdated or antiquated; especially a person with outmoded ideas; a fogy (518)

frail *adj.* having a delicate constitution; physically weak; not robust (521)

fuddy-duddy *n.* one who is old-fashioned and fussy (531)

fussbudget *n.* a person who fusses over trifles (535)

fussy *adj.* given to fussing; easily upset; insistent upon petty matters or details; fastidious (535)

gaffer *n.* an old man or rustic (537)

galoot *n.* a clumsy, uncouth, or sloppily dressed person (540)

garrulous *adj.* habitually talkative; loquacious (544)

geezer *n.* an eccentric old man (547)

generation gap *n.* reference to supposed philosophical and ideological differences between young and old (divisive term)

geriatric generation *n.* elders as a group (derisive)

geriatric ghetto *n.* home for elders (*Maledicta* 5:340)

Geritol generation *n.* elders as a group (derisive). Geritol is a patent medicine marketed for this age group.

goat *n.* a lecherous man (564)

golden age *n.* a period when a nation or some wide field of endeavor reaches its height (565). Euphemism for OLD AGE.

goose *n.* a silly person, a simpleton (568)

granny (grannie) *n.* a grandmother; an old woman; a fussy person (Southern) (573)

graybeard *n.* an old man (576)

Gray Panthers *n.* Political organization (Consultation of Younger and Older Adults) founded by Maggie Kuhn. This is a humorous journalistic title for the organization.

grimalkin *n.* a shrewish old woman (579)

grouch *n.* a habitually complaining or irritable person (581)

grouchy *adj.* inclined to grumbling and complaint; ill-humored; peevish (581)

grump *n.* a cranky, complaining person (583)

grumpy *adj.* fretful and peevish; irritable; cranky (583)

hag *n.* an ugly, frightful old woman; termagant; crone; a witch, sorceress (592)

infirm *adj.* weak in body, especially from old age; feeble (674)

infirmity *n.* lack of power; bodily debilitation; frailty (674)

Lawrence Welk generation *n.* elders as a group (derisive). A reference to their supposed musical preferences.

little old lady *n.* a negative term, suggestive of impotency and frailty

maid *n.* a girl or unmarried woman; a virgin (786)

miser *n.* one who deprives himself of all but the barest essentials to hoard money. A greedy or avaricious person (838)

mummy *n.* any withered or shrunken body, living or dead, that resembles a mummy (862)

obsolete *adj.* no longer in use or in fashion (907)

old cornstalk *n.* an ineffectual old man (Fischer, 92)

old-fashioned *adj.* of a style or method formerly in vogue; outdated; antiquated; attached to or favoring methods, ideas or customs of an earlier time (915)

old fuck *n.* old man (vulgar slang)

old guard *n.* reactionary, corrupt and aged politician (Fischer, 91)

oldster *n.* an old or elderly person (informal) (915)

old-timer *n.* one who has been a resident, member, or employee for a long time. Something that is very old or antiquated (915)

old wives' tale *n.* a bit of superstitious folklore (915)

outmoded *adj.* not in fashion. No longer usable or practical; obsolete (933)

overage *adj.* beyond the proper or required age (935)

over the hill *adj.* no longer useful or functional

peevish *adj.* querulous; discontented; fretful; ill-tempered; contrary; fractious (967)

pop *n.* an older man (derisive)

rambling *adj.* lengthy and desultory (1097)

reprobate *n.* morally unprincipled, profligate (1104)

rickety *adj.* feeble with age; infirm (1116)

second childhood *n.* a period of foolish, childlike behavior allegedly experienced by the elderly

senile *adj.* pertaining to, characteristic of, or proceeding from old age; exhibiting senility (1180)

senile dementia *n.* progressive, abnormally accelerated deterioration of mental faculties and emotional stability in old age (1180)

senility *n.* the state of being senile; mental and physical deterioration with old age (1180)

senior citizen *n.* a person of or over the age of retirement (1180)

show one's age *v.* to have the physical appearance of an elder person; to act the way society expects a person to act at a given age

silly *adj.* showing lack of good sense; unreasoning; stupid (1206)

spinster *n.* a woman who has remained single behind the conventional age for marrying (1245)

superannuated *adj.* retired or discharged because of age or infirmity; persisting ineffectively despite advanced age (1290)

toothless *adj.* lacking teeth; lacking force; ineffectual (1354)

trot *n.* an old woman (archaic) (1376)

twilight years *n.* old age (euphemism)

witch *n.* an ugly, vicious old woman; hag (1470)

withered *adj.* dried up or shriveled up as if from loss of moisture; lacking in freshness; faded; droopy

wizen *adj.* shriveled or dried up (1471)

wizened *adj.* shriveled, wizen (1471)

wrinkled *adj.* drawn up; puckered (1477)

THE FAR SIDE

"Hey! . . . Six-eyes!"

COLORFUL SPEECH

Examples of colorful speech taken from written and oral sources: insults, slurs, curses, threats, blasphemies, similes, comparisons, etc. Contributions are welcome and credited. We prefer short, clever, witty, creative, concrete examples. Always identify your source (person or publication).

- **My cock was as straight and rigid as a Wehrmacht officer's spine.** (*NL*, Jan. 1985, p. 42)

- As one testicle said to the other: **Don't mind that asshole behind you. We're working for the prick up front.** (Heard by Ebert Waldorf)

- Humor consultant Malcolm L. Kushner, who has **a smile that could sell used snuff**, said that "data-processing managers are **dull schmucks.**" (*Time*, 25 March 1985, pp. 8, 10)

- **Noisier than two skeletons fucking on a hot tin roof, with brass bras on.** (Folklorist Steve Poyser. Contributed by Simon Bronner)

- John McEnroe, the bratty tennis champ pictured as cute on his BIC razor commercials, "is **as cute as a razor nick.**" (Melvin Durslag, *TV Guide*, 28 Jan. 1984, p. 28)

- In Letters from the Editors, those who say "I could care less" are advised either to use the correct form, "I couldn't care less", or to use alternatives, such as, **Who gives a rat's ass, you puke-faced gargoyle?** (*NL*, Oct. 1984, p. 80)

- **You're as plain as cornbread — You look like the cross between a booger and a haint** [bogeyman; ghost] — **You're as ugly as a mud fence stuck with tadpoles — You wouldn't last any longer than a snowball in hell**

— **You're as dull as a froe** [a wedge-shaped cleaving tool], and **You're as useless as a milk bucket under a bull.** (From W.K. McNeil's "Folklore from Big Flat, Arkansas" in *Mid-America Folklore* 12/2 [Fall 1984], pp. 27-30)

• In 1983, Louisiana Governor Edwin Edwards bragged that he could not lose the election to David Treen unless he was **caught in bed with a dead girl or a live boy.** (*Time*, 11 March 1985, p. 29)

• Comments about a female coal miner: **She's got dust on the bust and coal in the hole.** — When she smokes a cigarette, **her face looks like a pig's ass with a piece of straw on it.** (Overheard in a Michigan saloon by Fred R.)

• From an article by Dave Tynan about a Hollywood stars' dentist: "Without a good set of choppers, **you can't do dickshit** in this town, not even dog-food commercials." — "Starlets **so hot you couldn't fiddle them with an asbestos condom.**" — "He's a **doughnut poker.**" [homosexual] — "Cigarettes yellow your tooth enamel. In a few years those pearlies of yours will **look like fog lights on the freeway.**" (*NL*, Oct. 1984, pp. 29-30)

• Sister to her younger brother who had just spat at her: **Save the rest to grease your cock in case a skunk comes by you want to screw.** (From Ann Beattie's *Falling in Place*, 1980, p. 4. Contributed by Catherine Felgar)

• **Everyone uses me as a pissing post.** (Complaint by a Wisconsin journalist to the Editor, 1982)

• **That girl is uglier than a hatful of assholes.** (*NL*, June 1982, p. 40)

254 • Reinhold Aman

- **Your request is as welcome as a premature ejaculation.** (Editor to a pushy author who demanded that his article be published immediately)

- **The best part of you ran down your momma's leg.** (Lee Marvin in the movie *Death Hunt*, 1981. Contributed by Len Ashley)

- **She has a cunt like a torn overcoat pocket.** (Comment about a large woman by Kurt Schweitzer to the Editor at a Milwaukee ethnic festival, July 1982)

- **You're slicker than snot on a doorknob** and **She's hotter than a fresh-fucked fox in a forest fire.** (Contributed by Robert Parrott)

- **You're as slick as deer guts on a door knob.** (From a letter to the Editor, from Fred R.)

- Dana was back in town, **looking as greasy as a snake in a barrel of snot.** (Comment in a letter about a mutual friend. Contributed by Chris Starr)

- For a fellow who's supposed to be an engineer, S.W. is **as dumb as a hoe handle.** (Contributed by Chris Starr)

- **If she was any dumber, you'd have to water her.** (Leo Hayes about a barmaid. Contributed by Robert Balliot)

- **It's raining like a (double-cunted) cow pissing on a flat rock.** (Contributed by Scott Beach, David Hibbard, and Elbert Waldorf)

- **He's so dumb he thinks cunnilingus is an Irish airline.** (German author Arno Schmidt. Contributed by Basil

Schader. Also in use in the USA. The actual name of the airline is *Aer Lingus*.)

• **I wouldn't piss in his ass if his guts were on fire.** (Contributed by Tim Hawley)

• **I bet she could do squat thrusts on a fire hydrant.** (Comment about a "whorish-looking" woman at a bar, overheard by Gordon Wood)

• **Go blow your tits off!** Australian equivalent of U.S. "Stop shitting me! I don't believe you!" (Told to the Editor by an Australian fellow-traveler on the Orient Express, 1982)

• **He's loose as a whore's crotch** and **He plays as tight as a tomtit's arsehole.** (Heard during poker games in a Middlesex, U.K., hospital by Patrick Debenham)

• **He's balder than Buddha's balls.** (Contributed by David Govett)

• **You double-revolving, interlocking and interfornicating brass-bound son-of-a-bitch!** (Frequent utterance by a Chief Boatswain Mate, U.S. Navy; heard by William Wortman)

• **You illegitimate son of twin-retarded African bastards!** (North Carolina, early 1900s)

• Pete Hamill is **one of the vilest maggots ever to bore holes in carrion.** (Joe S., commenting on the anti-Hamill poem in MAL 5:45-46)

• **She can suck a golf ball through a garden hose.** (Comment about a fellatrix, overheard by Sanford Gorney)

• He's so dumb he couldn't talk a two-headed pig out of a corncrib. (Contributed by Fred R.)

• That truck couldn't pull a sick whore off a pisspot. (Current with long-haul truckers in the late 1940s. Contributed by George Monteiro)

• That's so bad it would gag a maggot in a gut wagon. (Used in the 1940s. Contributed by Tim Hawley)

• She's got tits like slaters' nail bags. [Two large, stiff, hard leather bags filled with a few pounds of nails, slung crosswise over each shoulder.] — She's got a cunt like a bill-poster's bucket. — She's got a face like a blind cobbler's thumb. (Describing a monumentally large and ugly woman. All heard in the British Army, ca. 1970, by Alan Bird)

• He's jumping around like a fart in a mitten. (Contributed by M.L. + T.L. Sherred)

• May you have the fattest geese and no teeth, the finest wine and no palate, the prettiest wife and no sex organ! (God forbid!) (From the Yiddish. Contributed by Sherri Pine)

• Smirking like the pig that et the baby's diaper. (Joyce Harrington in "Sweet Baby Jenny," in *The Year's Best Mystery & Suspense Stories 1982*, p. 107. Contributed by Bruce Rodgers)

• When I was twenty, my dick be hard as Chinese 'rithmetic. (Richard Pryor in HBO's "Comedy Store's 11th Anniversary Show," July 1983)

• I lived in a town so small **the only thing open all night**

was my girlfriend's legs. (From *Easy Rider* magazine, unknown date & page. Contributed by Al Pergande)

• **Your breath smells like wild wolf pussy.** (Favorite remark of Howard, a Chicago black, mid-1950s. Contributed by his barracks-mate Joseph Duchac)

• **She took directions like a pig takes to garbage.** (Steve Martin in the 1982 movie *Dead Men Don't Wear Plaid.*)

• **This sheila bangs like a shithouse door in a gale.** (Australian comment about a sexually capable woman, probably created by writer Barry Humphries. Contributed by Gareth Hughes)

• I know you are **busier than a toothless beaver in a log jam.** (From a letter to the Editor by Norman Handelsman)

• He was **busier than a one-armed paperhanger with crabs.** (Contributed by Robert Goodwin)

• **I'm as busy as a blind queer at a wiener roast.** (Clyde H., in his letter to the Editor)

• If I ordered a dozen sons-of-bitches and they just sent me Harold, I wouldn't feel that I had been shortchanged. (A professor discussing a colleague; overheard by James Walters)

• At other times [he] sounds **as outraged as a satyr with a suppressed orgasm.** (Donald Kramer, in his article on *Maledicta* in "Par for the Curse," *MD* magazine [Nov. 1983, p. 165], describing your Editor's writings)

• Anyone who says that the shark is not a dangerous

animal is **as full of shit as a blocked toilet in a Mexican bus station.** (*NL*, May 1983, p. 51. Contributed by Gert Raeithel)

• **We call him "scrotum" — he's something between a prick and an arsehole.** (Contributed by Robert Penprase)

• **A crow shit on a log, and the sun hatched him.** (Armenian expression of disdain. Contributed by Albert Kalo)

• He's such a chronic worrier that **the skin of his forehead is like that of a chilled scrotum.** (Contributed by Henry Moehring)

• That apartment was so dirty that there were **fart stains on the wall.** (Disgruntled landlord describing the condition of one of his vacated properties. Contributed by Robert Th.)

• I feel **as frustrated as a eunuch masseur.** (Comment by Bob Buckie, Saudi Arabia, in a letter to the Editor)

• **I want it so quiet in here I could hear a rat pissing on cotton.** (Army officer to his men. Contributed by Stephen Gregory)

• **He's got a nose like somebody's elbow.** (From Lindsay Maracotta, *The Sad-Eyed Ladies: Life, Love & Hard Times in the Singles Scene*, 1977, p. 29. Contributed by Martha Cornog)

• **A blowjob is the sincerest form of penis envy.** (The Wiz, Flushing)

• The size of the screen on the Osborne computer can best

be described as **cretin-friendly**, but as I always say, **a bird in the hand is better than a pustule on your glans.** (Jerry Cerwonka, in a letter to the Editor)

• Most computer programs and their manuals are **as "user-friendly" as a syphilitic whore.** (Editor, to colleague upset by idiotic manuals)

• **I would drag my bare balls over forty miles of ground glass to finger-fuck her shadow!** (College student, 1958, leering lustfully at a photograph of Kim Novak. Contributed by Peter L.)

• The Australian price of my *Bawdry* book is $A14-95, which is currently about US$13.60 — but the exchange rate is **up and down like a whore's drawers** at the moment. (Don Laycock, in a letter to the Editor)

A BIG COCK AND A LEAKING MOUTH

It is a bad habit for children to have a meal walking about with a rice bowl and dropping grains of rice here and there.
This colour picture story book of children's life is written down for the purpose of helping the children to get rid of this bad habit. The illustrator vividly expresses the contents with plenty of children's interest and temperament.

大公鸡和漏嘴巴

姚正平写　　朱延令画

少年儿童出版社出版

40 开　　15 页

0.11 美元

(From the 1981 catalog of the Shanghai Publishing Company)

ADS FOR TV EXECUTIONS

Charles Chi Halevi

The recent efforts by a condemned criminal to get his execution televised gave rise to a plethora of protests and support — but all for the wrong reasons.

The problem with positions urged by both bleeding heart liberals and right wing neanderthals is that they fail to take into account the victims of capital crimes, whose death leaves them unable to support their families. Revenge may be sweet but it doesn't buy meat.

But what if we televised executions, and then sold the advertising spots to the highest bidders? The profits could provide an annuity for the victim's family, thus enabling the criminal to repay society and his victim.

Of course this would require some enabling legislation. The bill we envision could be called *Gory Advertising Sells Products*, better known by its initials: **GASP**.

Under **GASP** a condemned criminal's execution would be televised and ads sold to those companies that would benefit the most from such a market. If the execution is by electrocution, one natural advertiser would be the local electric company. If it's by gas chamber, then of course the gas company would get the nod. Should a firing squad be required, then the Winchester and Colt companies will want to get a shot at it.

There would be other advertisers, certainly. Funeral homes would find a natural market, and so would insurance companies who even now take great delight in reminding us to take care of our loved ones after we're gone. No doubt organized religions will want to discuss life after death.

Once GASP catches on, strange phenomena will be observed in American society. Calvin Klein will come out with a line of designer blindfolds, and more shaved heads will be seen on Main Street USA than can be accounted for by Krishna converts. Shrouds will be chic, just as camouflage outfits gained popularity again after the invasion of Grenada.

A regular TV series of executions could be launched, perhaps entitled "Saturday Night Dead." A music video by Michael Jackson would be the perfect accompaniment; with minor alterations, "Beat It" could be changed to "Heat It" and include the chorus:

> *It doesn't matter*
> *If you broil or fry,*
> *They'll watch it on TV*
> *And then buy, buy, buy.*
> *So heat it, heat it...*

For mass executions the Beach Boys could sing that surfing standard "Hang Ten."

Naturally these "live" shows will have some inherent problems. Ponder the plight of the poor producer whose star performer gets a last-minute reprieve, leaving the show with a lot of dead air to fill.

One way to solve this dilemma is to have a spare condemned person waiting in the wings. Soon, however, even they would be used up and advertisers looking for new blood will put pressure on legislators and judges to dispense the death penalty for shoplifting, making an illegal U-turn and keeping library books overdue.

They'll also petition to have executions made as colorful as possible, which means a return to burning at the stake and guillotining. Besides a renewed audience interest and higher Nielsen ratings, such a move would open the way for still more advertisers, such as Open Pit BBQ Sauce, Gillette and Head & Shoulders Shampoo.

True, the fainthearted will decry this solution, but their protests will die down as audiences are treated to theatrical entertainment reminiscent of the good old days of public hangings, when people brought their children and picnic lunches to enjoy the show and learn a lesson.

Constitutionally, there may be only one flaw in **GASP** — the "cruel and unusual punishment" experienced by the executed "performers."

After all, what could they possibly do for an encore?

TO MY CRITICS

When I am in a sober mood
    I worry, work, and think.
When I am in a drunken mood
    I gamble, fight, and drink.
But when all my moods are over,
    And the worst has come to pass,
I hope they bury me upside down,
    So the world can kiss my ass.

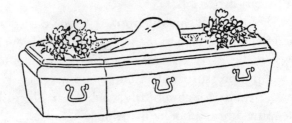

OFFENSIVE LANGUAGE
VIA COMPUTER

Reinhold Aman

Computer networks can be used to gather information from throughout the world. Unlike in traditional fieldwork, one does not have to interview informants personally but simply posts a query, or an entire questionnaire, on the electronic *bulletin board* (BB), and the users respond. BB's make this novel way of collecting data and responding easy: one calls the BB's number and leaves one's response. The quality and range of the responses depend on the precision of the questions asked, as well as on the type of user. Naturally, one can ask only those who have a computer and modem, which severely restricts the field of informants. However, these informants can gather information locally from those lacking such equipment and send it to the BB.

Henry Birdseye's "The Unknown BBS" (see MAL 7:276-77) is such a system for collecting information. It runs at 300 and 1200 baud and contains about one-quarter million characters' worth of kakological riddles, jokes, and other offensive language. It can be reached 24 hours a day by calling (303) 988-8155.

To test the usefulness of his system, Mr. Birdseye asked his BB users about terms for masturbation, urination, and vomiting. He did not request other essential information from the informants, such as their sex, age, geographic location, education, profession, etc., but the simple data below prove that such a BB system can be used successfully. To transmit the information gathered to others, one can either call up the BB and download it (have it sent by telephone to one's own computer), or ask for a printout, which I did.

Following below are the terms, after organizing and alphabetizing the raw data.

to masturbate (of females): beat the beaver, buttonhole, clap your clit, cook cucumbers, grease the gash, hide the hotdog, hit the slit, hose your hole, juice your sluice, make waves [from "the (little) man in the boat" = clitoris?], pet the poodle, slam the clam, stump-jump.

to masturbate (of males): beat the bishop, beat your little brother, beat the meat, burp the worm, butter your corn, choke the chicken, clean your rifle, consult Dr. Jerkoff, crank your shank, dink your slinky, feel in your pocket for your big hairy rocket, file your fun-rod, fist your mister, flex your sex, flog the dolphin, flog your dog, grease your pipe, hack your mack, hump your hose, jerkin' the gherkin, milk the chicken, Onan's Olympics (n.), one-stick drum improvisation (n.), pack your palm, paint your ceiling, play a flute solo on your meat whistle, play the male organ, please your pisser, point your social finger, polish your sword, pound the pud, pound your flounder, prompt your porpoise, prune the fifth limb, pull the pope, pull your taffy, run your hand up the flagpole, shine your pole, shoot the tadpoles, slakin' the bacon, slam your hammer, slam your Spam, slap your wapper, spank the monkey, spank the salami, strike the pink match, stroke the dog, stroke your poker, talk with Rosy Palm and her five little sisters, tickle your pickle, thump your pumper, tweak your twinkie, unclog the pipes, varnish your pole, walk the dog, watch the eyelid movies, wax your dolphin, whip your dripper, whizzin' jizzum, wonk your conker, yang your wang, yank the yam, yank your crank.

to urinate: bleed the liver, drain the dragon, drain the (main) vein, get rid of the bladder matter, siphon the python, visit Miss Murphy.

to vomit: drive the big white bus, hug the porcelain, kneel before the porcelain throne, pray to the porcelain gods, school lunch rerun (n.), technicolor rerun (n.), upchuck.

A CONTINUATION OF
A GLOSSARY OF ETHNIC SLURS
IN AMERICAN ENGLISH

Sterling Eisiminger

It has been nine years since my update of Abraham Roback's *A Dictionary of International Slurs* (1944) appeared in *Maledicta* 3 (1979). Four works have been especially helpful in updating and expanding the original glossary: Bruce Rodgers's *The Queens' Vernacular: A Gay Lexicon* (1979), Frederic G. Cassidy's "Unofficial Sectional City Names" (*Verbatim*, Autumn 1980), and Jacob Edward Schmidt's *Dictionary of Medical Slang* (1959) and *Libido* (1960). These works are cited as [R], [C], [D], and [L] respectively; [OED] is the *Oxford English Dictionary*.

As in the 1979 glossary, words and phrases which are merely descriptive, regionalisms, proverbial expressions, and terms for racial and national groups themselves have not been included.

To aid the user of this glossary, each main entry begins with the word which identifies the national or ethnic group being maligned. Whenever a comma appears in a main entry, the second element should be read first. Terms like *Zulu princess* and *Tijuana racetrack* have been cross-referenced. Thus *Zulu princess*, for example, is found in its proper alphabetical position among the *z*'s, but the full entry is found after *blacksmith's shop* since *Zulu* maligns blacks.

Further additions to this list will be gratefully received (English Department, Clemson University, Clemson, SC 29631).

African Railroad see listing after **blacksmith's shop**
Apache see listing after **Indian**
Athenian see listing after **Greek side**

black bagging *n* [L] Pudendum of black women; used
  collectively
Black Belt; Black Bottom; Black Town *n* [C] Black community within an urban area
black bezer *n* [D] Face of a black person
black jack *n* [R] Black man's penis; homosexual slang
black joke *n* [L] Pudendum of a black woman
blackleg *n* [L] Penis of a black man
black man choke, enough to make a *adj phr* [D] Very
  unpalatable; said of food and medicines
black Maria *n* [L] 1: Black prostitute 2: Pudendum of a
  black woman
black meat *n* [L] Pudendum of a black woman
black mouth *n* [L] Pudendum of a black woman
black pencil *n* [L] Black man's penis
blacksmith's shop *n* [L] House of prostitution run by black
  woman
  African Railroad *n* [R] San Francisco municipal bus line
    which is principally used by blacks
  **Colored Quarters; Colored Section; Colored Settle-
    ment; Colored Town; Colored Valley** *n* [C] Black
    community within an urban area
  Coon Bottom; Coon Town *n* [C] Black community
    within an urban area
  Ethy meat *n* [D] Black woman; *Ethy* is a clipped form
    of *Ethiopian*
  Hottentots *n* [D] Buttocks; from the nakedness of these
    African natives
  Jemima *n* [L] Black woman's pudendum
  Jig Town *n* [C] Black community within an urban area
  jungle meat *n* [R] Black man's penis; homosexual slang
  Nigerian *n* [R] Black man; homosexual slang

Nigger Hill; Nigger Quarters; Nigger Section; Nigger Town *n* [C] Black community within an urban area

Nubian *n* [R] Black man; homosexual slang

pumpernickel *n* [D, ca. 1924] Black prostitute, especially a mulatto

Zulu bingo *n* [R] Weekend dancing; homosexual slang

Zulu princess *n* [R] Young, handsome black man; homosexual slang

britannia metal see listing after **English sentry**

Canadian; Canadian bacon *n* [R] uncircumcised penis; homosexual slang

Chinese evil *n* Leprosy; from the prevalence of the disease in China

Colored see listing after **blacksmith's shop**

Comanche see listing after **Indian**

Coon see listing after **blacksmith's shop**

Copenhagen see listing after **Danish pastry**

Corsican *n* [L] Small but effective penis; allusion to Napoleon

Cuban pumps; Cubans *n* [R] Heavy boots; homosexual slang

Dago see listing after **Italian letter**

Danish pastry *n* [R] Transsexual; homosexual slang; from the pioneering operation undergone by Christine Jorgensen

Denmark, something's rotten in *cl* [R] Said of a sex change; homosexual slang

    Copenhagen capon *n* [R] transsexual; homosexual slang; from the pioneering operation undergone by Christine Jorgensen

    Copenhagen, go; go to Denmark *v phr* [R] Have sex change operation; homosexual slang

Dutch *n* [D] Wife

Dutch courage, dry *n* [D] Narcotics; contemporary play on *Dutch courage*

Dutch dumplings *n* [R] Buttocks; homosexual slang

Dutch fumigation *n* Resuscitation method learned from American Indians whereby smoke, blown into an animal's bladder, was forced into a victim's rectum to revive him; introduced in England in 1767

Dutch girl *n* [R] Lesbian; homosexual pun relating *dike* to the dikes of Holland

Dutch, go *v phr* [D] Commit suicide

ebony chick see listing after **blacksmith's shop**

ebony pidgeon see listing after **blacksmith's shop**

Egyptian queen *n* [R, late 1960s in San Francisco] Homosexual black man, particularly if he is stately and proud

English martini *n* [R, late 1960s in San Francisco] Tea, especially when spiked with gin

English method *n* [R] Homosexual intercourse against the thighs

English muffins *n* [R] Boy's buttocks; homosexual slang

English sentry *n* [D] Erect penis

britannia metal *n* [R] Sham

Ethy meat see listing after **blacksmith's shop**

European accentuation *n* [R] Tapered body with jutting buttocks; homosexual slang

French *v* [R] To perform fellatio

French, speak *v phr* [D, ca. 1914] Indulge in unconventional sexual play

French aches *n* [D, ca. 1700] Syphilis

French article *n* [L] French prostitute

French art; French head job; French love *n* [R] Fellatio; homosexual slang

French bathe *v phr* [R] To use perfumes as a deodorant in lieu of bathing; homosexual slang

French by injection *adj* [R] Said of a first-class fellator

French dip *n* [R] Vaginal precoital fluid; homosexual slang

French dressing; French-fried ice cream *n* [R] Semen; homosexual slang

French embassy *n* [R] YMCA with homosexuality running unchecked; homosexual slang

Frencher *n* [L] Male with a perverse sexual appetite

Frenchery *n* [L] House of prostitution

French fare *n* [L] Pudendum of a French woman

Frenchified *adj* [D] Sexually talented; said of a woman

Frenchie; French lady; French language expert; French woman *n* [R] Fellator; homosexual

French joke, tell a *v phr* [R] Oral stimulation of anus; homosexual slang

French kiss filter *n* [R] Any filter-tipped cigarette; homosexual slang

French language training *n* [R] Teaching fellatio; homosexual slang

French lessons, take *v phr* [D] Contract venereal disease

French marbles *n* [D, ca. 1700] Syphilis

French measles *n* [D, ca. 1600] Syphilis

French mole *n* [D, ca. 1700] Syphilis

French photographer *n* [R] homosexual photographer; homosexual slang

French postcard *n* [R] Exciting, prospective sexual partner; homosexual slang

French prints *n* [R] Unusual heterosexual pornography; homosexual slang

French revolution *n* [R] Revolution for homosexual rights; homosexual slang

French screwdriver *n* Hammer

French stuff *n* [R] 1: pornography 2: unusual sex activity

Gallic disease *n* [D] Syphilis

Paris brothers *n* [R] Homosexuals, esp. twins; homosexual slang

Galilee stompers *n* [R] Sandals; homosexual slang
Gallic disease see after **French stuff**
German helmet *n* [R] Glans penis; homosexual slang
German marching pills *n* [R] Amphetamines esp. methedrine; homosexual slang
German silver *n* [Roget] Sham
Greek *v* [R] Engage in pederasty; homosexual slang
Greek, low *n* [D] Sexual intercourse
Greek love; Greek way *n* [R] Pederasty; homosexual slang
Greek side *n* [R] Posterior; homosexual slang
    Athenian *n* [R] Pederast; homosexual slang
    Trojan horse *n* [R] Manly façade; homosexual slang

Hawaiian disease *n* [R] Absence of women, or "lakanuki"; homosexual slang
Hawaiian eye *n* [R] Anus; homosexual slang
    pineapple princess; pineapple queen *n* [R] Hawaiian homosexual
Hindustani jig *n* [L] Anal intercourse
Hottentots see listing after **blacksmith's shop**

Indian, dead as a wooden *adj phr* [D] Dead
    Apache *n* [R] Man who uses cosmetics; homosexual slang
    Commanche *n* [R] Man who uses cosmetics; homosexual slang
    Indian rug *n* [R] Cheap wig done in braids; homosexual slang
    Indians, give it back to the *v phr* said if anything fails or breaks
    Injun *n* [D] Junior intern
Irish *n* [L] Sexual temperament or fury
Irish beauty *n* [D] Woman with black eyes

Irish clubhouse *n* [L] Refined house of prostitution

Irish confetti *n* [L] Semen spilled extravaginally

Irish dip *n* [L] 1: "Cure for bashfulness with the girls"
2: Sexual intercourse

Irish draperies *n* [L] Pendulous breasts

Irish fairy *n* [R] Homosexual from the old sod[omy];
homosexual slang

Irish horse *n* [L] Impotent penis

Irish legs *n* [L] Heavy female legs

Irishman, potato-fingered *n* Clumsy person; from the
alleged predilection of the Irish for potatoes and the
stereotype of their awkwardness

Irish marathon *n* [L] Extended session of lovemaking

Irish pasture *n* [L] Pudendum of an Irish woman

Irish promotion *n* [L] Masturbation

Irish rise *n* [L] Sexual detumescence

Irish toothpick *n* [L] Erect penis of a sodomite

Irish wedding *n* [L] Masturbation

Italian airlines *n* [R] Walking; homosexual slang

Italian fig *n* [OED] Poisoned fig used as a secret way to
destroy an obnoxious person

Italian letter *n* [D, ca. 1870] Condom

  Dago Center; Dago Town *n* [C] Italian or Puerto Rican
community in an urban area

  Neapolitan disease see listing after **Italian letter**

  Spaghetti Corner *n* [C] Italian community within an
urban area

  Wop Flat; Wop Town *n* [C] Italian community within
an urban area

Jamaica discipline *n* [L] Wife's denial of sexual favors to
her husband

Jemima see listing after **blacksmith's shop**

Jew sheet *n* [R] Account, often imaginary, of money lent
to friends

Jew's lance *n* [L] Jewish circumcised penis

Jew Town *n* [C] Jewish community within an urban area

Jewish airlines *n* [R] Walking; homosexual slang

Jewish by hospitalization; Jewish by operation not by nation *adj phr* [R] Circumcised but not Jewish; homosexual slang

Jewish compliment; Jewish National *n* [R] Circumcised penis; homosexual slang

Jewish corned beef *n* [D] Circumcised penis of a Jew

Jewish dilemma *n* Free ham

Jewish foreplay *n* Extended pleading without any physical contact

Jewish lightning *n* [R] Fire insurance; an insurance term for a payment made to someone suspected of torching his own establishment

Jewish Renaissance *n* [R] Overelaborate furniture of doubtful taste; homosexual slang

    kipper, young *n* [D] Inadequate meal; play on *Yom Kippur*

    kosher; kosher style *adj* [R] Circumcised; homosexual slang

    kosher delicatessen *n* [R] Israel; homosexual slang

    kosher dill *n* [R] Circumcised penis; homosexual slang

jig see listing after **blacksmith's shop**

jungle meat see listing after **blacksmith's shop**

kipper, young see listing after **Jewish Renaissance**

kosher see listing after **Jewish Renaissance**

Latin mystery *n* [D] Doctor's prescription

Mexican airlines, to fly *v phr* [R] Smoke marijuana; from the fact that much marijuana smoked in the U.S. is grown in Mexico

Mexican cigarette *n* [R] Poorly made marijuana cigarette; homosexual slang

Mexican hairless *n* [D] Bald head
Mexican jumping bean *n* [R] Amphetamine; homosexual
slang
Mexican nightmare *n* [R] Gaudy ceramic crockery; homosexual slang
Mexican schlock *n* [R] Any art in poor taste; homosexual
slang
    Taco Town *n* [R] Nickname for San José; homosexual
    slang
    tamale *n* [R] Gaudy ceramic crockery; homosexual slang
    Tamaleville *n* [R] Nickname for San José; homosexual
    slang
    Tijuana Bible *n* [R] Lurid pornography
    Tijuana racetrack *n* [R] Diarrhea run; homosexual
    slang

Neapolitan disease see listing after **Italian letter**
Nigerian see listing after **blacksmith's shop**
nigger see listing after **blacksmith's shop**
Nubian see listing after **blacksmith's shop**

Paris brothers see listing after **French stuff**
pineapple see listing after **Hawaiian eye**
Polack see listing after **Polish handball**
Polish airlines *n* [R] Walking; homosexual slang
Polish disease *n* [D, ca. 1700] Syphilis
Polish handball *n* [R] Dried nasal mucus; homosexual
slang
Polack Town *n* [C] Polish community within an urban area
pumpernickel see listing after **blacksmith's shop**

Quaker guns *n* Logs painted to look like guns during U.S.
Civil War; so named because of Quaker pacifism

redneck see listing after **white-meat**

Roman candle *n* [R] **1**: Italian-American penis **2**: Any Italian; homosexual slang

Roman engagement *n* [R] Anal intercourse with a virgin girl; homosexual slang

Roman historian *n* [R] Orgy enthusiast; homosexual slang

Roman night *n* [R] Orgy; homosexual slang

Rome, fountains of *n* [R] Urinals; homosexual slang

Russian, high *n* [R] Simultaneous fellatio and anal intercourse; homosexual slang

Russian salad party *n* [R] Orgy in which all participants are greasy; homosexual slang

Russian, white *n* [R] Oral exchange of semen; homosexual slang

Scotch screw *n* [D] Nocturnal emission

Spaghetti see listing after **Italian letter**

Spanish cure *n* [D] Treatment of drug addiction by forced, total abstinence

Spanish fig *n* [OED] Poisoned fig used as a secret way to destroy an obnoxious person

Spanish rice *n* [R] Lumpy semen; homosexual slang

Sweden, product of *n* [R] Artificial blond homosexual; homosexual slang

Taco see listing after **Mexican schlock**

tamale see listing after **Mexican schlock**

Tijuana see listing after **Mexican schlock**

Trojan see listing after **Greek side**

Turkish delight *n* [R] Pederasty; homosexual slang

Turkish disease *n* [D, ca. 1500] Syphilis

Viking queen *n* [R] **1**: blond **2**: Blond male homosexual; homosexual slang

white-man's disease *n* Relative inability of Caucasians to jump; blacks' term of derision usually used in a basketball context

white meat; white owl *n* [R] White man's penis; homosexual slang

redneck foreplay *n* Complete absence of any preliminary physical contact

Yankee *n* [R] Masturbation; homosexual slang; from *yank off* meaning "to masturbate"

Yankee's yawn *n* [R] Open mouth of climaxing male; homosexual slang

Wop see listing after **Italian letter**

Yankee see listing after **white-meat**

Zulu see listing after **blacksmith's shop**

STATE OF CALIFORNIA
PROPOSITION 63

That English — you know, *English*, the language? O.K. That it, I mean English (the language) would be, like the totally *official* language. I mean, in California. And everybody would have to, like, speak it and everything. In California.

☐ Fer shure! ☐ No way, José!

(Xeroxlore · 1986)

DON'T CLOG UP THE LOVE CURRENT IN HER BRAIN

MARRIAGE COUNSELING, BLACK MUSLIM STYLE

The following document is *not* a spoof. It is a handout distributed by Black Muslims to blacks only in New York City (August 1987). Professor David B. of the City University of New York was able to obtain a copy, sent to us by one of his colleagues.

The typewritten original is reproduced below with all its typing, spelling, and punctuation idiosyncrasies. It strikes me as strange that the relatively difficult word *conscious* is spelled correctly, while more common words, such as *penis, sexual, sissy*, and *quicker* are misspelled. It is also noteworthy that all apostrophes are lacking (*thats, dont, womans*) and that capitalization follows no discernible pattern.

After having studied the advice below, all you selfish, mess-shooting, current-clogging fellows will know why your belovèd doesn't have any feelings for you any more. — *Ed.*

ISLAMIC CULTURAL PROGRAM
FREE MARRIAGE COUNSELING

UNDERSTANDING YOUR WOMAN

Brothers dont ever put your pennus in your womans mouth because this spoils your woman. When you put your pennus in your womans mouth or in her rectum, you are misusing your woman,And what you are doing to her is, you are starting your woman out on A sexual habit. And you are not conscious of what you are doing to her.

This is what cause all of our young peoples marriage to go sour. This is the reason that all of our young people start fussing and fighting like cats and dogs six months to A year after their marriage.

Now, the reason that all of our young people marriage start messing up in about 3 to 6 months is because, It takes about 3 to 6 months before that mess, that you shoots in her mouth, begins to take an affect on her brain.

Now, it mess you up to, but, it mess your woman up quiker then it mess you up, because shes got the thing in her mouth, and she gets the full load every time, and you are licking A hole, so you are missing most of yours so thats why it mess her up quiker then it mess you up.

And the afects that this mess have on your woman is, it clogs up the love current in her brain, and she dont have any feelings for you any more. And the more of this mess she eats the less feelings she have for you.

And it works the same way on you, as it works on her. You see, when you eat this mess, It makes you hard headed, and rebellus, and cold blooded, It kills the love in you, It makes you selfish, and small minded, and you cant reason with your woman any more, because all she can think of is, sex sex sex, just like A sisey. And, thats why all the arguements start.

If that young man new, that when he starts puting his pennus in his womans mouth that, that was the begining of the end, of his love afair, he would cut off his right arm, before he would ask her to do that to him. But he is not conscious of what he is doing to her, if he loves her.

So then after he mess her up, They finely come to the conclusion, That love dont last. But, thats A Lie. Love do last. Love will last you A life time, if you dont miss use it. And when you put your pennus in your womans mouth, or in her rectum. you are miss useing your Love. And thats why it turns sour on you. So dont miss use your woman, and she will Love you the rest of your Life.

And if you and your woman have this problem. Now. What you have to do is this. You and your woman will have to get your heads together, and Kick, That Sexal Habit. And once you have Kicked, your Sexal Habit, You can get your Love Life back together again.

Courtesy Of AL ISLAM

Copyright © 1987 by Larry Feign, Hong Kong

AUSTRALIAN MALEDICTA

Reinhold Aman

A feature story about this journal in *The Sydney Morning Herald* by David Dale (30 Oct. 1987, p. 15) brought letters from down under with current Australian maledicta. Here is a sampling.

Dr. Vernon T., who is compiling a dictionary of Australian prison lingo, contributed **baggy-arse**, a naïve, "green" prison officer, **mirror-man**, a prison official who responds to requests by saying, "I'll look into it" but does nothing, and **rock spider**, a child molester.

The Rev. Dr. David C. submitted slang used by medical personnel: segments of retirement villages and nursing homes are known as **Alzheimer's Avenue, Dementia Drive**, or **Senility Street**. Two types of patients unwelcome in "casualty rooms" are those whose health problems are not emergencies: the **N.O.F.**, an old patient with a fracture of the *Neck Of Femur*, and the **P.F.O.**, a drunk; from *Pissed, Fell Over*; *pissed* = drunk. A patient who is stupid or demented is **suffering from FITH Syndrome**; from *Fucked In The Head*. One with a negative personality **has a disease of the 13th cranial nerve**; there are only 12 genuine cranial nerves, and the fictitious 13th is the **opto-rectal nerve** which connects the eyes to the rectum, thus giving the patient "a shitty outlook on life."

Stephen W. reports a disgruntled friend's chain-type invective against a businessman in Sydney: **The cunt was a fucking spastic motherfucking shitfaced fucking cunt Jew arsehole fucking moron!**

Claudio A. contributed two sarcastic questions (see MAL 1:77-82) used in Australia but not in the U.S.A.: **Are the Kennedys gun-shy?** and **Does Rose Kennedy have a black dress?.** He comments as follows:

> I've never met an American who has heard these sarcastic questions; also, no American I've met found them funny but quite tasteless. They are complex insults, involving a non-American using a traditional American form of insult to offend Americans. Here the Kennedys are very well known and are seen by many as the American version of a Royal Family. They are also perceived by outsiders as having a special place in American society and history. By making fun of one of the better-known aspects of their history, i.e., the tragedy of the number of deaths, violent or otherwise, in their family, the insulter is acknowledging their revered place in the American ethos yet trivialising their tragedy.

John G. explains **bush pig** and **T.T.B.P.R.** heard currently in New South Wales: in Australia, a very ugly woman is called a **bush pig.** When such a female enters a pub or bar, one fellow says to his mates, "**T.T.B.P.R!**," meaning: **Turn That Bush Pig 'Round!** (and send her out into the street).

Most correspondents comment how much their language of abuse is influenced by American movies and television programs seen there, e.g., **The best part of you ran down your mother's leg!** or **He's a sandwich short of a picnic**, but as Dr. David C. points out, there are many colorful terms used in Australia that have not yet been collected. Examples: **May your chooks** [chicken] **turn to emus and kick your dunny** [outhouse] **down!, Go stick it up your bum...sideways!**, and the threat, **I'll rip your bloody arms off and beat you to death with the sloppy ends!**

TERMS OF ABUSE, TERMS OF ENDEARMENT, AND PET NAMES FOR BREASTS AND OTHER NAUGHTY BODY PARTS

Reinhold Aman

I. INTRODUCTION

The "nice" and "nasty" terms for breasts and genitals, as well as pet names for these organs presented here, are the first result of my *Maledicta Onomastic Questionnaire*. With this MOQ, I am collecting onomastic and semantic material deemed unfit for study by the cowardly and prudish establishment philologists and linguists. The acronym MOQ also mocks the University of Wisconsin's castrated and undaring DARE questionnaire and *Dictionary of American Regional English*.

My questionnaire consists of several hundred items organized by various categories. The number of items, about 500, seems to be the main reason why only 5% of the 6,000 recipients of the MOQ filled it out. Still, the terms collected so far in this ongoing project are overwhelming and will be presented in various articles like this one.

This article deals only with one short section from the MOQ, namely "Terms of Abuse and Endearment." There is a much longer, detailed section called "Body Parts" in the questionnaire that so far has yielded over 3,000 terms for *breasts, penis, vulva* and *vagina* alone and tens of thousands of terms for other topics—from excretions to angry utterances—familar to the most prudish professor but deemed too vulgar to investigate.

The terms are divided into various groups: in *general* and *descriptive* ones which, in the case of penis, show the designations for all kinds of such organs—whether they be big or small, thick or thin, long or short, soft or hard, straight or bent, wrinkled or smooth, and whatever else penes look like and are given names to characterize their appearance and functions. As to female breasts, the descriptive terms are designations for every conceivable type: big and small, hard and soft, pendulous, leathery, asymmetrical, and more. There are far too many terms to be included in this article; they will be presented later and, ultimately, in my DRAT, the *Dictionary of Regional Anatomical Terms*.

Another two groups, collected through Part 6 of the MOQ, are presented below. They cover *endearing* and *abusive* terms for sexual body parts, as well as *pet names* for bawdy body parts used by individuals and their spouses or friends.

The terms gathered for this study can be organized in many ways. Rather than boring you with too many statistics and tables, I will present some general comments on the findings and list the most commonly-cited endearing and offensive names, with a few remarks about my informants.

The personal information provided by participants in the ongoing MOQ survey includes their level of education, profession, and other matters. For this study, I have limited the personal data to geographic location, age, religion, race, and sex. The last item is very precise, thanks to the courage of my informants who indicated whether they are heterosexual, homosexual, or bisexual, which should make a difference in their vocabulary, especially in language dealing with sexuality.

The *sex* of the informants was the only significant factor as to whether they considered certain body-part terms "nice" or "nasty." The other characteristics did not, neither *age*, which ranges from 14 to 76 years, nor *race*, whether white, black, American Indian, Hispanic, Asian or mixed. *Religion* also shows no influence, ranging from Orthodox Jews and Roman Catholics to Greek Orthodox and Atheists. Finally, the *geographic background* of informants shows little difference in nice and nasty terms, whether they are from the United States, Canada, Great Britain, South Africa, Australia, or New Zealand. However, in the "Body Parts" section of the MOQ mentioned earlier, there are great differences in terms collected so far, especially those from Great Britain and Canada. Also, the foreign-language material received, in Dutch, French, German, Italian, Polish, Spanish, and Yiddish, provides interesting insights.

So that you get an idea of who my helpful informants are, a few numbers are necessary: as to *sex*, of the 318 total replies 86 are female and 232 are male; or, more specifically, 196 are heterosexual males, 22 homosexual males, and 14 bisexual males, as well as 78 heterosexual females, 2 lesbians, and 6 bisexual females. As to *race*, 308 are white, 8 are black, and 2 are of mixed background. By *religion*, 84 are Catholic, 35 Jewish, 35 Methodist, 108 practice no religion, and the remaining 56 are of various persuasions.

II. TERMS OF ENDEARMENT AND ABUSE

A. Breasts: "Nice" Terms

Regarding *terms of endearment and abuse for women's breasts*, of the 318 informants 291 provided nice terms, while 29 did not; 251 provided nasty terms, but 67 use no nasty terms. The most common nice terms for breasts are, by decreasing frequency: **breasts** (110, or about one-third of the respondents), **tits** (73), **boobs** (65), **titties** (30), and **boobies** (13). Other multiple entries are **bosom** or **bosoms** (8), knockers (8), jugs (6), 4 each chest and melons, tomatoes (3), and 2 each bazooms, bust, globes, hooters, mammaries, and teats.

The remaining nice terms were single occurrences, sometimes given with preceding adjectives: beautiful chest, beautiful pair, blossoms, boobulars, borstjes (Dutch, "breasts"), bubbies, bumpers, cantaloupes, chichis (Spanish, "tits"), chichitas (Spanish, "titties"), cycuszki (Polish, diminutive of cycki, cf. German Zitze, "teat"), dairy farm, diddies, dugs, figure, frontage, groodies, headlights, juicy peaches, love-pillows, mazoomas, mounds, mountains, Möppchen (German, diminutive, unknown meaning), nay-nays, nice handful, nice puppies, nice set, norks, pair, peaches, pechitos (Spanish, "breasties"), pretty lungs, procelain spheres (reported by a bisexual male), rising beauties, set of jugs, soft cadaby (unknown meaning), sweat-glands, sweetest valley, tetinas and tetitas (Spanish, "titties"), the girls, tsitskelakh (Yiddish, "titties"), and the warmest valley.

B. Breasts: "Nasty" Terms

While *tits* was commonly cited as a nice term (73 times), it was also considered a nasty term for breasts, 116 times, sometimes even by the same informants. Many qualified their responses in such cases by saying that it depends on the context, that is, who uses the term *tits* under what circumstances, with what tone of voice, facial expression, and the like. Also, they noted that the nice or nasty connotation is established by the preceding adjective. For example, in "You have great tits" or "What a lovely pair of tits!" the word is positive, nice, whereas in "ugly tits" or "Look at her sagging tits," the word *tits* has negative connotations. Still, in absolute terms, *tits* is considered by almost twice as many people nasty rather than nice.

Negatively-valued or nasty terms for breasts, in order of frequency, are: **tits** (116), **jugs** (23), **dugs** (20), **boobs** (18), **knockers** (13), **udders** (9), **bags** (7), 4 each **cans** and **melons**, 3 each **cow-tits, mosquito-bites, sagging tits,** and **titties.** Two responses each: **balloons, breasts, fried eggs, fuckin' tits, knobs, pancakes,** and **saggy tits.**

The following nasty terms were reported once each. In several cases, I have included the adjectives that were given with the nouns: "anything besides *breasts*," **bazooms, beaver-tails, bellys, body, boulders, chest, draggy udders, dried-up titties, droopers, dzwony** (Polish, "bells"), **Euter** (German, "udder"), **fat ugly wrinkled bottles, fat-sacks, fatty breasts, flab hangings, flabby melons, flapjacks, floppers, floppy tits, floppy whites, flops, globes, hairy stubs, hanging tits, Hänger** (German, "hangers," "hanging ones"), **honkers, lumps, lung-nuts, massive mammaries, milkers, milk-buckets, milk-glands, milk-sacks, molehills, no tits, old saggy tits, paps, peanuts, pimientos fritos** (Spanish, "fried green peppers"), **pimples, pimples on chest, pus glands, rocks, sagging summer squash, saggy pig tits, scar-crossed prunes, shitbags, skin, slugs, sweater-meat, teats, tieten** (Dutch, "teats"), **tired old tits, tube-socks with a golfball, ugly fat knockers, ugly jugs, waterbags,** and **wrinkled tits.**

Bosoms is used quite often, even though this plural is wrong, because *bosom* means both breasts. A woman can't have *bosoms*, unless she has a second set of breasts (preferably on her back, for dancing). The only woman I can think of who had *bosoms* was the Greco-Roman goddess Artemis or Diana of Ephesus who, as shown on a statue, sported at least 19 breasts—the ideal patron saint of the typical American mammophile.

Comparing *boobs* with *tits*, 65 informants think *boobs* is a nice term, while 18 think it is a nasty one. This 3:1 ratio shows that *boobs* is considered by most people to be a nice term. In the case of *tits*, and remembering the earlier comments about context, 73 respondents consider it a nice term, whereas 116 think it is a nasty word. As to the gender of informants, 14 females say that *boobs* is a nice term, but 10 think it is nasty. Eleven females think *tits* is a nice term, but twice as many, 22, consider it nasty. Eight homosexual and bisexual men think *boobs* is nice, while 2 say it is nasty. Seven gay males say that *tits* is nice, and 10 think it is nasty. As to lesbian and bisexual females, 2 think *boobs* is nice, but not one thinks it is nasty. Two of them say *tits* is nice, but 5 consider it nasty. See **Appendix** for details on region, sex, age, religion, and race of informants for this section.

C. Penis: "Nice" Terms

Of our informants, 252 provided nice terms for penis, 66 did not. The most frequently-cited nice name is **cock** (86), followed by **dick** (37), 17 each **pecker** and **penis, prick** (15), 8 each **love-muscle** and **peter, rod** (5), 4 each **pee-pee, sausage, tool, wang, weenie,** and **willy,** 3 each **dong, meat** and, **shlong** (Yiddish, "snake"), 2 each **dickie, dink, goober, little friend, love-stick, manhood, member, thing,** and **wanger.**

All others are cited only once: **baldheaded candidate, bat, best friend, big one, big piece of meat, big wand, cock of death, dinghy, dog, doohicky, dork, ducky-bird, dyduś** (Polish, no lit. meaning), **fat peter, friend, hacker, hampton, hampton wick, hard-on, horse's cock, hunky, jelly-bean, John Thomas, John Willie, johnson** (a black term, named after a large railroad brake lever), **joint, jolly roger, jongeheer** (Dutch, "young fellow"), **joystick, knob,** lingam (Sanskrit, from the *Kamasutra*), **little man, lollipop, love machine, love-gun, love-wand, mały** (Polish, "little one"), **member virile, muscle, nob, oak tree, one-eyed trouser-trout, organ, parts, penie, pet snake, pichita de oro** (Spanish, "golden cock"), **Piephahn** (German children's language, "dicky-bird," lit. "peeping cock"), **pink torpedo, pitonguita** (Spanish, "little python"), **privates, pud, puss, pussy, rig, Schniedelwutz** (German, unknown meaning, but dialectal *Wutz* means "pig" and "rolled object"), **Schniepel** (German children's language, lit. "tip, point"), **schwanger** (unknown meaning; perhaps from German, "pregnant"), **shmok** (Yiddish, lit. probably "snake"), **silky appendage, snatch pointer, soft, steel-rod, sugar-stick, third leg, throbbing member, throbbing muscle of pure love, tool of pleasure, trout, unit, wiener,** and **yang fella**.

D. Penis: "Nasty" Terms

Now we come to nasty names for the penis. Of the 318 total, 246 informants provided nasty terms, but 72 had none. As can be expected, about a dozen of the nasty terms for penis also show up in the nice column. Here are the nasty terms, again by decreasing frequency of citation: **prick** (81), **cock** (54), **dick** (21), **shlong** (8), **pecker** (6), 5 each **needle-dick, dong** and **dork**, and 3 times each **pencil-dick, penis, salami, shmok,** and **wee-wee**. There were 2 mentions each of **fuck-stick, thing, tool, weenie,** and **worm**.

The following terms appear once each as nasty terms for the penis, several times prefixed with *little*: **big clit, bitte** (French, "dick"), **blood-breaker, bug-fucker, capullito** (Spanish, "little [plant] bud"), **chuj** (Russian and Polish, "prick"), **cod, colostomy, crank, cunt-stabber, dangle-dong, dead worm, dimple-dick, dink, dipstick, dog, dribble-cock, dust cover for cunt, flaccid prick, fuckpole,**

God's revenge on a woman (submitted by a female), **gourd, green-colored dick, half a cob, joy-stick, lifeless, limp-dick, limp-prick, little dick, little peter, little pinkie, little sliver of flesh, little stick, little wiener, little worm, lul** (Dutch, "prick"), **man-meat, middle leg, millimeter-peter, minus a pinus, nothin' cock, old goat-peter, old warty cod, organ, pee-wee, penal dick, pichicorta** (Spanish, "short dick"), **piddler, pimple, pimple-prick, pine, piss-pipe, pisser, pissworm, poker, pots** (Yiddish), **puny prick, pus-rod, rod, rotten meat, scorz** (unknown meaning), **scrawny piece, shaft, shmendrik** (Yiddish, "little nobody, nincompoop"), **shorty, shriveller, shvants** (Yiddish, "tail"), **small, stupid dink, syphilitic prick, teeny, tossergash, ugly little dog-dick, unit, useless, verga** (Spanish, "dick"), **wet noodle, wet spaghetti, wimpy dick,** and **wrinkled dick.**

E. Vulva: "Nice" Terms

In this section I'll present names for vulva and vagina considered nice. Many informants, as also the general population, do not distinguish between *vulva* (the outer parts) and *vagina* (the channel, sheath).

As in the case of penis, many terms for vulva considered nasty also appear as nice terms in this collection. Of the 318 informants, 234 provided nice terms for vulva, while 84 had no nice name for it. Those who did not provide a nice name were all sexual persuasions, by the way. Nasty terms were provided by 274 respondents, but 44 have no negative terms. By frequency, here is a list of nice names for vulva and vagina: the most frequent name was **pussy** (125), followed by **cunt** (20 times, including by 4 females), 9 each **snatch** and **vagina, twat** (8), **honey-pot** (6), 5 times each **beaver** and **muff,** 4 times each **love-tunnel** and **puss,** 3 times each **cunny, fanny, hole, love-box,** and

quim, and twice each **cooze, furburger, love-nest,** and **rosebud.**

Other nice names mentioned once are: **baby-factory, belle chose** (French, "beautiful thing"), **box, bush, centric-part, chochito** (Spanish, "pussy"), **conchita** (Spanish, "little shell"), **dessert, Döschen** (German, "little box"), **fascinating furpiece, fount of femininity, fun-zone, fur-pie, fuzzy-muzzy, garden of love, Gizelle** (name), **hairy Mary, Holiday Inn, honeydew, inner self, inside, jelly-roll, joy-furrow, kitty, kitty-kat, kuciapka** (Polish, no literal meaning), **li'l pussy, lips, little kitten, love-cleft, love-organ, love-sheath, lovely flower, lunch, mick, Muschi** (German, "kitty-cat" and woman's name), **nookie, parts, peach-fish, play-pen, pocket, poo-poo, poontang, poozle, pud, slit, snackbar, sneetje** (Dutch, "little slit"), **soft furry mound of love, spread, sweet cunt, sweet pussy, tee-tee, thing, tight snatch, treasure-box, tunnel of love, vag, vertical smile, warm place, wazoo, wily,** and **yoni** (Sanskrit, from the *Kamasutra*).

F. Vulva: "Nasty" Terms

In his *1811 Dictionary of the Vulgar Tongue*, Captain Grose wrote that C**t is "a nasty name for a nasty thing." The most commonly-cited nasty word for the female organ of lust is still **cunt**, 179 times out of 318 responses, plus 14 instances where it is preceded by a specific adjective. Next in frequency is **gash** (20), **hole** (17), **twat** (14), **pussy** (13), 9 each **slit** and **snatch**, 3 each **canyon, smelly cunt,** and **stinkhole**, 2 each **box, crack, dirty cunt, fish,** and **stinky cunt.**

The remaining terms appear once each: "anything related to fish or smell," **ass, bayonet wound, bearded clam, beaver-trap, big cunt, big, cave, cheese factory, chocho gordo** (Spanish, "fat cunt"), **clit, cow-cunt, crater, dirty** hole, empty tunnel, envy-city, face, fanny, fat rabbit, fish-box, flabby cunt, foul-smelling cunt, fuck-hole, greedy pussy-lips, kut (Dutch, "cunt"), man-eater, man-entrap-ment, man-trap, Möse (German, "twat"), open well, open wound, panocha (Spanish, lit. "coarse brown sugar"), pee-hole, pestosa (Spanish, "diseased, stinky one"), piss-flaps, pizda (Polish, "cunt"), podrida (Spanish, "rotten, putrid one"), pox-ridden cunt, prat, rat-hole, rotten crotch, sardine can, scabby cunt, Schlabberfotze (German, "slob-bery, watery cunt"), scum-twat, scumbag, siffed-up cunt-hole (from *syphilis*), slash, slime-hole, slippery slut, sloppy bot, smell-hole, smelly pussy, snapper, something crawled in and died, sperm-canal, split-tail, stink-pit, tuna, vag, vagina, Votze (German, "cunt"; also spelled Fotze), wet-mop, wound, wrinkled cunt, and yeast-mill.

III. GENITAL PET NAMES

After this litany of nasties, I'll present some comments on pet names for sexual organs. There were fewer than expected actual pet names, which was a surprise. Even many homosexuals, many of whom appear to be very much in touch with their genitals, as it were, have fewer pet names than expected. One should think that now as we are entering the Golden Age of Masturbation—no thanks to AIDS—people would be paying more attention to their only truly safe sex partner and have more appealing names than "my thing" or "the old fella."

Martha Cornog has published several articles on genital pet names, including "Tom, Dick and Hairy" in *Maledicta* 5 (1981), pp. 31-40 (followed by my "What Is This Thing Called, Love?" pp. 41-44) and "Names for Sexual Body Parts: Regularities in 'Personal' Naming Behavior" in the *Festschrift in Honor of Allen Walker Read*, DeKalb, Ill.,

1988, pp. 133-151. This topic also pops up in unexpected places, such as in the Sex & Health advice column in *Glamour*, "Why would a woman nickname her lover's penis?" (Sept. 1987, p. 412, sent by Bruce R.), where some dorky guy is "troubled by the fact that she's [his lover] given my penis a nickname." In *Maledicta* we also feature from time to time updates on new genital pet names. Doris L., Chicago, informed me that Henry Miller called his penis "John Thursday" in *Opus Pistorum*.

There are also jokes about penis pet names. Ingrid B. told me a German joke about what European women call a penis: German women call it "Curtain" (comes down after every act); English women call it "Gentleman" (rises in front of a lady); French women name it "Chanson" (goes from mouth to mouth); and Russian women call it "Guerrilla" (you never know if it's coming from the front or the rear).

There were some surprises in the genital pet name section of the MOQ. Informants not only have pet names for their own and their friends' sexual organs, but also for other body parts and related equipment. For example, one woman calls her left breast "Alice" and her right breast "Phyllis." Another woman names her breasts "Judo" and "Jello." An 18-year-old calls hers *Tasty* and *Delicious*. Several years ago, when I was introduced to the wife of a New York friend and sex researcher, I was tempted to ask her whether she calls her breasts "Schleswig" and "Holstein," respectively, as her ancestors came from the German state called Schleswig-Holstein. Considering the importance of breasts in many cultures, mammaries ought to produce playful mammonyms, such as *Tutti Frutti*, *Lo & Behold*, *Frick & Frack*, or *Sweet & Low*.

Two males have pet names for their **hands**: one calls his right hand "Rosy Palm," after the well-known "Rosy Palm and her five daughters," and another calls it "Little Jo-Jo," after his girlfriend's name. One lady wrote me that she calls her right hand "Little Reinhold." Speaking of which, a lawyer in Seattle is such a fan of *Maledicta* that he and his girlfriend have pet-named his penis after me, calling it "Rey." Such honor!

Testicles also have pet names. One professor of biology calls his testes "John Henry." Bill A.'s 24-year-old wife calls his penis "Little Buddy" and his testicles "Little Buddy's buddies."

Interestingly, **vibrators** also have pet names. In their article in this volume, Salmons & Macaulay reported "Steely Dan" (in William Burroughs's *Naked Lunch*). One of our New York informants calls her vibrator "Charlie," and a Wisconsin musician calls hers "B-flat," after the sound it emits at low speed. She also has a second pet name for it, the German "Wunderorgasmusmaschine."

To stimulate readers into pet-naming their privates, I have suggested several pet names in *Maledicta* 5, such as *Sumer* (it's *icumen in*), or *My Prince* (someday he'll come) or *The South* (it will rise again), as well as *Trouble* (many men like to get into it), but my efforts seem to have been largely wasted. Still, in personal correspondence, some confide in me what they call their own or their partner's organ. For example, a London educator calls the penis of her husband, an actor, "Yorick" (from *Hamlet*'s "Alas, poor Yorick, he is dead"). And a lady in Chicago suggested that I call my appendage *Bavarian Bratwurst*.

A. Penis Pet Names

Of the 204 pet names for penis collected so far, 117 are used by heterosexual men for their own organ, and 49 by their wives or girlfriends. Pet names used by homosexuals are discussed later.

Many of the penis pet names used by males are common terms, such as **dick** (15), **cock** (13), **pecker** (6), **prick** (5), **willie** (4), and twice **boy**, but there are very specific ones, of which the cleverest is by an Ohio physician who calls his penis "His Royal Highness, Prince Everhard of the Netherlands." Other pet names are often prefixed with *my* or *my little.* Here is the list of penis pet names gathered so far: **ace** (as in "ace in the hole"), **ascent, baby's arm, banger, big fella, big log, blue-steel, boy** (as in "You hungry, boy?"), **chachiporra** (Spanish, "big stick"), **Charlie, chinchin** (Japanese childrens' language), **o-chinchin** (the same, with the honorific prefix *o-*), **crank, dong, Elmer Pudd, flip** (from Philip), **Fred, friend, godgiven groover, Harvey** (after the giant rabbit in the movie), **husky, il mio amico** (Italian, "my friend"), **it,** John, **John Henry Longfellow** (*John* and *Henry* are pet names for his testicles), **John Thomas, joy-stick, junior, knob, leather cigar, little boy blue** (as in "come blow my horn"), **little buddy, little dickie, little guy with the German helmet** (from *German helmet,* a term for glans), **little guy, little John, love-muscle, love pump, love scepter, ma bitte** (French, "my dick"), **mack, mate, Milton, Mr. Happy, Mr. Johnson, Mr. Penis, my friend, my little friend, my thang, oak tree, old baldy, Opie, oral tube** (as in "Talk to me through this tube"), **Oscar, Ozymandias** ("...and despair," from Shelley's sonnet), **Pedro, pee-dee, pee-pee, penis, Percy, Pete, Peter, Pogo, purple throbber, rhythm and blues, rod, Roger, Roscoe** (twice), **Rufus, Schniepel** (German, 'dicky,' lit. "point, tip"), **simba, spunky, tally-whacker, tarzoon, teenager, the ever-famous, thing, Thomas Jefferson** (as in "all men are created equal"), **Throckmorton, tiddelly pod, Tom, tool of pleasure, toy, unit, Vivitar** (after the enlarging camera lens), **Walter, wang, war-head, weapon, wee-wee, Pwicked Willie, Winston** (as in "tastes good, like a cigarette should"), and **Yogi** (after the cartoon character).

Women use pet names for the penis of their husbands

or male friends, too, sometimes the same names as their male partners use. **Dick** was most frequent, with 4 listings, followed by 2 each **cock, Fred, him, John Thomas, little friend, tool, weenie,** and **whang.** The remaining occur once each: **ace, bat, big hard hot throbbing dick, cutums, deck, Freddie** (after her husband), **goober, good buddy, himself, his highness, junior, little dickie, little Elvis, little one, lollipop, Lou** (husband's name), **love-wand, Matthew** (husband's name), **moby** (from *Moby Dick*), **mouse, Mr. Happy, Mr. Microphone** (as in "I'll be back to pick it up"), **Mr. Wang, my fella, my friend, panchito** (Spanish, "little belly" and man's name), **pecker-mine, pee-pee, peeper, Pete, rod, Russell the love muscle, sausage & eggs** (for penis and testes), **special friend, super-dong, tally-whacker, the indicator, toy, Walter, Willie, Willy, winger,** and **woofer.**

B. Vulva and Vagina Pet Names

Out of the 86 women participating in the MOQ survey, 34 have pet names for their own vulva, and 101 males use pet names for their wives' or female friends' genitals.

The women's most frequent pet name is **pussy** (13), but terms considered nasty by others also appear in this listing, often preceded by *my*: twice each **box, pussy,** and **vulva,** and once each **coochy, cunny, cunt, friend, furry bits, good pussy, herself, hot wet pussy, junioress, Little Debbie, Little kitty, Matthilda, mouse's hole, my burger, peach-fish, precious pudenda, Priscilla, pussy galore, pussy, sex, snatch, tesorito** (Spanish, "little treasure"), **Virginia,** and **womanhood.**

The most frequent pet name for vulva by males also is **pussy** (41 times), followed by **cunt** (7), **vagina** (4), **twat** (3), and 2 each **bush, honey-pot, lips, muffy, peach-fish, rosebud, snatch,** and **sweet cunt.** Other pet names mentioned are: **belle chose** (French, "beautiful thing"), **box, buggy, cave, chatte** (French, "cat"), **chochito mío** (Spanish, "my little pussy"), **cock, coño** (Spanish, "cunt"), **coral, cunnie, cunny, Delores, Döschen** (German, "little box"), **fanny, flaps, furburger, fuzzy-bunny, Gizelle, hair-pie, home sweet home, honey-pie, jelly cave, jelly-roll, junioress, Kathy's pink surprise** (after a dish named thus, and his wife's name), **kitty, lei** (Italian, "she, her"), **li'l pussy, liesje** (Dutch, Lizzie and *lies*, "groin"), **Louis, love-box, love-nest, lunch, Magdalena** (after a very religious girl-friend), **Mary, Maxine, mick, money-pot, mouse, Ms. Mary, muff, Muschi** (German, "kitty-cat" and woman's name), **nether lips, pencil-sharpener, poussé** (fake French), **pretty little thing, princess, pussy cat, pussy-lips, Sally, Satchmo, satin doll, snutchie, squeeky, sugarbush, the Beave** (from *beaver*), **the Deep** ("she doesn't like it," he added), **thing, tukso** (Tagalog, "temptation"), **tunnel of love, tush, warm fuzzy, ying-yang,** and **zouzoune** (his wife is French).

C. Genital Pet Names Used by Homosexuals and Bisexuals

The remaining pet names are those provided by male and female homosexuals and bisexuals. Of 36 informants, 21 *homosexual and bisexual men* have pet names for their *own penis*, namely: **Baby Huey, best friend, Chester, big dick, cock** (2), **cunt-leg, dick** (2), **John Henry** ("the steel-driving man"), **John Thomas, Junior, little thing, my ten inches, Omar, pee-pee** (2), **Peter, piece, pinky weenie, prick, Schwanz** (German, "tail") and **willy.**

Pet names by *homosexual males* for their *friends' penis*: **cock, dick, handsome, little** (plus man's name), **love tool, Omar Junior, pee-pee, Peter, piece, pretty-dick, pussy, Schwanz, shlong, tally-whacker,** and **tiny tot.**

Pet names by *bisexual men* for their *friends' penis*: **cock** (2), **cute little pee-pee, dingus, joy-stick,** and **junior.**

One *lesbian* reported a pet name for her *own vulva*: **Penelope** (she's of Greek origin).

Pet names by *bisexual women* for their *own vulva* are: **clit, my pussy-cat, pussy** (2), **tee-tee,** and **vagina.**

Pet names by *lesbians* for their *friends' vulva*: **Fifi, little baby,** and **Monique.**

Finally, pet names by *bisexual females* for their *friends' vulva*: **clit, flower, fur-patch, love-nest, pussy, tee-tee,** and **vagina.**

IV. CONCLUDING REMARKS

So much for a first look at abusive, endearing, and pet names for body parts that *all* people have, including hypocritical scholars, journalists, book reviewers, and popular word gurus.

As is the case with human beings who are attacked with derogatory names if they deviate from the norm—fat, skinny, short, tall, ugly, smelly, useless ones—body parts, too, are given deprecatory names if they deviate from the norm of a society or an individual.

Also, as in the case of people, there are many more negatively-valued (nasty) than positively-valued (nice) terms for body parts. From these large collections of negatively-valued data one can establish what the ideal, "normal" person and body parts look like. From the nasty terms for penis and breasts, for instance, one can see what the ideal body parts should look like. As the nasty terms for penis predominantly deal with shortness, smallness, softness, uselessness, and illness, one knows that a so-called normal penis should be long, thick, hard, useful, and healthy. Similarly, the negatively-valued term for breasts tell us that "normal" breasts should not be small, flat, dried up, fat, wrinkled, floppy or saggy.

The norms for people and body parts vary from culture to culture, from epoch to epoch, but some characteristics are probably universal. I say "probably" because nobody has studied or even collected negative terms from most languages. This is where *Maledicta* comes in, to some degree continuing the frank work of late 19th-century and early 20th-century European researchers of folklore and offensive language whose work was also discredited by the hypocritical, brainless, repressed, prudish, intellectually dull establishment. Many of those earlier researchers who published their findings in *Am Ur-Quell*, *Kryptádia* and *Anthropophyteia* happened to be Jewish, which did not help much in anti-Semitic Europe. They were physically abused, driven out of the countries, or worse. I won't be driven out of the country, but I certainly "don't get no respect"— from the mousebrains, that is, whether they are cacademics or the general public. Luckily, enough intelligent people see the deeper significance of what I am doing, helping me carry on my lonely but cheerful uphill struggle. The easiest way to help me continue is to fill out questionnaires. Thus, when the revised MOQ appears in a future *Maledicta*, please don't give me excuses for failing to complete the questionnaire and don't be so bloody lethargic. Unlike certain shameless cacademics, I am not asking you for money, just for your time.

A much shorter version of this material was presented at the annual meeting of the American Name Society in Chicago, 16 October 1988.

V. APPENDIX

Nasty Terms for Women's Breasts
(MOQ Nr. T- 06)
by Geographic Distribution

It would take many pages of this publication to print out the results of MOQ information gathered so far. All of that material will appear, one day, in my *Dictionary of Regional Anatomical Terms*. The following list is just a sample of what can be done. The data can be extracted, sorted and arranged in any way needed, by age, sex, religion, race, profession, geographic location, and any combination thereof. For this list, I arranged the information by geography: first the USA, alphabetically by state (not all states are represented because of the lethargy of our readers), and within each state by postal ZIP code. Then follow English-speaking foreign countries, then other foreign countries.

The informant's confidential code shows the *region* where the terms are in use. It consists of abbreviated names of states or countries, postal codes, and initials.

The next column lists the *terms*. Missing terms (-) indicate that the informant did not supply any.

The next column shows the *sex* of the informant: **m** = male heterosexual; **f** = female heterosexual; **g** = gay male; **l** = lesbian female; **x** = bisexual female; **z** = bisexual male.

The *age* is indicated by year of birth (new method) or by the actual age or by a letter indicating the age group: **t** = 11-20 years; **y** = 21-35; **m** = 36-50; **e** = 51-65; **o** = over 65 years.

The informant's *religion* shows the current affiliation; where two are given (separated by a hyphen), the first is the religion in which the informant was brought up, the second is the current affiliation, if any.

Race: **b** = Black, **i** = American Indian, **w** = White

ABBREVIATIONS FOR RELIGIONS

agnos	= agnostic	mo.syn	= Missouri Synod
amer	= American	ortho	= orthodox
bapt	= Baptist	pract	= practicing
cath	= Catholic	presb	= Presbyterian
ch	= church	prot	= Protestant
congr	= Congregationalist	ref	= reform(ed)
cons	= conservative	sev.day	= 7th-Day Adventist
denom	= denominational	south	= southern
episc	= Episcopalian	unit	= Unitarian
meth	= Methodist	witch	= witchcraft

Region / Code	Term	Sex	Age	Religion	Race
Alabama					
AL36106JT	tits	m	m	south bapt - atheist	w
Arizona					
AZ85201LT	-	f	e	cath - none	w
AZ85741DL	-	m	o	bapt - none	w
California					
CA90000LF	jugs	m	y	atheist - agnos	w
CA90006DV	-	g	y	presb - christian	w
CA90024LL	knockers	f	y	jewish ref - agnos/atheist	w
CA90025PK	boobs	f	y	jewish ref - atheist	w
CA90028RS	tits	l	m	jewish -none	w
CA90036JS	jugs	z	e	bapt - none	b
CA90039AN	tits	x	m	bapt - taoist	b
CA90046RD	tits	g	m	meth - none	w
CA90057RM	boobs	m	o	prot	w
CA90069AN	tits	z	y	cath - none	w
CA90069AR	breasts	g	e	ch of england - atheist	w
CA90069MM	lumps	m	y	atheist	w
CA90210JK	saggy tits, knockers	m	y	cath - non-pract	w
CA90210RR	-	g	y	disciples of christ - none	w
CA90403RW	jugs	m	y	jewish cons - jewish	w
CA90405BR	-	m	m	jewish ref	w
CA91214GT	fatty breasts	f	y	mormon - agnos	w
CA91326SF	boobs	f	m	agnos	w
CA91403ET	dried-up titties	m	y	cath - none	w
CA91423RC	-	m	e	meth - unit	w
CA91604GL	bazooms	m	e	prot - atheist	w

Region / Code	Term	Sex	Age	Religion	Race
CA91605MG	slugs	m	m	jewish cons - jewish ref	w
CA91701CR	tits	f	m	agnos	w
CA91786DM	tits	m	y	episc	w
CA91786KM	knockers	f	y	episc	w
CA92083GR	boobs	f	1961	none - pagan	w
CA92109DF	tits	l	y	greek ortho - none	w
CA92120RD	-	m	e	presb - atheist	w
CA92277PS	breasts	z	1936	cath - atheist	w
CA92624NL	bags, tits	m	m	south bapt - prot	w
CA92703MA	knockers	f	y	lutheran - cath	w
CA92705EC	boobs	f	o	prot - deist/agnos	w
CA92706PK	shit-bags	m	y	agnos - pantheist	w
CA92715LH	jugs	m	m	meth/presb - none	w
CA93639FS	cans	m	y	cath	w
CA93726GK	tits	m	e	jewish - atheist	w
CA94025DW	dugs, udders	g	m	south meth - agnos	w
CA94101AN	tits	z	1959	none	w
CA94115MP	floppers	m	y	cath - none	w
CA94115MT	-	g	y	episc - agnos	w
CA94117SB	knockers	z	e	agnos	w
CA94702MZ	-	m	1950	jewish - none	w
CA94703BB	dugs	g	1947	meth - agnos	w
CA94704RS	dugs	m	m	jewish ref	w
CA94705MJ	tits	m	y	agnos	w
CA94707RS	tits	m	m	prot - none	w
CA94903DW	dugs	m	m	atheist	w
CA95008LT	anything besides breasts	f	1954	jewish atheist - none	w
CA95050JJ	cow-tits	g	e	cath	w
CA95128LC	boobs	f	y	none	w
CA95628RR	jugs	f	1948	meth/presb - neo-paggan /witch	w
CA95671JG	udders	m	y	cath	w
CA95671JL	jugs	m	1957	atheist	w
CA95696DC	body	z	1957	cath - none	w
CA95719RM	tits	m	e	prot - agnos	w
CA95827JA	knobs, tits	m	m	presb - none	w

Colorado

CO80207DB	-	m	e	bapt - none	b
CO81612MS	tits	m	o	none	w

Connecticut

CT06071JS	bellys	m	m	cath - christian	w
CT06239RG	mosquito bites	m	y	none	i
CT06430AN	sagging	m	e	jewish ref - agnos	w

Region / Code	Term	Sex	Age	Religion	Race
District of Columbia					
DC20002KC	hairy stubs	f	y	meth - none	w
DC20007SG	tits	m	t	jewish ref - agnos	w
DC20024KP	-	m	m	meth - atheist	w
DC20560CS	boobs	m	m	quaker - atheist	w
Florida					
FL32347JG	udders	m	m	bapt - atheist	w
FL32804AP	tits	m	y	lutheran	w
FL33040KJ	tits	m	y	prot - agnos	w
Georgia					
GA30067MO	tits	m	e	jewish	w
GA30318CW	jugs	f	t	bapt - holiness	b
Hawaii					
HI96813BB	-	m	m	episc	w
Illinois					
IL60047DW	tits	f	e	presbterian	w
IL60047WW	bags	m	e	cath	w
IL60060MM	jugs	m	y	lutheran	w
IL60201EW	(all but *breasts* are nasty)	m	1935	jewish	w
IL60202RF	milkers, udders	m	1945	lutheran - agnos	w
IL60302LM	-	f	y	atheist - theist	w
IL60304MF	titties	m	y	cath - agnos	w
IL60426SW	flab hangings	m	t	satanist	b
IL60542LS	tits	m	m	presb - lutheran	w
IL60600FF	tits	m	m	meth - atheist	w
IL60610GF	dugs	g	1951	dutch ref - presb	w
IL60613ER	floppy whites	m	y	jewish	w
IL60613SW	tits	g	y	cath - none	w
IL60614ER	tits, jugs	f	m	jewish	w
IL60614MH	lung-nuts	m	e	sev.day - none	w
IL60615AN	knockers	f	1962	cath	b
IL60626CW	dugs	f	1953	cath - agnos	w
IL60626SI	-	m	y	cath - christian	w
IL60643DM	dugs	m	1931	presbterian	w
IL60656DM	sagging tits	m	m	cath - none	w
IL60657CH	tits	f	y	jewish cons - agnos	w
IL60657FP	droopers, sweater-meat	m	1942	cath	w
IIL60658RS	tits	m	y	cath	w

Region / Code	Term	Sex	Age	Religion	Race
IL60660AS	tits	m	e	cath - meth	w
IL60660GS	tits	m	y	agnos - atheist	w
IL60660RZ	-	f	y	meth - none	w
IL61277DW	tits	m	y	meth	w
IL62704TS	jugs	m	m	lutheran - agnos	w

Indiana

IN46220EK	bags	f	y	agnos	w
IN46802LC	tits	f	20	prot - none	w
IN47150DC	dugs	z	e	presb - agnos	w
IN47401JB	tired old tits	g	1942	disciples of christ	w
IN47905TG	boobs	f	1957	atheist	w
IN47907ANON	sagging tits	f	1950	cath	w
IN47907MA	boobs	f	1934	christian (non-denom)	w

Kansas

KS64131TW	jugs	x	m	bapt	w

Kentucky

KY40031MA	tits	x	y	cath - none	w
KY40031WW	titties	m	y	bapt	b
KY40205TH	tits	m	m	presbterian	w
KY41101RB	-	m	m	meth - agnos	w

Louisiana

LA70360NL	-	m	e	cath	w
LA70502JH	bags	m	1955	cath	w
LA71058EA	saggin' tits	m	m	south bapt - none	w

Maine

ME04064DP	balloons	g	e	jewish ortho - jewish refo	w
ME04401TK	honkers	f	1949	cath - not practicing	w

Maryland

MD20740DH	sagging tits	m	y	meth - none	w
MD20741WK	tits	m	y	cath	w
MD20782KL	knockers	f	1970	cath - witch	w
MD20783AN	boobs	f	y	meth - episc	w
MD20815KM	tits	m	m	ch of christ - none	w
MD20912EB	peanuts,bags	z	1952	meth - agnos	w
MD20912GP	cow-tits	m	y	greek ortho	w
MD21157PS	tits	m	y	cath	w
MD21204MF	tits, jugs	f	y	cath - none	w
MD21204RS	tits	m	m	cath - not practicing	w
MD21206GD	tits	f	y	cath - presb	w
MD21212GB	-	m	e	bapt- none	w
MD21214MK	pimples	m	m	cath - atheist	w

Region / Code	Term	Sex	Age	Religion	Race
MD21214TB	jugs, udders, pancakes	x	25	bapt/mormon/cath - agnos	w
MD21225WW	scar-crossed prunes	m	m	meth - agnos	w
MD21228WS	-	m	e	episc (low) - none	w

Massachusetts

MA02172MA	tits	m	y	jewish - neo-pagan, hindu	w
MA01570BF	tits	m	t	cath - none	w
MA01588DC	bags, tits	m	t	none	w
MA01614DB	tits	m	y	cath - atheist	w
MA01821SM	-	f	1957	cath - agnos	w
MA02115CP	-	f	m	prot - atheist	w
MA02129AL	-	m	y	jewish agnos - atheist	w
MA02129CP	-	x	y	meth - none	w
MA02144MT	tits	m	1958	episc - none	w
MA02155EA	-	m	y	jewish/agnos - agnos	w
MA02155PP	-	f	y	presb - none	w
MA02766MB	tits	f	1968	jewish cons - atheist	w

Michigan

MI48043DD	udders	m	y	christian	w
MI48047LL	-	m	e	prot	w
MI48047ML	-	f	m	meth - none	w
MI48072MK	tits	f	e	presb - belief in force	w
MI48103JM	-	m	y	agnos - atheist	w
MI48152GF	tits	f	y	universalist unit	w
MI49204WF	-	m	y	prot - none	w

Minnesota

MN55407JC	-	m	y	presb - atheist	w
MN55409	tits	m	y	prot (congregat) - none	w
MN55414DL	-	m	y	cath	w

Mississippi

MS39531PR	-	m	1962	lutheran (mo.syn) - none	w

Missouri

MO63100TS	tits	m	1954	prot - undecided	w

Nebraska

NE68377HG	milk buckets	m	e	lutheran	w

Nevada

NV89102RT	jugs	m	e	meth - unit/inactive	w

Region / Code	Term	Sex	Age	Religion	Race
New Jersey					
NJ07011MC	saggy pig tits	m	m	cath - russian ortho	w
NJ07424WL	flapjacks, mosquito bites	z	y	cath - atheist	w
NJ07885OB	no tits	m	o	congr - none	w
NJ08553WB	tits	m	m	presb - none	w
NJ08628DS	-	m	y	cath - none	w
NJ08854TS	knockers	g	y	south bapt - none	w
NJ08903AM	-	m	m	atheist - none	w
New Mexico					
NM87119RW	tits	m	m	meth	w
New York					
NY10000AN	-	m	e	meth - agnos	w
NY10000BN (NL)	-	g	m	jewish - zen-buddhist	w
NY10000JS	tits	m	e	jewish ref	w
NY10011MB	jugs	m	m	episc - none	w
NY10012RB	boobs	g	e	jewish - none	w
NY10014AN	boobs	g	m	cath - none	w
NY10019AS	udders	f	m	cath - none	w
NY10023GR	pus glands	f	y	greek ortho - none	w
NY10025JF	tits	z	o	cath - atheist	w
NY10032LT	boobs	m	m	jewish ortho - jewish	w
NY10128RM	tits	m	e	south bapt - unit	w
NY10475WR	tits, boobs	m	m	cath - agnos	w
NY10583RL	knockers	m	o	jewish ref	w
NY10591JW	bags	m	t	cath	w
NY10707JM	tits	m	41	cath	w
NY10952RK	tits	m	e	presb	w
NY11200HL	-	m	e	jewish - none/buddhist	w
NY11230RC	boobs	f	y	jewish ref - jews for jesus	w
NY11377JS	tits	m	m	cath	w
NY12123JC	tits	m	m	meth - none	w
NY13681JB	tits	m	o	cath - none	w
NY14063EL	tits	m	e	jewish - none	w
NY14075WK	udder	m	o	cath	w
NY14301EL	tits	m	e	cath - agnos	w
NY14411LT	paps	f	y	prot - atheist	w
NY14411TT	-	m	m	episc - agnos	w
NY14845JH	dugs	m	y	cath - atheist	w
NY14847AW	-	f	e	cath - episc	w

Region / Code	Term	Sex	Age	Religion	Race
North Dakota					
ND58368BE	boobs	f	y	united meth - none	w
ND58368JE	-	m	y	assembly of god - none	w
Ohio					
OH44113DR	-	m	e	ch of england - atheist	w
OH44504MH	tits	m	t	lutheran	w
OH44511CH	knobs	m	e	lutheran - unit	w
OH45324MR	tits	f	t	presb - none	w
OH45341LH	tits	m	1955	pentecostal	w
OH45371DH	massive mammaries	m	o	meth	w
OH45387RF	-	m	m	jewish atheist - jewish agnos	w
OH45701MM	tube-socks w. a golfball	m	m	meth - agnos	w
Oklahoma					
OK73115TR	-	m	e	meth - none	w
Oregon					
OR97202CR	tits	m	t	swiss ref prot - agnos	w
OR97310JW	fuckin' tits	m	y	cath - none	w
OR97331IP	dugs	m	1950	presb- christian (non-spec)	w
Pennsylvania					
PA15206SM	tits, boobs	f	1962	episc - uncertain	w
PA15226JM	tits, jugs	m	1960	cath - none	w
PA15537DN	dugs	m	m	prot - atheist	w
PA15857JS	saggy tits, draggy udders	m	m	cath - none	w
PA16602KD	globes	m	m	cath - none	w
PA16803DK	-	m	m	cath - none	w
PA17201SS	hanging tits	m	e	jewish cons	w
PA17601SG	-	m	1959	lutheran - none	w
PA18062RW	dugs	m	e	jewish - agnos	w
PA19087JT	-	m	e	meth - agnos	w
PA19144DD	tits	m	y	jewish - agnos	w
Tennessee					
TN37204JK	dugs	m	o	presb - unit	w
TN38343JQ	tits	f	y	bapt	w
Texas					
TX77349PR	-	z	y	lutheran - pentecostal	w
TX78217JF	jugs	f	y	presb - zen	w
TX78703AN	tits	f	m	south bapt - secular	w
TX78723AC	tits	f	1954	cath - none	w

Region / Code	Term	Sex	Age	Religion	Race
TX78758DA	tits	m	m	presb - none	w
TX78765AN	tits	g	y	fundamentalist - agnos	i
TX78765BM	boobs	f	1959	ch of christ - buddhist	w
TX78840RW	beaver-tails	f	y	meth	w

Virginia

VA22012TS	summer sqash, sagging	f	1960	cath	w
VA22075EC	tits	f	y	cath - agnos	w
VA22180HC	tits	g	y	disciples of christ - none	w
VA22203BK	tits	g	y	meth - none	w
VA22203RT	tits	m	m	episc - atheist	w
VA22205AK	molehills	f	m	cath - none	w
VA22310EG	-	f	y	christian - pagan/taoist	w
VA23464AN	fuckin' tits	m	y	united meth	w
VA23868DR	chest	g	1962	bapt	b

Washington

WA98133RH	-	m	m	jewish	w
WA98272LB	fat-sacks	m	y	christian - satanism	w
WA99205BS	milk-sacks	m	t	none	w
WA99208VB	tits	m	m	agnos - ch of god	w

Wisconsin

WI53005JY	cans, jugs	f	1936	prot	w
WI53151DR	-	f	m	cath - none	w
WI53186RA	udders	m	1936	cath - agnos	w
WI53211CP	dugs, teats	f	y	atheist	w
WI53211GP	tits, jugs	m	y	cath - none	w
WI53211RP	boobs	m	e	prot	w
WI53211RR	tits	m	m	cath - none	w
WI53703DG	flaps	m	1946	atheist	w
WI53703LP	milk-glands	f	1948	presb - none	w
WI53703TM	-	m	1956	cath lapsed	w
WI53704GV	jugs	m	y	none - atheist	w
WI53704JM	titties	f	1963	united ch of christ - none	w
WI53704MS	knockers, melons, mosquito-bites	f	1961	prot - none	w
WI53711RO	cow-tits, water-bags, fried eggs	m	o	lutheran - none	w
WI53713EL	tits	f	y	amer bapt - don't go to ch	w
WI53713SC	dugs	m	y	agnos	w
WI54157JM	tits	m	y	cath	w
WI54912DT	fat ugly wrinkled bottles	z	1948	bapt - atheist	w

Region / Code	Term	Sex	Age	Religion	Race
Australia					
AUS 2086DM	-	m	y	ch of england - none	w
AUS 2601DL	tits	m	1936	ch of england - none	w
AUS 5081AR	tits, dugs	m	o	atheist/agnos	w
AUS SW	dugs	g	1947	cath - aquarian	w
AUS VT	-	m	1943	congr - non-religious	w
Canada					
CAN A1B1P1FW	-	m	e	anglican	w
CAN B0J3J0PC	jugs	m	m	anglican - atheist	w
CAN BC AN	tits	x	m	prot, united - atheist	w
CAN H2W1B7DP	boobs	m	27	agnos - atheist	w
CAN H3B4P1DM	dugs	f	30	united presb - atheist	w
CAN J0E1J0MC	-	m	y	cath/unit/sev.day - none	w
CAN J0E1J0PK	dugs	f	y	prot	w
CAN J8V1N2WD	rocks, flops, skin, melons, fried eggs	m	m	prot - agnos	w
CAN J8X1C7DC	cans	m	y	none	w
CAN K1R7T2RG	ugly fat knockers	m	e	episc	w
CAN K2B5R8BD	tits	m	e	united ch - atheist	w
CAN L2T1J5LB	tits	m	y	prot - none	w
CAN L3K1Y6PL	tits	m	y	cath - none	w
CAN L3K2M2PB	udders	m	y	bapt	w
CAN L3P3K2MJ	tits	m	m	anglican	w
CAN L5J4J9PD	wrinkled tits	m	y	greek ortho - atheist	w
CAN L6T2Y1JB	cans	f	y	cath - none	w
CAN M1T1R8SA	-	m	e	meth - atheist	w
CAN M4M3E8JA	jugs, old saggy tits, balloons	m	76	meth	w
CAN M5M2J2AU	tits	m	1950	jewish cons - none	w
CAN M5R2M5GR	tits	f	1956	cath - lapsed	w
CAN M9B4Z5GW	tits	m	y	anglican - atheist	w
CAN M9R3T5RJ	-	g	e	prot	w
CAN R8N1W1MC	-	m	t	cath	w
CAN R8N1W1PC	tits	m	m	anglican - none	w
CAN T0J0Y0JC	pancakes	f	m	presb - united ch of canada	w
CAN V5V2H2AB	knockers	f	m	atheist - none	w
CAN V6R2R5JD	-	z	e	prot - none	w
CAN V9R1W6JH	ugly jugs	f	m	none - agnos pantheist	w
England					
UK M68BTRW	dugs	m	y	ch of england - none	w
UK OXFORD JL	tits	m	1965	ch of england - agnos	w

Region / Code	Term	Sex	Age	Religion	Race
Ireland					
IR DUBLIN FM	flabby melons	m	1962	cath - atheist	w
IR DUBLIN GG	tits	m	1966	cath lapsed	w
IR DUBLIN JA	tits	f	1966	cath - atheist	w
IR DUBLIN MO	tits, melons, boulders	f	1964	cath	w
IR DUBLIN MP	-	f	1966	cath	w
IR DUBLIN NC	tits	f	1961	moslem - atheist	w
IR DUBLIN NM	-	f	1963	cath - atheist	w
IR DUBLIN RE	-	f	1966	cath	w
IR DUBLIN RM	tits	z	y	cath - atheist	w
IR DUBLIN SC	melons	f	1962	cath	w
IR-N	tits	m	1951	cath	w
IRE-SR	-	f	y	cath - none	w
New Zealand					
NZ GM	-	m	1935	bapt - none	w
NZ IRM	pimples on chest	m	1965	none	w
NZ JG	knockers	m	1953	anglican - agnos	w
NZ JR	-	f	1937	presb agnos - buddhist	w
NZ PB	floppy tits	m	65	none - anglican	w
NZ SG	tits .	f	1923	none - cath	w
South Africa					
SA 1460JE	dugs	m	1935	anglican - meth	w
SA 1500 CVDB	tits	m	1970	meth - agnos	w
France					
FR 75665JB	-	m	1955	atheist - agnos	w
Germany					
GERM 5300RS	Euter	m	y	lutheran - none	w
GERM 6203PS	Hänger	m	1964	cath - none	w
GERM (USA))ET	-	m	m	meth - atheist	w
GERM (USA) KT	-	f	m	prot - pagan	w
GERM (USA) RK	tits	m	y	episc - south u.s. charism	w
Mexico					
MEX (IL) TS	-	m	m	lutheran - agnos	w
Netherlands					
NL LV	tieten	m	1922	netherlands ref - anglican	w

Region / Code	Term	Sex	Age	Religion	Race
Poland					
POL 61689WS	dzwony	m	y	atheist	w
Spain					
SP 41700RR	pimientos fritos	m	1941	ch of england - atheist	w

Copyright © 1986 by Neil Crawford

OFFENSIVE ROCK BAND NAMES
A LINGUISTIC TAXONOMY[1]

Joe Salmons *and* Monica Macaulay

INTRODUCTION

Rock music has always been a form of rebellion, and as such has always been intended to shock those who do not count themselves among its followers. The outward manifestations of such rebellion have become more outrageous with each succeeding generation. Appearance and behavior have always played a part, although the *Beatles'* "long" hair seems mild next to the day-glo mohawks, funereal makeup and safety pin earrings of more recent youth fashion. Elvis's hips have given way to slam dancing and spewing green vomit from stage. Screamin' Jay Hawkins climbing out of a coffin to open his shows in the 1960s may sound strange even today, but it is mild next to Ozzy Osbourne biting the heads off bats on stage or the use of chainsaws during live performances.

Lyrics have also played a part—witness the increase in explicitness from *Tommy James and the Shondells'* "(My Baby Does the) Hanky-Panky" (recorded in 1963-1964 and a number one hit in 1966) by way of the *Beatles'* "Why Don't We Do It in the Road" (November 1968) to the *Dead Kennedys'* "Too Drunk to Fuck" (1981).

Only in the last ten years or so, however, have many bands given themselves *names* that participate in this development. To be sure, trends in band names have always been observable. Among the more notable:

a) **insect names** in the early 1960s, beginning with Buddy Holly's *Crickets* and the takeoff on that by the *Beatles*;

b) **psychedelic names** of the 1960s, such as *The Strawberry Alarm Clock, Jefferson Airplane* and **light/heavy oxymorons**, for instance, *Iron Butterfly* and *Led Zeppelin*;

c) **literary names,** which have long been popular, such as *The Droogs* (from *Clockwork Orange*) and Hesse's *Steppenwolf.*

However, offensive band names remained very rare until the late 1970s. The most famous early example is, of course, the British band the *Sex Pistols,* formed in 1976 by promoter Malcolm McLaren, whose explicit goal was to offend the public (cf. Hebdige 1979 and Robbins 1983). Since then, offensive band names have proliferated on both sides of the Atlantic.

A look at well over 150 such band names from the alternative rock scene in the 1980s—gathered from alternative/college radio play lists, *fanzines*[2], and personal experience in the alternative rock scene—shows clear patterns of preference for particular types of offensive, shocking, and/or insensitive names over others. This article gives an annotated taxonomy of a corpus of such names.

We can touch on only a fraction of the possible topics, but a few other areas deserve mention. First, the explosion in the number of small, independent record companies (*indies*) has given us offensive, often humorous record company names, e.g., *Toxic Shock, Psycho, Self Immolation, Braineater, Slash, Doo Doo Productions, Roadkill Records, Stiff*[3] and *Rabid Cat.* Second, rock pseudonyms play an important role, such as *Sid Vicious* and *Johnny Rotten* (both *Sex Pistols*), *Richard Hell* (*Voidoids*), *Jello Biafra* (*Dead Kennedys*) and *Venus Penis Crusher* (*Cycle Sluts from Hell*).

Finally, we have concentrated only on the British and American scenes, reflecting our experience and knowledge. These phenomena are, however, international. From the German-speaking countries, for instance, come bands such as West Germany's *Geile Tiere* ("horny animals")[4] and *Schleimkeim* ("slime-seed") from the German Democratic Republic, as well as the West German record labels *Totenkopf* ("skull, death head") and *Giftplatten* ("poison records").

THE TAXONOMY

In the taxonomy which follows (and in the alphabetical list of the entire corpus found in the appendix), we have tried to exclude bands not part of the alternative rock scene, e.g., metal (be it heavy metal, speed metal, etc.) and rap/hip-hop.[5] The lines between genres are notoriously difficult to draw, however, especially since many alternative musicians consciously seek to break down such distinctions, and since bands evolve over time—e.g., *The Cult*, which began as an alternative band, *Southern Death Cult*, but which has gained a more metal-oriented audience. As a result of the fuzziness of some boundaries, we realize that some readers may well disagree with our inclusion or exclusion of particular items.

"Alternative music" is extremely difficult (if not impossible) to define, but some characteristics should be noted. It has been defined simply as "any kind of rock music not found on commercial radio."[6] Alternative certainly includes the various genres and subgenres of punk (from the late 1970s: *Sex Pistols*, *Ramones*, etc.) and thrash (generally, a later development: *Angry Samoans*, *Black Flag*), both of which are often classed under the broader heading of "hardcore." Closer to the mainstream but still clearly alternative are the "garage rock" bands of the early 1980s (*Green on Red*, *Vandals*, *Cramps*), which emphasized rawer production and sound than "new wave," although much of the latter is also widely considered alternative. Numerous hybrids have also grown up in the alternative scene:

surf-punk, cow-punk, metal-core and speed metal (the last two existing on the boundary between alternative and heavy metal), etc.

Musically, key features often include simple instrumentation (of the genres mentioned, only new wave regularly included keyboards), simple song structure (often two or three chords), high volume and a very fast beat. In general, one finds a "raw" sound, in conscious opposition to the highly produced sounds of commercial bands.

The corpus is broken down into four major categories: **Sex, The Body, Death,** and **Society**, with subdivisions as appropriate. As might be expected, many items fit into more than one category, and in such cases, we have included bands under both or all headings.

I. SEX

Sexual allusions, ranging from euphemistic to explicit, figure prominently throughout the language of alternative rock. For example, "cover bands" (bands that play popular songs rather than original music) are known within the alternative scene as *cover whores*, referring to the fact that cover bands can earn far more money than original bands, who often play for free even in established clubs. That is, they are motivated by money and not simply by the desire to play. *To jerk off* or *to masturbate* means to play long and unstructured solos, i.e., to indulge oneself at the expense of other musicians and the audience. Musicians who are particularly eager to play (often working with several bands at once, plus jamming with others on the side) are called *sluts*. *Jazz fags* are players who show too much musical sophistication and are seen as lacking aggression and regarded as soft.[7]

We have divided this category into four subgroups:

Genitalia; Acts, Positions, etc.; Homosexuality; and *General and Other.*

A. Genitalia

Both male and female genitalia are among the most popular sources for taboo band names.

HIS

Big Balls and the Great White Idiot
Buzzcocks[8]
Cocks in Stained Satin
Dicks
Hard-ons
Man-Sized Action
Penetrators
Raw Meat. This Indianapolis band uses as its logo a spurting penis, removing any potential ambiguity about the meaning of its name. Meat references are generally common in band names, for instance *Meatpuppets* and *Meatmen.*
Revolting Cocks
Sex Pistols
Throbbing Gristle

HERS

Several of these bands are entirely or predominantly female.

Clit Boys
C*nts
Killer Pussy
Les Blank's Amazing Pink Holes
Pussy Galore. Named after the character in the James Bond movie *Goldfinger.*
Slits

B. Acts, Positions, etc.

Bob on This
Circle Jerks
Doggy Style
Lubricated Goat. We may have miscategorized this, but we doubt it.
Meat Beat Manifesto

Strangulated Beatoffs
Tupelo Chain Sex
Vibrators. A far subtler but parallel name was the 1970s band *Steely Dan*, named after a vibrator in William Burroughs's novel *Naked Lunch*.

C. Homosexuality

1,000 Homo DJs
Art Phag
Fudge-packers
Gay Cowboys in Bondage
Gaye Bykers on Acid
Homo Picnic
Homosexuals. This is not overtly offensive, but is striking for its choice of the most general, least marked name for an often stigmatized group, and for its clinical tone.
Lesbian Dopeheads on Mopeds
Pink Fairies
Violent Femmes. *Femme* meant "queer, fag" in Wisconsin— where the *Violent Femmes* come from—when one of the authors was growing up there. It is reported to be archaic or obsolete within the gay community itself, except in classified ads.

D. General and Other

Alien Sex Fiend
Crucifucks. This name manages to combine more offensive references than virtually any other: *Sex* (general/other), *Society* (religion), and *Society* (profanity).
Cycle Sluts from Hell
Deviants
Gigolo Aunts
Necropolis of Love
Root Boy Slim & the Sex Change Band
Sex Boys
Sex Gang Children
Sic F*cks
Soviet Sex

II. OTHER PHYSICAL

A. The Body

Note that all non-genital body parts and related topics taken together are far less common than genitalia-based band names alone.

4-skins
Afterbirth
Bollock Brothers. This band was started by Johnny Rotten of the *Sex Pistols*. Note the allusion to the *Sex Pistols'* first album "Never Mind the Bollocks," a title considered offensive by many in the United Kingdom. U.K. *bollocks* = U.S. *balls*.
Butthole Surfers
Cancerous Growth
Carnivorous Buttock Flies
Cramps
Contractions
Lost Cherees
Mighty Sphincter
Neurotic Arseholes. This may be a social rather than a physical reference.
Sarcastic Orgasm
Severed Heads
Stretch Marks

B. Bodily Fluids and Excretions[9]

Excretion and various other bodily fluids (and related topics) also appear. It is perhaps surprising, however, how few references there are to feces and how many there are to vomit.

Bloody Mess and the Skabs
Bulimia Banquet
Discharge
Fartz
Johnny Vomit
New Roger Diarrhea
Seemen

Smegma
Specimen
Spermbirds
Spit
Stains
Strangulated Beatoffs
Technicolor Yawns. This is a euphemism for throwing up.
Thrownups
Vomit and the Zits
Vomit Launch
Vomitorium
Yeastie Girls. Rap fans will instantly recognize the takeoff on
the *Beastie Boys*.

C. Abortion, Fetuses, etc.

Aborted at Line 6. This is actually a computer reference, i.e.,
a program that failed to run past line 6.
Dayglo Abortions
Fetus Productions
Foetus Interruptus
Freddy Fetus & the Abortions
Fried Abortions
Scraping Foetus Off the Wheel. This band has also released
records under other names: *You've got Foetus on your Breath*,
Foetus über Frisco, etc.
Screaming Fetus
Sharon Tate's Baby

III. DEATH[10]

There is a genre of alternative rock known as "death rock,"
but the names of its best-known purveyors (e.g., *Bauhaus*
and *Joy Division*[11]) surprisingly do not include references to
death. This category is so well-represented among non-
death rock band names that we can present only a very incomplete list here.

Bone Orchard
Capital Punishment
Christian Death

Condemned to Death
Corpse Grinders
Dead Can Dance
Dead Hippies
Dead Kennedys
Dead Milkmen. This name incorporates reference both to the *Dead Kennedys* and the well-known "Monty Python" sketch.
Death of Samantha. This band appeared after Samantha Smith, child goodwill ambassador to Russia, was killed in an airplane crash.
Death Piggy
Heads on Sticks
Hollywood Autopsy
Killing Joke
MDC. These initials have been glossed as *Multideath Corporation*, *Millions of Dead Cops*, and *Millions of Dead Children*.
My Dad is Dead
My Life with the Thrill Kill Kult
Napalm Death
Necropolis of Love
Necros
Rotting Corpses
Screaming Dead
Severed Heads
Southern Death Cult. This band is now known simply as *The Cult*, after a transitional stage as *Death Cult*.

IV. SOCIETY

Note how often these names are topical, usually focussing on death or other misfortune covered in the news media, e.g., *Death of Samantha, Jerry's Kids, Boat People, Battered Wives*.

A. Ethnicity

In diverse musical circles, references to African-American culture play a complex role. For example, common insults about musicianship (even among white musicians) include

"to play white," "they're too white," "white boys," etc.
This is motivated, at least in part, by an attempt to identify
with African-American musical culture. Furthermore,
punks (and many others in the alternative scene) see themselves as marginalized by the rest of society and thus attempt to identify with other marginalized groups. Note, in
this context, Richard Hell's famous quote "Punks are niggers" (Hebdige 1979: 62). For more information, the reader
is referred to Hebdige's 1979 study, much of which is devoted to tracing the complex relationship between British
punk rock and West Indian culture in Great Britain.

17 Pygmies
Beat Nigs. This band makes clear on its album cover that *nig*
    is a positive word for them, a general term for all op-
    pressed groups, consistent with the discussion above.
Boat People
Clive Pig & the Hopeful Chinamen
Closet Negros
Coolies
Drunk Injuns
Inca Babies
Tar Babies
Tragic Mulatto

B. Politics

Note how many of the bands in this category refer directly
to the Kennedy assassination, largely no doubt as a result
of the influential band, *Dead Kennedys*.

Baby Jesus Hitler
Bhopal Stiffs
Capital Punishment
Dead Kennedys
Dead Oswalds. This is probably a direct takeoff on the *Dead
    Kennedys.*
Elvis Hitler
Fearless Iranians from Hell. According to Robbins (1989),
    this band actually has an Iranian member.

Flaming Mussolinis
Jack Rubies. Reference to Kennedy assassination.
Naked Raygun. Cf. *Ray & the Guns* as another reference to
 Ronald Reagan.
Peace Corpse
Single Bullet Theory. Reference to Kennedy assassination.
Trotsky Icepick

C. Religion

Agnostic Front
Baby Jesus Hitler
Bad Religion
Blind Idiot God
Blessed Virgins
Catholic School Boys from Hell
Christian Death
Crippled Pilgrims
Crucifucks
False Prophets
Jesus and Mary Chain
Jesus Chrysler
Part-time Christians
Pope Paul Pot. This name represents a blend of two rather
 unlikely characters: *Pope Paul* and *Pol Pot*.
Vatican Commandos

D. Profanity

In order to avoid even more censorship than they would
already encounter, several bands have used asterisks for
vowels in particularly taboo words (*C*nts, Sic F*cks*). Similarly, some taboo words occur with non-standard orthog-
raphy (*Scumfucs*) and a few other groups have chosen
euphemistic forms (*FU's, F-word*). Notice the predominance of *fuck* over all other vulgarities, and the complete
absence, throughout the corpus, of *shit*.

Bitch Magnet. In contemporary youth culture, this refers to males who are considered particularly attractive by females. The figure of speech finds full expression in the description of how to pick up women: Tie a rope around the leg of a *bitch magnet* and throw him out a car window while cruising slowly through a crowded area. Pull him back in and pick the women off.

Cheetah Chrome Motherfuckers
Crucifucks
C*nts
F-word
FU's
Flaming Fuckheads
GG Allin and the Scumfucs
Reverb Motherfuckers
Richard Hell & the Voidoids
Sic F*cks

E. Violence

Battered Wives
Chainsaw Dawg
Deep Wound
Impulse Manslaughter
My Bloody Valentine
Nurse with Wound
Rapeman[12]
Stranglers
Suicidal Tendencies
Tex and the Horseheads. This "cow-punk" band's name combines cowboy imagery and the violent imagery typical of punks. This probably explains the use of the word *horseheads*, as a subtle reference to the movie *The Godfather*.
Verbal Abuse
Violent Apathy
Violent Children
Violent Femmes

F. The Handicapped

Autistics
Crippled Pilgrims
House of Freaks

Th' Inbred. The fact that this band comes from West Virginia lends its name particular significance, given stereotypes about Appalachian culture.
Jerry's Kids
Phantom Limbs
Poster Children
Retarded Elf
Slow Children

G. Children

Black Market Babies
Catholic School Boys from Hell
Death of Samantha
Inca Babies
Jerry's Kids
Peter and the Test Tube Babies
Poster Children
Sex Boys
Sex Gang Children
Slow Children
Tar Babies
Violent Children

NAMING PATTERNS

There are a few patterns that deserve comment here. First, there is the consciously derivative name: *Celibate Rifles* (*Sex Pistols*), *Lesbian Dopeheads on Mopeds* (*Gaye Bykers on Acid*), *Yeastie Girls* (*Beastie Boys*). Oxymorons are also popular: *Violent Femmes*, *Violent Apathy*, etc., as are puns: *Jesus Chrysler* (also, naturally, a euphemistic form of the exclamation *Jesus Christ*), the *Thrownups*, *Peace Corpse*, *Slow Children*.

One of the most time-honored traditions in rock music is the formula [*Proper Name*] *and the* -s. Among offensive names, many are distinguished by the choice of last name and/or the plural noun phrase: *Richard Hell and the Voidoids*, *Clive Pig & the Hopeful Chinamen*, *GG Allin and the Scumfucs*. A recently popular twist on this is to have an initial noun phrase that is not a name replace the proper name: *Bloody Mess & the Skabs, Vomit & the Zits, Big Balls & the Great White Idiot* (in this item, note also the inversion of singular and plural from the usual pattern). Also, [NP(plural)] *from Hell* occurs frequently: *Catholic School Boys from Hell, Cycle Sluts from Hell, Fearless Iranians from Hell.*

[*Proper Name*] + [*Proper Name*], often with clashing images, is another recent naming strategy: *Elvis Hitler, Baby Jesus Hitler, Jesus Chrysler, Pope Paul Pot*, etc.

Finally, one syntactic trend that has intensified in the last decade is that of sentences as names—cf. *The Teardrop Explodes, They Might be Giants, Frankie Goes to Hollywood, Gene Loves Jezebel*, etc. This goes back at least to the early 1970s band, *It's a Beautiful Day*. So far, however, only a few offensive sentence-names have surfaced: *Bob on This, My Dad is Dead, Dead Can Dance*.

CONCLUSION

Why this pattern of offensive names, extending beyond the bands to record labels, pseudonyms, etc.? The answer lies no doubt in the fact that the aesthetic of the alternative scene has, in no small part, evolved out of the punk movement. That working aesthetic and its rhetoric were "steeped in irony" according to Hebdige (1979: 63), who describes the scene in terms of "darkly comic signifiers" and "gutter-snipe rhetoric." What one finds today in the alternative scene is a dual motivation to offend. On the one hand, the overtly political bands consciously exploit offensive material politically. This is particularly common for much early English punk and hardcore in general; from bands in our list, take for example the following titles: *Dead Kennedys* "Nazi Punks Fuck Off," *MDC* "John Wayne Was a Nazi," *Dicks* "Bourgeois Fascist Pig," *Crucifucks* "Hinkley

Had a Vision." On the other hand, some bands such as *Dead Milkmen* are not as clearly political, aiming more for humor or general shock value. Usually, however, in practice this line cannot be clearly drawn—both politics and humor play significant roles.

As a result of their efforts to shock and offend, members of the alternative scene have been the target of much censorship. For example, the *Dead Kennedys'* 1985 album "Frankenchrist" contained a poster by H.R. Giger (*Landscape #20*, featuring numerous rather abstract genitalia) that was deemed obscene by the state of California (cf. Wishnia 1987 for details). This happened despite a warning on the album that "the inside foldout to this record cover is a work of art by H.R. Giger that some people may find shocking, repulsive, or offensive. Life can be that way sometimes." Lead singer Jello Biafra was arrested in 1986 on charges of "distribution of harmful matter to minors," after a 14-year-old San Fernando Valley girl gave her younger brother a copy of the album. Biafra and the *Dead Kennedys'* record label, "Alternative Tentacles," a leading force in the alternative scene, were ultimately cleared when a mistrial was declared, but it ended the band, according to Robbins (1989).[13] A motion for retrial was denied by the judge.

The *Circle Jerks'* classic "Golden Shower of Hits" was banned from some radio stations as obscene although it only contained a medley of very well-known pop songs done in thrash style tracing a relationship from beginning to end: "Afternoon delight," "She's having my baby" and "D-I-V-O-R-C-E," etc. Presumably it was the name of the record that caused the reaction.

The band *Rapeman*—named after a Japanese comic — has recently broken up because of controversy surrounding the name (*Spin*, June 1989: 24). *Spin* also reported in the same issue (73) that the name *Fine Young Cannibals*—which we had deemed too mild for inclusion in our corpus—is being abbreviated to *FYC* to increase their pop appeal.

We do not pretend to have presented the definitive taxonomy of offensive band names, nor a complete list, nor to have even scratched the surface of potential areas of investigation within the rock scene. We hope that this brief article suggests some further avenues of interest and stimulates further research in the area.

FOOTNOTES

1. The authors thank, first of all, John Kirby, for inspiring this piece by his questions about offensive band names. *Phrogs*—Rick Rogers, Kendel Tilton, and The King—all helped with their detailed knowledge of the alternative scene. Thanks also to Frank Dent and Evan Finch of Bored Records. Any and all errors are naturally ours alone.

2. Fanzines are small-circulation publications focussing on science fiction, comics, or the alternative scene or some part of it. From *fan* + [maga]*zine*.

3. *Stiff's* motto is "If it ain't STIFF, it ain't worth a fuck."

4. Robbins (1983, 1989) mistranslates their name as 'wild animals,' although their album cover shows one horse mounting another and the band calls itself an 'electronic sex band.'

5. The research potential of the latter area is evidenced by the Los Angeles-based rap band *NWA* (*Niggers with Attitudes*) and their recent song "Fuck the Police."

6. Mass Giorgini, bassist for the band *Rattail Grenadier* (Roadkill Records), personal communication.

7. This clearly reflects a white and very *a*historical perspective about the position of jazz in American culture.

8. We have deleted initial definite articles from band names because of the tremendous variation in their use by the bands themselves.

9. Fluids can, of course, flow into the body as well as out, cf. *Claude Coma & the IVs*.

10. Note again that we do not deal with heavy metal, which deals extensively with death imagery (as well as Satanic imagery, etc.—rare in the alternative scene) and could be a study in itself.

11. *Joy Division* has become *New Order* since their lead singer killed himself, according to alternative scene legend, by putting his head in a

noose and standing on a block of ice until it melted. Death rock might be loosely characterized by relatively amelodic sound, slow heavy beat, often a predominately bass-oriented mix, and lyrics usually about death and dying.

12. The band which is most brought to mind by the word *rape* is the West Coast band, *The Mentors*, whose work has been called *rape rock*, based on their lyrics and stage show.

13. Wishnia (1987) points out that the choices of band and record label for prosecution were crucial. Major record labels have certainly released material equally worthy of attention, cf. e.g., *Judas Priest*'s "Eat Me Alive." Such labels commonly spend over $50,000 to record an album and could have comfortably spent far more than the $60,000 spent by *Alternative Tentacles* on Biafra's defense. Wishnia also cites sources involved in that case who think the prosecution did not reckon with Biafra's intelligence and articulateness, expecting rather "a bunch of blue-haired kids who didn't know what they were doing."

WORKS CITED

Hebdige, Dick. 1979. *Subculture: The Meaning of Style*. New York: New Accents/Methuen.

Robbins, Ira A. (editor). 1983. *The New Trouser Press Record Guide*. New York: Scribners. Most recent revised edition, 1989.

Wishnia, Steven. 1987. "Rockin' With the First Amendment: Of Punk and Pornography." *The Nation*. October 24: 444-446.

APPENDIX
Alphabetical List of Band Names

4-Skins
17 Pygmies
1,000 Homo DJs
Aborted at Line 6
Afterbirth
Agnostic Front
Alien Sex Fiend
Art Phag
Autistics
Baby Jesus Hitler
Bad Religion

Battered Wives
Beat Nigs
Bhopal Stiffs
Big Balls and the Great White
   Idiot
Bitch Magnet
Black Market Babies
Blessed Virgins
Bloody Mess and the Skabs
Blind Idiot God
Boat People

Bob on This
Bollock Brothers
Bone Orchard
Bulimia Banquet
Butthole Surfers
Buzzcocks
C*nts
Cancerous Growth
Capital Punishment
Carniverous Buttock Flies
Catholic School Boys from Hell
Chainsaw Dawg
Cheetah Chrome Motherfuckers
Christian Death
Circle Jerks
Claude Coma & the IVs
Clit Boys
Clive Pig & the Hopeful China-
  men
Closet Negros
Cocks in Stained Satin
Condemned to Death
Contractions
Coolies
Corpse Grinders
Cramps
Crippled Pilgrims
Crucifucks
Cycle Sluts from Hell
Dayglo Abortions
Dead Can Dance
Dead Hippies
Dead Kennedys
Dead Oswalds
Dead Milkmen
Death of Samantha
Death Piggy
Deep Wound
Deviants
Dicks
Discharge
Doggy Style
Drunk Injuns
Elvis Hitler

F-word
False Prophets
Fartz
Fearless Iranians from Hell
Fetus Productions
Flaming Fuckheads
Flaming Mussolinis
Foetus Interruptus
Freddy Fetus & the Abortions
Fried Abortions
Fudge-packers
FU's
GG Allin and the Scumfucs
Gay Cowboys in Bondage
Gaye Bykers on Acid
Geile Tiere
Gigolo Aunts
Hard-ons
Heads on Sticks
Hollywood Autopsy
Homo Picnic
Homosexuals
House of Freaks
Impulse Manslaughter
Inbred
Inca Babies
Jack Rubies
Jerry's Kids
Jesus Chrysler
Johnny Vomit
Killer Pussy
Killing Joke
Leather Nun
Les Blank's Amazing Pink Holes
Lesbian Dopeheads on Mopeds
Lost Cherees
Lubricated Goat
Man Sized Action
MDC
Meat Beat Manifesto
Mighty Sphincter
My Bloody Valentine
My Dad is Dead
My Life with the Thrill Kill Kult

Naked Raygun
Napalm Death
Necropolis of Love
Necros
Neurotic Arseholes
New Roger Diarrhea
Nurse with Wound
Part-time Christians
Peace Corpse
Penetrators
Peter and the Test Tube
  Babies
Phantom Limbs
Pink Fairies
Pope Paul Pot
Poster Children
Pussy Galore
Rapeman
Raw Meat
Retarded Elf
Reverb Motherfuckers
Revolting Cocks
Richard Hell & the Voidoids
Root Boy Slim & the Sex Change
  Band
Rotting Corpses
Sarcastic Orgasm
Schleimkeim
Scraping Foetus Off the Wheel
Screaming Dead
Screaming Fetus
Seemen
Severed Heads
Sex Gang Children

Sex Pistols
Sharon Tate's Baby
Sic F*cks
Single Bullet Theory
Slits
Slow Children
Smegma
Southern Death Cult
Soviet Sex
Specimen
Spermbirds
Spit
Stains
Stranglers
Strangulated Beatoffs
Stretch Marks
Suicidal Tendencies
Tar Babies
Tex and the Horseheads
Throbbing Gristle
Thrownups
Tragic Mulatto
Trotsky Icepick
Tupelo Chain Sex
Vatican Commandos
Verbal Abuse
Vibrators
Violent Apathy
Violent Children
Violent Femmes
Vomit and the Zits
Vomit Launch
Vomitorium
Yeastie Girls

SLOGANS TO PROMOTE NATIONAL CONDOM WEEK

Reinhold Aman

The following list is a composite of Xeroxlore received from our readers. Most sheets had 20-25 slogans. The first copies arrived in May 1988 from Roy M., Ohio, and Brian P., Illinois. The next batch was sent in October by Roberta U., Michigan, and Michael F., Illinois. Two came in November, from Chas. H., Illinois, and Joe S., Arizona (in prison). In December, three more versions: from Tom M., Kansas, Jackie Y., Wisconsin, and George K., Connecticut. In February 1989, from Michael W., Washington; in March from Frank N., Kentucky, and the last one in July 1989 from John M., Canada.

In March 1989, *Playboy* magazine (pp. 43-44) published 20 common slogans.

The German news magazine *Der Stern* (No. 14, 30 March 1988: 74) shows a photo of the red-light district in Kiel with the poster: NUR EIN DUMMI MACHT OHNE GUMMI, "Only a dummy does [it] without [a] rubber."

- Cover your stump before you hump.
- Before you attack her, wrap your whacker.
- Don't be silly, protect your willy.
- When in doubt, shroud your spout.
- Don't be a loner, cover your boner.
- You can't go wrong if you shield your dong.
- If you're not going to sack it, go home and whack it.
- If you think she's spunky, cover your monkey.
- It will be sweeter if you wrap your peter.
- If you slip between the thighs, be sure to condomize.
- She won't get sick if you wrap (cap) your dick.
- If you go into heat, package (wrap) your meat.
- While you are undressing Venus, dress up that penis.
- When you take off her pants and blouse, suit up your trouser mouse.

- Especially in December, gift-wrap your member.
- Never (never) deck her with an unwrapped pecker.
- Don't be a fool, vulcanize your tool.
- The right selection? Check (sack) your erection.
- Wrap in foil before checking her oil.
- A crank with armor will never harm her.
- Before you blast her, guard your bushmaster.
- Before you bag her, sheath your dagger.
- To save embarrassment later, cover your 'gator.
- She'll be into fellatio, if you wrap your Horatio.
- There's still cunnilingus with a shielded dingus, but she'll pass on fellatio if you've wrapped up Horatio.
- Befo' da van start rockin', be sho' yo' cock gots a stockin'.
- Before you let it all hang out, be sure to wrap your trouser trout.
- Before you bang her, engulf your wanger.
- Encase your porker before you dork her.
- If you really love her, wear a cover.
- Don't make a mistake, muzzle your snake.
- Sex is cleaner with a packaged wiener.
- If you can't shield your rocket, leave it in your pocket.

The last version received, circulating on a campus in Newfoundland, had additional, different slogans:

- No glove, not love.
- Urge for a f**k, reach for a latex.
- When in doubt, leave it out.
- Want to activate the cock, put on the sock.
- When you are in charge, collect your discharge.
- When there is a flutter in your pants, get the rubber in your hands.

WHAT -*IST* ARE YOU?
A GUIDE
TO COMMON PREJUDICES

Reinhold Aman

You know the two most common labels hurled by the PC Creeps and the Socially Sensitive Thought Police: **racist** and **sexist**. What you may not know is the fact that many of those who accuse others of racism and sexism are closet racists and closet sexists themselves, just like the busybody heterosexuals and pornography-hunters who publicly attack homosexuality and pornography but who in private get their jollies from the lifestyle and literature they attack.

A **racist** is one who discriminates against others on the basis of their race. A **sexist** discriminates on the basis of sex. In recent years, a few other -*ist* labels have been added to these two standard terms, for example, **ageist**, one who discriminates against, ridicules, fears, or hates old people.

During the past few years, new terrorizing tools of oppression have appeared, most often on college campuses (places once known for Tolerance, Free Speech and Brave Thoughts). Among such terms are **sizeist** (one who discriminates against persons because of their size—mainly fat women and dwarfs), **lookist** (one who discriminates against persons because of their looks and appearance—mainly ugly folks), and **ableist** (one who discriminates against persons because of their physical or mental conditions—mainly crippled and retarded persons). Even our animal brethren and sistren now have sensitive spokeshumans who accuse you of being a **speciesist** if you prefer one species of animal over another. You are a **speciesist** if you prefer a cuddly kitten over a creepy spider or if you speak unkindly of, are repulsed by, or kill ear wigs, fleas, or divorce-lawyer-like filthy sewer rats.

Humans, like other animals, are innately wary of, fear, are hostile towards, hate, or ridicule those who are "different," those who look, dress, eat, walk, talk or behave not like themselves. People all over the world always have reacted—and always will react—negatively towards those who deviate physically, intellectually, or behaviorally from their own norms.

Knowing that sooner or later the fanatical Sensitive Ones will tongue-lash and label us for our genetic self-preserving cautions and inborn survival mechanisms ("prejudices") toward others who deviate from our norms, I now present a *reductio-ad-absurdum* glossary of some of the *-ist* labels with which the utopian zealots will oppress us insensitive brutes.

GLOSSARY

In order to shorten the definitions, I am using *one who dislikes* for the more comprehensive and accurate *one who discriminates against, is wary of, ridicules, fears, dislikes, or hates.*

accentist one who dislikes those who speak with a regional, social or foreign accent

agnuphilist one who dislikes men who copulate with lambs and sheep. From Latin *agnus* "lamb" and Greek *philos* "loving"

angusto-anusist one who dislikes those who have an inflexible, tight anal sphincter. From Latin *angustus* "tight." Vulgarly called **tight-assist**

angusto-vaginist one who dislikes women who have a tight, prepuce-chafing vagina. Vulgarly called **tight-pussyist**

artificial-denturist one who dislikes those who have false teeth

baldist one who dislikes bald men

bareist one who dislikes those who are naked

belchist one who dislikes those who belch frequently

big-ballist vulgar synonym of **macro-testist**

big-cockist vulgar synonym of **macro-penist**

big-tittist vulgar synonym of **macro-breastist**

boxerist one who dislikes those who wear boxer shorts

brillo-paddist one who dislikes those who have hard, abrasive pubic hair. From Brillo® pad, a pot scourer made of steel wool or hard plastic

bulldykist one who dislikes masculine man-hating lesbians

broad-nosist one who dislikes those who have a broad nose

bumist one who dislikes bums. Same as **homelessist**

caecusist one who dislikes those who are visually catastrophically challenged. From Latin *caecus* "blind"

caeruloculist one who dislikes those who have blue eyes. From Latin *caeruleus* "blue" and *oculus* "eye"

castor-dontist one who dislikes those who have buckteeth. From Latin *castor* "beaver" and *dens* "tooth." Same as **eleanor-rooseveltist**

cerumist one who dislikes those who frequently pick wax from their ears. From Latin

cera "wax"

circumcist one who dislikes men who have a circumcized penis. Same as **cuttist**

coitus-interruptist one who dislikes men who withdraw their penes before ejaculation

coughist one who dislikes those who cough during musical or theatrical performances

crepitist one who dislikes those who loudly pass intestinal gas. From Latin *crepitus* "loud fart"; from *crepitare* "to crackle"

cuntist vulgar synonym of **vaginist**

cuttist one who dislikes men who have a circumcized penis. From gay slang *cut* "circumcized"

dildoist one who dislikes women who satisfy themselves sexually with a dildo

dowager-humpist one who dislikes those who copulate with dignified elderly women. From colloquial *hump* "to copulate"

dowager's-humpist one who dislikes dignified older women who suffer from an abnormal curvature of the upper back and spine

drapist one who dislikes men who have an uncircumcized penis. From gay slang *drapes* "foreskin"

droolist one who dislikes those who frequently let saliva flow from their mouths

dry-vaginist one who dislikes women who have an unlubricated, penis-chafing vagina
dumboist one who dislikes those who have large floppy ears. From the Disney elephant *Dumbo*
earist one who dislikes those who have jug-handle ears
effluvist one who dislikes those who smell offensively of perfume or deodorants. From Latin *effluere* "to flow out"
eleanor-rooseveltist one who dislikes those who are bucktoothed. Same as **castor-dontist**
epilepsist one who dislikes those who suffer from epilepsy
erectionist one who dislikes men who are able to maintain an erection
expectorist one who dislikes those who spit frequently. From Latin *expectorare* "to expel from the chest"
fat-assist vulgar synonym of **steatopygist**
fingerist one who dislikes those who have knobby or stubby fingers
flaccidist one who dislikes men who cannot maintain an erection. From Latin *flaccus* "flabby"
flatfootist one who dislikes those whose arches of the instep are flattened
flatulist one who dislikes those who quietly pass intestinal gas. From Latin *flatus*

"wind, silent fart"; from *flare* "to blow"
frigidist one who dislikes women who are sexually unaroused. From Latin *frigus* "frost, cold"
furrist one who dislikes those who wear animal furs
fuscuoculist one who dislikes those who have brown eyes. From Latin *fuscus* "brown" and *oculus* "eye"
gaptoothist one who dislikes those who have a wide gap between their incisors
gingivist one who dislikes those who show too much gum when smiling. From Latin *gingiva* "gum"
goiterist one who dislikes those who have an enlarged thyroid gland
gourmandist one who dislikes those who are excessively fond of eating and drinking
hairy-leggist one who dislikes women who have unshaven, hairy legs
hattist one who dislikes men who wear hats, especially cowboy hats
high-voicist one who dislikes women who have an annoying high-pitched voice
hirsute-armpitist one who dislikes women who have unshaven, bushy armpits. From Latin *hirsutus* "hairy, bristly"
homelessist one who dislikes panhandlers and other bums
homunculist one who dis-

likes dwarfs and other short people. From Latin *homunculus* "small human"; diminutive of *homo* "human being"

hunchbackist one who dislikes spinally challenged people. Same as **quasimodist**

hymenist one who dislikes female virgins. From Greek *hymen* "membrane"

hypertensionist one who dislikes those who suffer from high blood pressure. Term actually used by some companies to deny employment to people with hypertension

impotentist one who dislikes men who suffer from sexual impotence. Vulgarly called **limp-dickist**

irvingist one who dislikes men named *Irving*

jockey-shortist one who dislikes men who wear silly sissy underwear

kneeist one who dislikes those who have knobby knees

knock-kneeist one who dislikes those whose legs curve inwards at the knees

kumquatist one who dislikes those who eat yellowish citrus fruits with sweet spongy rinds. From Chinese *gam* "gold" and *gwat* "citrus fruit"

labia-majorist one who dislikes women who have large, flappy vulvar lips

leprosist one who dislikes those who suffer from Hansen's disease

limp-dickist vulgar synonym of **impotentist**

limpist one who dislikes those who walk with a limp

little-dickist vulgar synonym of **micro-penist**

long-hairist one who dislikes men who have long hair

long-nosist one who dislikes those who have a long nose

loose-vaginist one who dislikes women who have a loose, non-gripping, cathedral vagina

low-fibrist one who dislikes those who eat food with low fiber content

macro-areolist one who dislikes women who have large colored rings around their nipples. From Greek *makros* "big" and Latin *areola* "small open space"

macro-breastist one who dislikes women who have large breasts. Vulgarly called **big-tittist**

macro-clitorist one who dislikes women who have a large clitoris

macro-femurist one who dislikes women whose thighs are as chunky as Hillary Clinton's. From Greek *makros* "large" and Latin *femur* "thigh." Also called **thighist**

macro-lippist one who dislikes those who have large facial lips

macro-nipplist one who dislikes women who have large nipples

macro-penist one who dislikes men who have a large penis. Vulgarly called **big-cockist**

macro-pubic-hairist one who dislikes those who have bushy pubic hair

macro-scrotumist one who dislikes men who have a large scrotum

macro-testist one who dislikes men who have large testes. Vulgarly called **big-ballist**

menstruist one who dislikes menstruating women

micro-areolist one who dislikes women who have small dark rings around their nipples

micro-breastist one who dislikes women who have small breasts

micro-clitorist one who dislikes women who have a small clitoris

micro-lippist one who dislikes those who have narrow facial lips

micro-nipplist one who dislikes women who have small nipples

micro-penist one who dislikes men who have a small penis. Vulgarly called **little-dickist**

micro-pubic-hairist one who dislikes those who have little or no pubic hair

micro-scrotumist one who dislikes men who have a small scrotum

micro-testist one who dislikes men who have small testes. Vulgarly called **small-ballist**

mumblist one who dislikes those who habitually mumble

nameist one who dislikes others because of their names. General term. *See* **irvingist**

nasal-pickist one who dislikes those who frequently extract nasal mucus with their fingers

neckist one who dislikes those who have a short or no neck

nosebuggist one who dislikes those who have dried or moist nasal mucus on their faces

obeso-abdomenist one who dislikes those who have a big belly

orgasmist one who dislikes others on the basis of the speed of reaching an orgasm. General term. *See* **quick-orgasmist, slow-orgasmist**

penist one who dislikes men on the basis of the size of their penes. General term. *See* **big-cockist, little-dickist, macro-penist, micro-penist**

pigeon-toeist one who dislikes those whose feet are not parallel but whose toes are turned inwards

plaid-sockist one who dislikes those who wear plaid socks

porkist one who dislikes those who eat porcine meat

premature-ejaculist one who dislikes men who suffer from premature ejaculation

prepucist one who dislikes men on the basis of the lack or possession of a foreskin. General term. *See* **circumcist, cuttist, drapist**

pubic-hairist one who dislikes persons on the basis of their pubic hair. General term. *See* **brillo-paddist, macro-pubic-hairist, micro-pubic-hairist**

quasimodist same as **hunchbackist**. From Quasimodo, the hunchbacked bellringer of Nôtre Dame in Paris

quick-orgasmist one who dislikes those who reach orgasm too quickly. Not to be confused with **premature-ejaculist**

red-hairist one who dislikes those who have red hair. From the ancient prejudice linking redhaired people with the devil

red-meatist one who dislikes those who eat red meat

rubophallonasist one who dislikes men whose noses resemble Bill Clinton's proboscis. From Latin *ruber* "red," Greek *phallos* "penis" and Latin *nasus* "nose"

saltist one who dislikes those who salt their food

sandalist one who dislikes those who wear sandals

scratchist one who dislikes those who scratch themselves frequently, especially their crotches

scrotumist one who dislikes men on the basis of the size of their scrota. General term. *See* **macro-scrotumist, micro-scrotumist**

short-hairist one who dislikes those who wear their hair short

short-pantsist one who dislikes men who wear short pants

shrill-voicist one who dislikes women who have a high-pitched piercing voice

sinister-manist one who dislikes those who are left-handed. From Latin *sinister* "left" and *manus* "hand." Also called **southpawist**

sloppy-vaginist one who dislikes women who produce excessive vulvar and vaginal secretions during copulation and cunnilingus

slow-orgasmist one who dislikes those who reach orgasm too slowly

small-ballist vulgar synonym of **micro-testist**

smegmaist one who dislikes those who have a smegma-soiled penis or vulva

smellist one who dislikes those who emit offensive odors

smokist one who dislikes those who smoke tobacco

smuggist one who dislikes those who are highly self-satisfied

snorist one who dislikes those who snore

southpawist same as **sinister-manist**

spindly-leggist one who dislikes women who have thin, spindly legs

spotted-owlist one who dislikes those who protect the *Strix occidentalis*

stammerist one who dislikes those who stammer

steatopygist one who dislikes those who have immense buttocks. From Greek *stear* "fat, tallow" and *pyge* "buttocks." Vulgarly called **fat-assist**

strabismist one who dislikes those who are cross-eyed. From Greek *strabos* "squint-eyed"

stutterist one who dislikes those who stutter

surdist one who dislikes those who have damaged tympanic membranes. From Latin *surdus* "deaf"

swarthist one who dislikes dark-complexioned persons

temporarily-ableist one who dislikes those who are temporarily abled, i.e., not yet blind, deaf, crippled, or dead

testist one who dislikes men on the basis of the size of their testes. General term. *See* **big-ballist, macro-testist, micro-testist, small-ballist**

thighist one who dislikes

women who have large thighs. Same as **macro-femurist**

tight-assist vulgar synonym of **angusto-anusist**

tight-pussyist vulgar synonym of **angusto-vaginist**

toe-cheesist one who dislikes those who have cheesy excretions between their toes

turtleneckist one who dislikes those who wear turtleneck sweaters

twattist vulgar synonym of **vaginist**

urinist one who dislikes those who urinate frequently

vaginist one who dislikes women on the basis of the condition of their vaginas. General term. *See* **cuntist, dry-vaginist, loose-vaginist, sloppy-vaginist, tight-vaginist, twattist**

voicist one who dislikes persons on the basis of their voice. General term. *See* **accentist, high-voicist, shrill-voicist**

volvoist one who dislikes those who own a Volvo car

wartist one who dislikes those who have horny projections on their skin

yellow-teethist one who dislikes those who have yellow teeth

you-knowist one who dislikes those who frequently say "you know."

DEBUNKING KENNEDY'S
"I AM A JELLY-FILLED DOUGHNUT"

Reinhold Aman

I must put an end to a well-known canard spread by an ignorant language professor and widely disseminated by ignorant journalists and their equally ignorant copycats.

About seven years ago, an American language professor claimed that President John F. Kennedy's exclamation *Ich bin ein Berliner!* really means "I am a jelly-filled doughnut!" This nonsense was reprinted widely, including in *The New York Times* of April 30, 1988, where the ignoramus also claimed that "such citizens never refer to themselves as 'Berliners'" and that the residents of Berlin "tittered among themselves" when J.F.K. uttered his immortal words.

When the 16th edition of Bartlett's *Familiar Quotations* (Little, Brown) appeared in 1992, its general editor, Justin Kaplan, rehashed the *N.Y.T.* story (footnote, p. 742) and even implied in a newswire interview published in the *San Francisco Chronicle* and *The Los Angeles Times* that he himself had discovered the "real" meaning, chuckling heartily about Kennedy's alleged *faux pas*.

As a former professor of German, a native speaker of German blessed with *Sprachgefühl*, a German dialectologist, and a researcher of the semantics and onomastics of aggressive language, I am qualified to debunk and kill off that idiocy promulgated by tittering and chuckling ignoramuses.

Ich bin (ein) Berliner means "I am a Berliner" or "...a male person/native of Berlin" and absolutely nothing else! A female from Berlin would say, *Ich bin (eine) Berlinerin.* Most northern Germans normally do not use the indefinite article *ein(e)* with place-name origins and professions (e.g., *Ich bin Berliner. Ich bin Professor.*), whereas most southern Germans, Austrians, and Swiss Germans do use it (*Ich bin ein Schweizer. Ich bin eine Österreicherin. Ich bin ein Professor.*).

Haven't those chuckling ignoramuses ever heard of polysemy? Even though *Berliner* is also used in northern Germany to mean "jelly-filled doughnut," when someone says, *Ich bin (ein) Berliner*, it means "I am a male person from Berlin" only. (Let's ignore the possibility of an unemployed German-language professor or general editor wearing a doughnut costume to make a few bucks advertising that food.)

No intelligent native speaker of German tittered in Berlin when J.F.K. spoke, just as no native speaker of German, or one who does know this language, would titter if someone said, *Ich bin ein Wiener* or *Hamburger* or *Frankfurter.* Only a chuckling chucklehead would translate *Ich bin ein Wiener* ("I am a male Viennese") as "I am a sausage (*or* penis *or* ineffectual person *or* jerk *or* very serious student)." Only a tittering twit would translate *Ich bin ein Hamburger* ("a male person from Hamburg") as "I am a meat patty (*or* hobo *or* beggar *or* scarred prizefighter *or* inferior racing dog *or* mixture of mud and skin nutrients)." And only a babbling bubblebrain would translate *Ich bin ein Frankfurter* ("a male person from Frankfurt") as "I am a long, smoked, reddish sausage (*or* weenie *or* dead Supreme Court judge)."

As a male native of *Bayern* (Bavaria), it is correct for me to state, *Ich bin ein Bayer*, "I am a Bavarian." If some ignoramus chuckles that it *really* means "I am an aspirin," I'll shove a wiener up his nose!

DOOR WHORE
AND OTHER NEW MEXICO
RESTAURANT SLANG

Ben Radford

The following deprecatory terms are used by employees at restaurants in Corrales and Albuquerque, New Mexico:

amateur night   a night when the tips are very low. Reference to amateurs who are unfamiliar with the customs of good tipping

AC or **alzheimer's candidate**   a customer, usually elderly, who repeatedly asks the same questions concerning the menu or forgets what he or she ordered

breast check   a walk through the restaurant to check female customers for particularly large or attractive breasts. Also called **tit run**

camper   a customer who stays for an unusually long time at a table

Damien   a particularly difficult or messy child at a table. From the satanic child in the film *Damien*

door whore   a hostess who stands near the entrance door and seats customers

farmer   a customers who, through behavior or appearance, seems to be from the country; a hick

farsighted, to be   to ignore customers by pretending not to see or notice them when one is busy doing something else

Griswolds a family of customers, usually a nuclear family, who are all bothersome, requesting extras on everything, complaining, dropping items, yelling, etc. Reference to National Lampoon's vacation movies, featuring the Griswold family. Also called **Simpsons**

immigrant a foreign customer, especially one who doesn't speak English. Sometimes used contemptuously

planet BoDean a fictional planet where irritating customers come from. Usage: "I've got a guy at my table who wants to know what a burrito is. Another guy from planet Bo-Dean." Frequently used with farmer-type customers

sheep tables a group of tables where customers all arrive and leave at the same time

shmeg or **smeg** same as **spooge**. Reference to smegma

Simpsons same as **Griswolds**. Reference to the television cartoon show featuring uncouth characters

spooge an offensive substance such as butter or Ranch salad dressing accidentally spilled on someone. Also used as a verb. Usage: "Damn it! I was carrying these plates and I spooged myself."

temper a customer who tips ten percent, especially a repeat customer. From *ten* + *per*(cent)

tit run same as **breast check**.

CANONICAL STRICTURES
AGAINST
SWEARING AND BLASPHEMING

Translated
by
Joseph S. Salemi

Prior to the major codifications of canon law in the Roman Catholic Church, many local churches had their own collections of ecclesiastical canons (from the Greek κανών; a rule, regulation, or stricture). These compilations sometimes took the form of "penitential books" or manuals for confessors, which set forth appropriate punishments for various sins. The text of the excerpts translated here comes from a Belgian manual of the 19th century, but the canons are clearly from a much earlier period—perhaps medieval. The following four are from a section dealing with sins against the Second Commandment: *Non assumes nomen Dei tui in vanum*, "Thou shalt not take the name of thy God in vain."

§

If anyone should swear by God's hair, or His head—if he should do it once unthinkingly let him repent by subsisting on bread and water for seven days; if after having been warned he should do it a second and a third time, let him suffer the same punishment for fifteen days.

Si quis per capillum Dei, aut per caput ejus juraverit, si semel
nesciens fecerit: poenitens aqua et pane septem dies victitet; si se-
cundo, ac tertio monitus idem fecerit, dies quindecim.

§

If he swears by heaven, or by any other created thing, let him
suffer in a like manner for fifteen days.

Si per coelum, aut per aliam aliquam creaturam: dies item quindecim.

§

If anyone blasphemes, he shall be penitent for just as long a
time as he remained impenitent.

Si quis blasphemat: tandiu poenitens erit, quandiu impoenitens
permansit.

§

If anyone should publicly blaspheme God, or the Blessed Virgin Mary, or any saint, let him stand in the open before the
doors of the church for seven Sundays while the solemnities
of the Mass are celebrated. And on the last of these days let
him stand with his head uncovered and his shoes tied with a
string around his neck. And for the seven preceding weeks let
him fast on bread and water on Fridays. On no account is he
to enter the church. On each of the seven Sundays, if he is
able, let him give food to one, two, or three poor men; in
other cases let some other penance be imposed upon him. If
he refuses, let him be forbidden entrance into the church, and
on his death let him be denied the rites of burial. A rich man
shall be fined forty solidi by the magistrate; in other cases let
the fine be thirty or twenty solidi.

Si quis Deum, vel beatam Mariam Virginem, vel aliquem sanc-
tum publice blasphemaverit: pro foribus ecclesiae diebus dominicis septem, in manifesto, dum missarum solemnia aguntur, stet: ul-
timoque ex illis die, sine pallio, et calcementis ligatus corrigia cir-

ca collum, septemque praecedentibus feriis sextis in pane et aqua jejunet, ecclesiam nullo modo tunc ingressurus: singulis item septem illis diebus dominicis, tres, aut duos, aut unum pauperem pascat, si potest; alioquin alia poenitentia afficiatur: recusans, ecclesiae ingressu interdicatur; in obitu ecclesiastica sepultura careat. Dives a magistratu mulctetur poena solidorum quadraginta, alioquin triginta seu viginti.

Source: J. Gaume, *Manuel des Confesseurs* (Bruxelles: H. Goemaere, n.d.), pp. 531-32. The Dutch writer Ed Schilders submitted the Latin excerpts.

MOZART'S BIZARRE
VERBAL BEHAVIOR
A CASE OF TOURETTE SYNDROME?

Rasmus Fog

Peter Shaffer's *Amadeus* left in its wake much curiosity about Mozart's behavior which has been described as erratic, disoriented, and bizarre (Kerman, 1988). In the memoirs by Caroline Pichler (Blümml, 1914) an example is found of the famous composer's behavior:

> Once I was sitting at the piano, playing "Non più andrai" from Figaro; Mozart, who happened to be present, came up behind me, and my playing must have pleased him, for he hummed the melody with me, and beat time on my shoulders; suddenly, however, he pulled up a chair, sat down, told me to keep playing the bass and began to improvise variations so beautifully that everyone present held his breath, listening to the music of the German Orpheus. But all at once he had had enough; he jumped up and, as he often did in his foolish moods, began to leap over table and chairs, miaowing like a cat, and turning somersaults like an unruly boy....

In many of Mozart's letters there are long passages of obscene words (Hildesheimer, 1982). Even in love letters—for example to his cousin Bäsle—such bizarre sentences are found:

Nun aber habe ich die Ehre, sie zu fragen, wie sie sich befinden und sich tragen? – ob sie noch offens leibs sind? ob sie etwa gar haben den grind? – – ob sie mich noch ein bischen können leiden? –	But now I have the honor to ask you how you are doing? – Whether you still have diarrhea? [lit., "if your body is still open"] Whether you even have scabies? – – Whether you still like me a little bit? –

ob sie öfters schreiben mit einer
kreiden? – ob sie noch dann und
wan an mich gedencken? – ob sie
nicht bisweilen lust haben sich
aufzuhencken? – ob sie etwa gar
bös waren? auf mich armen nar-
rn; ob sie nicht gutwillig wollen
fried machen, oder ich lass bei
meiner Ehr einen krachen! doch
sie lachen – victoria! – – unsre
arsch sollen die friedens= zeichen
seyn! – ich dachte wohl, dass sie
mir nicht länger wiederstehen
könnten. ja ja, ich bin meiner
sache gewis, und sollt ich heut
noch machen einen schiss, obwohl
ich in 14 Tägen geh nach Paris.
wenn sie mir also wolln ant-
worten, aus der stadt Augsburg
dorten, so schreiben sie mir baldt,
damit ich den brief erhalt, sonst
wenn ich etwa schon bin weck,
bekomme ich statt einen brief
einen dreck. dreck! – – dreck! – o
dreck! – o süsses wort! – dreck! –
schmeck! – auch schön! – dreck,
schmeck! – dreck! – leck – o char-
mante! – dreck, leck! – das freüet
mich! – dreck, schmeck und leck!
– schmeck dreck, und leck dreck!
– – Nun um auf etwas anders zu
kommen; haben sie sich diese fas-
nacht schon braf lustig gemacht.
in augsburg kann man sich der-
malen lustiger machen als hier.
ich wollte wünschen ich wäre bey
ihnen, damit ich mit ihnen recht
herumspringen könnte.

Whether you frequently write with a
stick of chalk? – Whether you occasionally think of me? – Whether you
don't sometimes feel like hanging
yourself? – Whether you even were
angry with me? With me, the poor
fool. Whether you won't willingly
make peace, or—by my honor—I'll
fart! [lit., "let one crackle"] But you
laugh – Victory! – – Our arses
should be the peace signs! – I
thought that you could no longer
resists me. Yes, yes, I'm sure of my
thing, and if I should today still take
a shit, even though in 14 days I'll
travel to Paris. If you want to write
to me, from the city of Augsburg,
then write soon, so that I'll get your
letter; otherwise—if I'll be gone by
then—I'll get crap instead of a letter
[i.e., nothing. *Dreck* literally means
"dirt, filth" and sometimes is used
as the short form of *Scheißdreck*,
"shit-dirt"]. Crap! – – Crap! – O
crap! – O sweet word! – Crap! –
Smack! ["smell" in Mozart's dialect,
used for rhyme] – Nice, too! –
Crap, smack! – Crap! – Lick [also
used for rhyme] – O charming one!
Crap, lick! – I enjoy that! – Crap,
smack and lick! – Smack crap, and
lick crap! – – Now, to turn to something else: have you enjoyed yourself during this carnival? In Augsburg one can have much more fun
than here. I wish I were with you, so
that I could really jump around
with you.

In many cases, the obscene and vulgar words do not seem

to have any connection with the content of the rest of the letter, and they seem to appear in bursts, i.e. tic-like. This has led to the theory that Mozart might have suffered from Tourette Syndrome (Fog & Regeur, 1983).

Tourette Syndrome = TS (or more correctly, Gilles de la Tourette's Syndrome) was described in 1884 by the French neuropsychiatrist George Gilles de la Tourette. It starts at the age between two and 15 years, and consists of multiple, involuntary muscular and verbal tics. These symptoms are in about 40 percent of all cases accompanied by coprolalia (involuntary uttering of obscene and scatological words) or copropraxia (involuntary obscene gestures). Other types of complicated, bizarre behavioral patterns have also been described (Robertson, 1989). Coprographia (obscene writing) seems very rare, but the author has seen a single case among Danish TS patients.

The symptoms may persist for many years, and in some cases TS is a lifelong illness. The symptoms do not lead to dementia, psychosis, or other types of mental deterioration. For many years it was thought that TS was a psychologically/psychodynamically explainable disease related to various neurotic states. Nowadays, most researchers feel that TS is a purely physical disorder, and a genetic transmission has been suggested. The symptoms (the tics as well as the bizarre behavioral patterns) can be repressed by neuroleptic drugs, which have a specific blocking effect upon certain (dopamine D-2) receptors in certain (basal ganglia) brain areas (Fog & Regeur, 1986).

Could Mozart have suffered from TS? Hildesheimer (1982) mentions that Mozart had tics, but he does not give any detailed description. It has not been possible for the author to find other clear descriptions of muscular tics concerning Mozart. There are, however, many descriptions of his outbursts of bizarre behavior. The coprographia has been thought of as a familiar tradition and also as a stereotype of the period. On the other hand, the obscene words appear in many cases as "tics," in sudden outbursts without relation to the context. It is not possible to find related phenomena in Mozart's music. It has been reported by his biographers that his bizarre behavior disappeared when he played the piano or when he played billiards. It is characteristic of TS patients that symptoms may disappear when "emotional" behavior is performed (singing, swimming, playing tennis, etc.).

It has been difficult to explain why the genial composer has such a poor social career. If Mozart suffered from TS (and this is, of course, only a hypothesis), his behavior might have been socially unacceptable in the long run. Nobody would have known that his involuntary bizarre behavior was an expression of a minimal brain dysfunction which did not affect his genius.

REFERENCES

Blümml, Emil K. (ed.) (1914). *Caroline Pichler: Denkwürdigkeiten aus meinem Leben.* Georg Müller, Munich.

Fog, Rasmus and Regeur, Lisbeth (1983). "Did W. A. Mozart Suffer from Tourette's Syndrome?" (Abstract). Seventh World Congress of Psychiatry, Vienna, July 11–16, 1983.

Hildesheimer, Wolfgang (1982). In: *Mozart.* Farrar, Straus and Giroux, New York.

Kerman, Joseph (1988). "The Residue of Genius." *The New York Review* 35, no. 13, pp. 50–52.

Robertson, Mary M. (1989). "The Gilles de la Tourette Syndrome: The Current Status." *British Journal of Psychiatry* 154, pp. 147–169.

NOTE

Reinhold Aman translated and annotated Mozart's archaic Austrian dialect (containing several orthographic errors). Mozart's many rhymes cannot be reproduced in English, alas.

YOU'RE UGLY, YOUR DICK IS SMALL, AND EVERYBODY FUCKS YOUR MOTHER!

THE STAND-UP COMEDIAN'S RESPONSE TO THE HECKLER

Andrew Conway

In performances by comedians in the USA it is not uncommon for a member of the audience to interrupt the performance by shouting a comment. The comedian must respond to this or lose face. This article discusses some of the responses that are currently in use[1] and defines the main categories of insult that are used.

The comedian's response to the heckler is called a *heckler line*. Usually the performer simply wants to silence the offender so that he[2] can continue with his act. The ideal heckler line leaves the victim feeling so crushed that he is not inclined to continue the dialog. If the comedian can, he will respond to whatever the heckler said, but he need not. A successful comedian will usually have a large repertoire of lines, and will attempt to choose one that fits the situation, as this will make the response appear to be improvised. A few performers will encourage hecklers, as responses that appear to be spontaneous will be funnier to the audience than a prepared routine. One commented that his job was to make whatever the heckler said seem funny, to make the heckler comfortable with what he had said.

It is normally considered very bad etiquette for a comedian

to use a joke written by another comedian without paying for it or "trading" another joke for it. If the author finds out about it, it can lead to more than merely verbal aggression. Many comedians make an exception for heckler lines, provided they are not used regularly or made part of a routine. The logic seems to be that if you really need to control a difficult member of the audience, you should be free to use whatever it takes. However, the authors of some of the lines below might not be happy to hear them used by another performer. Sometimes a comedian will take an existing joke and modify it to avoid stealing material, or to create a line that works better for his stage character or audience. This is referred to as a *switch*, and it is considered acceptable behavior, provided the change is large enough. Many of the jokes below are switches on some other line.

The main categories of heckler lines are variations on
- telling the heckler to be quiet
- calling the heckler *asshole*
- implying the heckler is drunk or drugged
- implying the heckler is childish
- implying the heckler is an idiot
- implying the heckler is ugly
- sexual insults
- insults to parents
- implying the heckler has a menial job

Each of these categories is briefly commented on below, and examples are given. Lines such as the title of this article which fall into more than one category have been assigned to one or the other by auctorial whim. Some lines are specifically directed at men, women, children, adolescents or people with beards. Where this is the case, it is indicated after the line. If a line which applies to a specific sex could be easily modified to apply to the other sex I have not bothered to give both versions or to indicate to which sex it applies. Obscure references are noted after the line.

Telling the Heckler to Be Quiet

A simple and popular approach is for the comedian to tell the heckler to be quiet.

Shut up!

Shut the fuck up!

Fuck off!

On a scale of one to ten ... fuck off!

Look man, I grew up in the ghetto, I've been through your wallet, I know where you live, shut up, sit down. The comedian is black.

Shut yer fucking face! Unless you have something intelligent to say.

I'm not really good with hecklers, but a friend who is good with hecklers wrote something down for me. The comedian then takes a piece of paper from his pocket and pretends to read from it: *Oh, yeah, "Fuck off!"*

Why don't you take a piggyback ride on a buzz saw? Said to a child.

Sir, if I said anything to offend you, please believe me.

You know, I think you've got nothing there.

I'll buy you a beer if you'll drink it in Oakland. The comedian is in San Francisco. Oakland is a largely black city on the other side of the Bay and the butt of many local jokes.

Hey, man, I like doing my act the way you like having sex ... alone.

Why don't you put your nose in your ear and blow your brains out?

Oh, yeah? Said to an aggressive group of hecklers who were walking away from the show. It was said quietly, so that the audience could hear it, but the not hecklers.

Do you know who I am? Not many people do. That's why I carry this. The comedian then makes the one-finger gesture considered crude in America. This is a parody of a series of American Express commercials in which this phrase precedes the display of a credit card.

Well, I don't know about you, but my sides are splitting. Aren't you glad you got out of bed to say that? Said sarcastically to a heckler who has just said something which is not funny.

Calling the Heckler "Asshole"

The word *asshole* seems to have a particular resonance in heckler lines. The heckler is behaving in a manner which is aggressive and unpleasant to the comedian, and by extension to the rest of the audience. This would normally justify the epithet. The insult has the right emotive content: it is strong enough to be funny, but not so powerful that the comedian loses the sympathy of the audience.

If I wanted to hear from an asshole I would have farted.

If you want to be on stage we'll switch places ... you come up here and be funny and I'll go down there and act like an asshole.

The difference between a comic and an asshole is ... about ten feet.

What an asshole. This line works best if the comedian first is polite to the heckler.

I'm sorry, I don't know how to deal with you. I'm a comic, not a proctologist.

Is that a heckler? ... No, it's an asshole. This is performed by two comedians, one of whom says the first line and the other the second.

Stereo assholes. Said to a pair of hecklers.

Seventeen more of you and we'd have a golf course. A golf course has eighteen holes.

On a scale of one to ten ... you're an asshole.

Excuse me, what was that? ... I like that, assholes with amnesia. The second part of this line is only used if the heckler fails to repeat what he just said.

Any more bright ideas, asshole?

Implying the Heckler Is Drunk or Drugged

Very often a heckler may be under the influence of alcohol or other intoxicants. Even if he is not, it is common for the comedian to suggest that he is (or should be).

It's all right. I remember the first time I had a beer.

It's all right. I remember the first time I had a quaalude.

Don't smoke marijuana; this could happen to you.

Go ask mommy for a valium. Said to a child.

Go ask mommy for a thorazine. Said to a child.

Had a little too much sugar this morning? Said to a child.

Children, just say "No." Children, look at this man ... just say "No!" This is a reference to an anti-drug slogan.

Here's an alcoholic who doesn't want to remain anonymous.

You shouldn't drink on an empty head.

Looks like the face on the bar room floor finally got up.

He's suffering from bottle fatigue.

One more word out of you and I'll put you back in your bottle of alcohol. This implies that the heckler is a biological specimen.

Isn't it amazing what a little kindness, patience and benzedrine can do?

I'm sorry, I don't speak alcoholic.

Implying the Heckler Is Childish

A comedian may suggest that heckling is childish behavior. Any further interruptions then become an admission of immaturity on the part of the heckler. The comedian will often adopt a patronizing or superior tone for this type of line.

Similar lines, but usually with a more gentle insult, are used if the heckler really is a child.

Isn't that special?

Thank you for sharing.

I hope your face clears up.

What's the matter, kid, didn't you get enough attention at home?

You go home and tell this joke to your mom, because you still live with her.

Everyone else here works and plays well with others.

Don't yell at me, I ain't your mother.

Now I know why some animals eat their young. Said to a child.

You make me wish I'd donated to Planned Parenthood. Said to a child.

I love kids ... lightly sauteed. Said to a child.

I love children. I eat one every day. Said to a child.

I have the heart of a child ... in a jar at home. Said to a child. As with all spoken comedy, timing of heckler lines is important. One comedian who reviewed an earlier version of this article was particularly concerned with the rhythm or meter with which the line is delivered. This is one of several lines he modified. The previous version was: *I have the heart of a small child ... in a jar in the kitchen.*

If you guys want to grow up you'll stop now, 'cause I'm bigger than you are and I carry hatchets, so deal with that. This comedian juggles hatchets in his act.

What are you going to be IF you grow up? Said to a child.

This year's poster child for zero population growth. Said to a child.

That was a pretty good joke, kid. What are you trying to do, top your parents? Said to a child who has just been funny.

You could get a job in a charm school ... as a bad example.

Implying the Heckler Is an Idiot

The comedian can insult the heckler's intelligence by suggesting a severe mental handicap, a taste for soap operas or just living in an unfashionable town.

I'm paid to act like a fool, what's your excuse?

What holds your ears apart?

I see your therapy's coming along just fine.

So what's the matter? Thirtysomething *was on reruns?* Thirtysomething is a popular television program.

What, was there no tractor pull on tonight, you had nothing to do? A "tractor pull" is a form of televised entertainment too stupid to explain.

Did you go to school on the big school bus or the little school bus? The little school bus would be used for handicapped children.

We'll have a telethon for you later. Telethons are long television programs which attempt to raise charitable contributions usually for the diseased or handicapped.

Were you in the special class at school? The special class is for mentally handicapped children.

Are you from the shallow end of the gene pool?

Do all your friends wear hockey helmets and go on a lot of field trips? Implies that the heckler is in a class of mentally handicapped children.

Every village has one.

There's a guy who'll never get cancer of the brain.

He's a legend in his own mind.

That's pretty good. Got another one? No? That's why I'm up here and you're down there. To a heckler who has just got a laugh.

Isn't it amazing that such a big head can hold such a small mind?

Hey, mind your own business ... or don't you own a business

... or a mind? The comedian I collected this line from was particularly concerned that I get the timing correct. As he put it, It's "Hey, mind your own business," one, two, three, "or don't you own a business?" one, two, three, "or a mind?"

Well, there's something penicillin won't cure.

Your parents must be cousins.

Isn't it a shame when cousins marry?

Aaaughhh! Said, as if imitating the heckler, to a heckler who has said something inaudible.

Where are you from? ... That explains it.

Where are you from? ... Sorry? ... No, I heard you, I'm just sorry.

Implying the Heckler Is Ugly

As usual, the content of the insult need have nothing to do with reality. It does not matter how good-looking the heckler is, calling him ugly can still get a laugh.

Is that really your face or did your neck just throw up?

Is that your face or did you just block a kick?

You're the only case where the baby died and the afterbirth lived.

On a scale of one to ten ... you're ugly.

You're ugly, your dick is short, no one likes you, shut the fuck up. Said to a man.

You look like Beaver Cleaver. Is your mom going to make us a swell pot roast today? Said to a man. "Beaver Cleaver" was a child character in *Leave it to Beaver,* a situation comedy

I've seen better faces on a clock, and even then a cuckoo came out.

I've seen better faces on an iodine bottle. An iodine bottle is labelled with a skull and cross bones to indicate poison.

Ah, the flower of womanhood! You look more like the stem. Said to an adolescent girl.

Is that a wart on your tongue, or did you bring your wife?

Give me a break, will you. After all, you'd still have the funniest lines in the place if you kept your mouth shut. Said to an older woman.

How many peeping Toms have you cured? Said to a woman.

Get a shave. Your face looks like an armpit. Said to a bearded man.

You could play a human being with a little rehearsing.

You've got just the right kind of looks for television. Two more legs and you could star in a western.

Oh, look, a C&R commercial just got let out. Said to men wearing suits. *C&R* make cheap suits.

Hey, you, Mr. Supercuts! Said to someone with an obviously expensive haircut. *Supercuts* are low-priced barbers.

Did you hear Jenny Craig is having a special? Usually said to a woman. *Jenny Craig* is a weight loss program.

Sexual Insults

A great range of sexual insults and slurs can be used. The classification of these would be enough for another article. Among other things the heckler can be accused of being impotent, gay, promiscuous, a masturbator, a prostitute, the relative of a prostitute, a transvestite, or of dating someone promiscuous.

You'd look good with a dick in your mouth. Just kidding, you'd look good with everyone's dick in your mouth. Usually said to a woman.

I don't have a lot of time for this so let's get it over quickly ... you're ugly, your dick is small and everybody fucks your mother. Said to a man.

Good to see you again, back in men's clothing. Said to a man.

Look, it's my old school master. How are you doing, Master

Bater? Said to a man. This can really get a laugh on stage, though it looks painful in writing.

So's your sister. Said to someone who has just said "That's easy."

Is that your boyfriend? ... Small world.

Is that your wife? ... Small world.

Said to a man who has just implied that the comedian is gay: *Only one way to find out if I'm gay ... suck my dick and see if I come.*

Or: *Only one way to find out if I'm gay ... suck my dick and see if I try to stop you.*

Or: *You want to know if I'm gay ... you and your girlfriend bend over and see who I fuck.*

Or: *Why, are you lonely?*

Eat me.

Save your breath, you'll need it to blow up your date later.... I don't know what happened, I bit her ear, she farted and flew out the window. Said to a man. This implies that the heckler uses an inflatable plastic doll for sexual purposes.

You're just bitter 'cause your parents wanted a boy. Said to a man or boy.

Said to a man, as if flirting with the heckler. It is particularly effective with Mormons who do not drink coffee: *Let's go somewhere and drink* lattes *and talk about it.*

Or: *Do you like espresso?*

You couldn't get laid in a whorehouse with a fistful of twenties. Said to a man.

Fuck me, you'll never go back to women. Said to a man who has just said "Fuck you!"

Sorry, that's a low blow.... Speaking of low blows, how's your wife? Said to a man whom the comedian has just insulted.

What's the matter? Got your tongue caught in a zipper? Said to a heckler who has failed to respond to an insult.

Where are you from? … You guys come together? … Oh really? Said to two men. "Oh really?" is asked in a tone of voice that implies the men are gay.

Did you folks hear about the good time that was had by all? Well, here she is! Said to a woman.

While you're down there, do an old friend a favor. Said to a woman standing at the edge of the stage.

Slap the bitch! Said to the boyfriend of a woman heckler. This would normally be too strong an insult to use on stage, but the comedian has a particularly aggressive stage character and built up to this with milder insults to which the heckler responded.

Insults to Parents

As many articles in *Maledicta* have indicated, it is not uncommon for an insult to be applied to the family members of the target. Heckler lines are no exception. Parents are the usual subject, particularly the heckler's mother.

I went to Baskin Robbins and the flavor of the month was your mother. I had two scoops. Baskin Robbins is a chain of ice cream parlors.

So's your mother. Said to a heckler who has just said, "That's easy."

Were your parents related? At least they had the same last name.

I could have been your father but my brother beat me to it 'cause he had change for a dollar.

Yo mama. The comedian is black, or performing to a black audience. This implies he is about to insult the heckler's mother.

People like you make me wish birth control was retroactive.

I'm glad you came. Too bad your father did.

Shut up or I'll put my hand in my pocket and strangle your father. Said to a child.

Implying the Heckler Has a Menial Job

A comedian will often state that the heckler is preventing him from doing his job and add that he does not interfere with the heckler at work. However, the job that the comedian claims not to be interfering with is always of a menial nature, usually prostitution or working in a fast-food restaurant.

This is my job. I don't come into McDonald's and give you a hard time when you're at work.

This is my job. I don't knock the shovel out of your hand when you're at work.

This is my job. I don't knock the dick out of your mouth when you're at work. Usually said to a woman.

This is my job. I don't come and put out your red light when you're at work. Said to a woman.

This is my job. I don't show up at your job and jump on the bed. Said to a woman.

This is my job. I don't show up at your job and unplug the Slurpee machine. The Slurpee machine serves an almost edible product in certain fast-food restaurants.

This is my job. I don't pee in the alley when you're giving blow jobs to transsexuals.

This is my job. I don't show up at your job at the sperm clinic and jerk the Playboy out of your hands. Said to a man.

This is my impression of you at work: "Do you want fries with that?"

Look chick, you made your expenses for the night. Let me make mine. This implies that the woman is a prostitute. The line is an old one, and the term *chick* might no longer be acceptable.

You work your side of the street and I'll work mine. Said by a street juggler to a woman.

Isn't platinum a precious metal? Or is it a common ore? Said to a platinum-blonde woman. Pun on *ore/whore*.

Finally, there are limits to the force of insult that a comedian can use and still remain funny. While a male comedian can call a female heckler *asshole*, he is unlikely to get a good response if he calls her *bitch* or *cunt*. The limits of acceptable bad taste depend on the audience and the setting, as well as the stage character that the comedian has established. A black comedian entertaining a rural white audience cannot say, "Shut up or I'm going to date your sister and make her pregnant," nor can a clown character performing at a children's birthday party say, "Shut the fuck up!" however much he may want to.

NOTES

[1] The majority of these lines were collected from Robert Nelson, Scott Meltzer, Ngaio Bealum and Dave Gomez. Many thanks for their creative maledictions.

[2] I use the masculine pronoun with apologies to include female comedians and hecklers.

NOMEN EST OMEN

Reinhold Aman

The Latin saying *nomen est omen*, "your name is your destiny" or "your name foretells what you are or will become," has been illustrated many times in popular collections.

One such list, "Medical Curiosities" by John Holgate, was published in *Word Ways* 22/2 (May 1989): 84–86, from which a few examples are presented below. Most of the personal names have no offensive meaning in their original languages. The names are listed alphabetically, followed by the specialties of their bearers.

> **Cockburn**: disease of penile and scrotal skin
> **Fick**: heat production during muscular activity.
>   (The German noun *Fick* means "fuck.")
> **Fukuda**: sex education
> **Fukuhara**: sex education
> **Raper**: gynecology
> **Schmucki**: testicular cancer
> **Semenova**: infertility
> **Shita**: hematoma of the rectus sheath
> **Shitov**: gastrointestinal hemorrhage
> **Shitskova**: acute intestinal infections
> **Soranus**: inflammation of the rectum during pregnancy.

In *American Name Society Bulletin* No. 82 (15 Aug. 89): 6, Dr. Arthur Bolz presents a list of 28 verified names of medical doctors whose last names match their professions. Examples:

> **Assman**: proctology
> **Crapp**: proctology
> **Crapper**: gastroenterology
> **Dick Finder**: urology
> **Dick Tapper**: urology
> **Footlick**: podiatry
> **John Wiener**: urology
> **Looney**: psychology
> **Peter Cockshot**: urology
> **Toothacher**: dentistry

LIST OF CONTRIBUTORS

Reinhold Aman, Ph.D. Philologist and publisher in California
Leonard Ashley, Ph.D. Professor of English in New York
Giuliano Averna, Poet, writer and translator in Italy
Simon Bronner, Ph.D. Professor of Folklore in Pennsylvania
Bob Burton Brown, Professor of Education in Florida
Merritt Clifton, Writer and publisher in Canada
Andrew Conway, M.A. Computer scientist in California
Martha Cornog, M.A. Librarian and sex researcher in Pennsylvania
Sterling Eisiminger, Ph.D. Professor of English in South Carolina
Margaret Fleming, Ph.D. Professor of English in Arizona
Rasmus Fog, M.D. Psychiatrist and hospital director in Denmark
Charles Halevi, B.A. Publicist and writer in Illinois
John Hughes, Film writer in California
Monica Macaulay, Ph.D. Professor of Linguistics in Indiana
James Matisoff, Ph.D. Professor of Asian Linguistics in California
Sandra McCosh, M.A. in Folk Life. Writer in California
Arthur McLean, M.A. Writer and poet in Alabama
George Monteiro, Ph.D. Professor of Portuguese in Rhode Island
Lois Monteiro, Ph.D. Professor of Medical Sciences in Rhode Island
Stephen Murray, Ph.D. Sociologist and linguistic researcher in California
Don Nilsen, Ph.D. Professor of English in Arizona
Frank Nuessel, Ph.D. Professor of Linguistics and Spanish in Kentucky
A. P. Cuban artist and illustrator in New York
Elias Petropoulos, Greek folklorist and writer in France
Benjamin Radford, B.A. in Psychology. Lives in New Mexico
Edgar Radtke, Ph.D. Professor of Romance Languages in Germany
Boris Razvratnikov, Ph.D. Professor of Slavic Languages in Illinois
Joseph Salemi, Ph.D. Professor of English and Classics in New York
Joe Salmons, Ph.D. Professor of Linguistics in Indiana
Grace Sardo, Librarian and publicist in Canada
Clifford Scheiner, M.D. Surgeon and erotica bibliographer in New York
Mario Teruggi, Ph.D. Professor of Geology. Lexicographer in Argentina
Robert Tierney, M.Ed. Professor of Education in Mexico
Laurence Urdang, Lexicographer and editor of *Verbatim* in Connecticut
Joan Vinyoles, Chemical Engineer and lexicographer in Spain